First World War
and Army of Occupation
War Diary
France, Belgium and Germany

61 DIVISION
182 Infantry Brigade
Royal Warwickshire Regiment
2/6th Battalion
1 September 1915 - 22 September 1919

WO95/3056/2

The Naval & Military Press Ltd
www.nmarchive.com
Published in association with The National Archives

Published by

The Naval & Military Press Ltd

Unit 10 Ridgewood Industrial Park,

Uckfield, East Sussex,

TN22 5QE England

Tel: +44 (0) 1825 749494

www.naval-military-press.com

www.nmarchive.com

This diary has been reprinted in facsimile from the original. Any imperfections are inevitably reproduced and the quality may fall short of modern type and cartographic standards.

© Crown Copyright
Images reproduced by permission of The National Archives, London, England, 2015.

Contents

Document type	Place/Title	Date From	Date To
Heading	WO95/3056/2		
Heading	61st Division 182nd Infy Bde 2-6th Bn R. Warwicks 1915 Sep 1919 Feb (1916 Feb, Mar, Apr Diaries Missing)		
Miscellaneous	Summary Of War Diary of 2/6th Battalion Royal Warwickshire Regiment	04/09/1915	04/09/1915
War Diary	Epping	01/09/1915	02/09/1915
War Diary	Maldon	03/09/1915	31/10/1915
Miscellaneous	Right Column Order No.24		
Miscellaneous	March Table		
War Diary	Maldon	01/11/1915	30/11/1915
Heading	War Diary of 2/6th Battalion Royal Warwickshire Regiment From 1st December 1915 To 31st December 1915 Volume 2		
War Diary	Maldon	01/12/1915	31/12/1915
Heading	Practice March 31st December 1915 182nd Brigade Operation Orders By Brigadier General E.X. Daubeney Commanding		
Miscellaneous	2/6th Battalion Royal Warwick Regiment Operation Orders	31/12/1915	31/12/1915
Operation(al) Order(s)	182nd Inf. Bde Order No 30	29/12/1915	29/12/1915
Miscellaneous	Instructions		
Miscellaneous	Practice March 2/6th Battalion Royal Warwickshire Regiment	31/12/1915	31/12/1915
Heading	War Diary of 2/6th Battalion Royal Warwickshire Regiment From 1st January 1916 To 31st January 1916 Volume 3		
War Diary	Maldon	01/01/1916	31/01/1916
Heading	War Diary of 2/6th Batt. R. War.R From May 21st To May 31st 1916 (Volume 5)		
War Diary	Perham Down	21/05/1916	21/05/1916
War Diary	France Le Havre	22/05/1916	23/05/1916
War Diary	Gonnehem	24/05/1916	31/05/1916
Heading	War Diary of 2/6th Batt. Royal Warwickshire Regt From June 1st 1916 To June 30th 1916 (Volume 3)		
War Diary	Gonnehem	01/06/1916	07/06/1916
War Diary	Bethune	08/06/1916	08/06/1916
War Diary	Beuvry	09/06/1916	10/06/1916
War Diary	Bethune	11/06/1916	12/06/1916
War Diary	La Gorgue	13/06/1916	22/06/1916
War Diary	Croix Barbee	23/06/1916	24/06/1916
War Diary	In The Trenches	25/06/1916	30/06/1916
Heading	War Diary of 2/6th Battalion Royal Warwickshire Regiment From 1st July 1916 To July 31st 1916 Volume 3		
War Diary	In The Trenches	01/07/1916	09/07/1916
War Diary	Riez Bailleul	10/07/1916	15/07/1916
War Diary	In Trenches	16/07/1916	20/07/1916
War Diary	Riez Bailleul	20/07/1916	22/07/1916
War Diary	In The Trenches	19/07/1916	19/07/1916

War Diary	Riez Bailleul	22/07/1916	23/07/1916
War Diary	Merville	24/07/1916	31/07/1916
Heading	War Diary of 2/6th Batt Royal Warwickshire Regt From 1st August 1916 To 31st August 1916 Volume 3		
War Diary	Riez Bailleul	01/08/1916	09/08/1916
War Diary	In The Trenches	10/08/1916	17/08/1916
War Diary	Riez Bailleul	18/08/1916	25/08/1916
War Diary	Le Grand Pacaut	26/08/1916	31/08/1916
Heading	War Diary of 2/6th Battalion Royal Warwickshire Regiment From September 1st 1916 To September 30th 1916 Volume 5		
War Diary	Le Grand Paquat	01/09/1916	02/09/1916
War Diary	In The Trenches	03/09/1916	11/09/1916
War Diary	Laventie	12/09/1916	19/09/1916
War Diary	Trenches	20/09/1916	26/09/1916
War Diary	Laventie	27/09/1916	30/09/1916
Heading	War Diary of 2/6th Battalion Royal Warwickshire Regiment From 1st October 1916 To 31st October 1916 Volume VI		
War Diary	Laventie	01/10/1916	01/10/1916
War Diary	Trenches	02/10/1916	08/10/1916
War Diary	Laventie	08/10/1916	13/10/1916
War Diary	Trenches	14/10/1916	15/10/1916
War Diary	Laventie	15/10/1916	25/10/1916
War Diary	Trenches	26/10/1916	28/10/1916
War Diary	Laventie	28/10/1916	28/10/1916
War Diary	Merville	29/10/1916	31/10/1916
Heading	War Diary of 2/6th Battalion Royal Warwickshire Regiment From 1st November To 30th November 1916 Volume VII		
War Diary	Merville	01/11/1916	01/11/1916
War Diary	Busnes	02/11/1916	02/11/1916
War Diary	Auchel	03/11/1916	03/11/1916
War Diary	Magnicourt	04/11/1916	04/11/1916
War Diary	Houvin	05/11/1916	05/11/1916
War Diary	Bonnieres	06/11/1916	14/11/1916
War Diary	Bernaville	15/11/1916	15/11/1916
War Diary	Bertaucourt	16/11/1916	16/11/1916
War Diary	Robemprre	17/11/1916	17/11/1916
War Diary	Warloy	18/11/1916	20/11/1916
War Diary	Bouzincourt	21/11/1916	27/11/1916
War Diary	Hedauville	28/11/1916	30/11/1916
Heading	2/6th Battalion R. Warwickshire Regt War Diary December 1st 1916 to December 31st 1916 (Volume 8)		
War Diary	Hedauville	01/12/1916	01/12/1916
War Diary	Martinsart	02/12/1916	10/12/1916
War Diary	Wellington Huts	11/12/1916	14/12/1916
War Diary	In The Line	15/12/1916	19/12/1916
War Diary	Martinsart	20/12/1916	21/12/1916
War Diary	Hedauville	22/12/1916	31/12/1916
Heading	War Diary of 2/6th Battalion Royal Warwickshire Regiment From 1st January 1917 To 31st January 1917 Volume IX		
War Diary	Martinsart	01/01/1917	05/01/1917
War Diary	Warwick Huts	06/01/1917	12/01/1917
War Diary	In Trenches	13/01/1917	15/01/1917

War Diary	Rubempre	16/01/1917	16/01/1917
War Diary	Candas	17/01/1917	17/01/1917
War Diary	Domleger	18/01/1917	18/01/1917
War Diary	Canchy	19/01/1917	31/01/1917
Heading	War Diary of 2/6th Battalion Royal Warwickshire Regiment From February 1st 1917 To February 28th 1917 Volume X		
War Diary	Canchy	01/02/1917	04/02/1917
War Diary	Yaucourt Bussus	05/02/1917	12/02/1917
War Diary	Canchy	13/02/1917	14/02/1917
War Diary	Marcelcave	15/02/1917	18/02/1917
War Diary	Harbonnieres	19/02/1917	24/02/1917
War Diary	In Support	25/02/1917	28/02/1917
Heading	War Diary of 2/6th Battalion Royal Warwickshire Regiment From March 1st 1917 To March 31st 1917 Volume XI		
War Diary	Support Trenches Vermandovillers	01/03/1917	03/03/1917
War Diary	Front Line	04/03/1917	08/03/1917
War Diary	Vauvillers	09/03/1917	14/03/1917
War Diary	Trenches	15/03/1917	17/03/1917
War Diary	Licourt	18/03/1917	27/03/1917
War Diary	Devise	28/03/1917	29/03/1917
War Diary	Tertry	30/03/1917	31/03/1917
Heading	War Diary of 2/6th Battalion Royal Warwickshire Regiment From April 1st 1917 To April 30th 1917 Volume XII		
War Diary	Tertry	01/04/1917	05/04/1917
War Diary	Villevecque	06/04/1917	06/04/1917
War Diary	In The Line	07/04/1917	09/04/1917
War Diary	Villecholles	10/04/1917	10/04/1917
War Diary	Ugny	11/04/1917	19/04/1917
War Diary	Savy	20/04/1917	22/04/1917
War Diary	Brown Line 52 Section	22/04/1917	23/04/1917
War Diary	Outpost Line	24/04/1917	25/04/1917
War Diary	Outpost Line S 23.b 9 5 To S12.a.7.6	26/04/1917	27/04/1917
War Diary	Savy	28/04/1917	29/04/1917
War Diary	Brown Line S.14.b.5.5. S.15.d.1.0	30/04/1917	30/04/1917
Heading	War Diary of 2/6th Battalion Royal Warwickshire Regiment From May 1st To May 31st 1917 Volume XIII		
War Diary	S.14.b.5.5 S.15.d.1.0 Brown Line	01/05/1917	05/05/1917
War Diary	Outpost Line S.23.b.9.3 To S12.a.7.6	06/05/1917	09/05/1917
War Diary	Savy	10/05/1917	13/05/1917
War Diary	Beauvois	14/05/1917	14/05/1917
War Diary	Herley	15/05/1917	16/05/1917
War Diary	Longeau	17/05/1917	17/05/1917
War Diary	Flesselles	18/05/1917	20/05/1917
War Diary	Gezincourt	21/05/1917	22/05/1917
War Diary	Ivergny	23/05/1917	23/05/1917
War Diary	Berneville	24/05/1917	31/05/1917
Heading	War Diary of 2/6th Battalion Royal Warwickshire Regiment From June 1st, 1917 To June 30th 1917 Volume XIV		
War Diary	Berneville	01/06/1917	11/06/1917
War Diary	Dainville	12/06/1917	23/06/1917
War Diary	St Georges	24/06/1917	30/06/1917

Heading	War Diary of 2/6th Battalion Royal Warwickshire Regiment From July 1st 1917 To July 31st 1917 Volume XV		
War Diary	St. Georges	01/07/1917	23/07/1917
War Diary	Ligny-sur-Canux	24/07/1917	25/07/1917
War Diary	Roubrouck	26/07/1917	31/07/1917
Heading	War Diary of 2/6th Battalion Royal Warwickshire Regiment From August 1st 1917 To August 31st 1917 Volume XVI		
War Diary	Roubrouck	01/08/1917	16/08/1917
War Diary	Brandhoek Area (Divisional Reserve)	17/08/1917	25/08/1917
War Diary	Ypres North	26/08/1917	31/08/1917
Heading	War Diary of 2/6th Battalion Royal Warwickshire Regiment From September 1st 1917 To September 30th 1917 Volume XVII		
War Diary	Field	01/09/1917	07/09/1917
War Diary	Query Camp	08/09/1917	12/09/1917
War Diary	Ridge Camp	12/09/1917	14/09/1917
War Diary	Clyde Camp	15/09/1917	24/09/1917
War Diary	Field	24/09/1917	30/09/1917
Heading	War Diary of 2/6th Battalion Royal Warwickshire Regiment From October 1st 1917 To October 31st 1917 Volume XVIII		
War Diary	Field	01/10/1917	31/10/1917
Heading	War Diary of 2/6th Battalion The Royal Warwickshire Regiment From November 1st 1917 To November 30th 1917		
War Diary	Field	01/11/1917	08/11/1917
War Diary	In The Field	09/11/1917	30/11/1917
Heading	War Diary of 2/6th Battalion The Royal Warwickshire Regiment From December 1st 1917 To Decr 31st 1917 Volume XX		
War Diary	Field	01/12/1917	31/12/1917
Miscellaneous	Appendix 'A' to War Diary for December 1917		
Heading	War Diary of 2/6th Battalion Royal Warwickshire Regiment From January 1st To January 31st 1918 Volume XXI		
War Diary	In The Field	01/01/1918	31/01/1918
War Diary	Field	01/02/1918	28/02/1918
Heading	182nd Brigade 61st Division 2/6th Battalion Royal Warwickshire Regiment March 1918 & April		
War Diary	Field	01/03/1918	23/03/1918
Miscellaneous	Appendix 'B' Brief Summary Of Operations By Surplus Personnel Of Battalion From Night Of March 21st		
War Diary	Field	24/03/1918	30/04/1918
Miscellaneous	Appendix 'A'		
Miscellaneous	XVIII Corps No.G.a.155/5	10/04/1918	10/04/1918
Map	Lacouture		
Heading	War Diary of 2/6th Battalion Royal Warwickshire Regiment From May 1st To May 31st 1918 Volume XXV		
War Diary	Field 36 A.S.E 1/20,000	01/05/1918	14/05/1918
War Diary	36a.S.E 1/20,000	15/05/1918	22/05/1918
War Diary	36a. 1/40,000	23/05/1918	27/05/1918
War Diary	36a.S.E. 1/20,000	27/05/1918	31/05/1918

Heading	War Diary of 2/6th Battalion Royal Warwickshire Regiment From June 1st To June 30th 1918 Volume XXVI		
War Diary	In The Field	01/06/1918	30/06/1918
Heading	War Diary of 2/6th. Battalion The Royal Warwickshire Regiment From July 1st To July 31st 1918 Volume XXVII		
War Diary	In The Field Ref 36A S.E 1/20,000 Of 36 A 1/40,000	01/07/1918	05/07/1918
War Diary	In The Field	06/07/1918	31/07/1918
Operation(al) Order(s)	2/6th Bn. Royal Warwickshire Regiment Order No.115 dated 7/7/16	07/07/1918	07/07/1918
Miscellaneous	Appendix 'A'		
Miscellaneous	Appendix 'B'		
Operation(al) Order(s)	2/6th Bn. Royal Warwickshire Regiment Order No.117 dated 11/7/16	11/07/1918	11/07/1918
War Diary	Sheet 36.a.1/40000	01/08/1918	05/08/1918
War Diary	Sheet 36.a.N.E 1/20000	06/08/1918	22/08/1918
War Diary	Sheet 36.a 1/40000	23/08/1918	31/08/1918
Operation(al) Order(s)	2/6th Bn. Royal Warwickshire Regiment Order No.118 dated 7/8/16	07/08/1918	07/08/1918
Heading	War Diary of 2/6th Battalion Royal Warwickshire Regiment From September 1st 1918 To September 30th 1918 Volume XXIX		
War Diary	Sheet 36a N.W. 1/20,000 Sheet 36 N.W. 1/20,000	01/09/1918	21/09/1918
War Diary	Sheets 36 & 36a 1/40,000	22/09/1918	30/09/1918
Miscellaneous	2/6th. Bn. Royal Warwickshire Regiment Reference Map Sheet 36 N.W.	06/09/1918	06/09/1918
Heading	War Diary From 1st October To 31st October 1918 2/6th Battalion The Royal Warwickshire Regiment (Volume XXX)		
War Diary	Sheet 36 N.W. 1/20,000	01/10/1918	02/10/1918
War Diary	Lens II 1/100,000	03/10/1918	08/10/1918
War Diary	Valenciennes 12 1/100,000	09/10/1918	19/10/1918
War Diary	Sheet 57B 1/40,000	20/10/1918	21/10/1918
War Diary	Sheet 51A S.E. 1/20,000	22/10/1918	31/10/1918
Miscellaneous	2/6th Battalion Royal Warwickshire Regiment issued in Connection with Order No. 149	23/10/1918	23/10/1918
Heading	War Diary of 2/6th Bn. The Royal Warwickshire Regt From November 1st To 30th 1918 Volume XXXI		
War Diary	Sheet 51A 1/40,000	01/11/1918	10/11/1918
War Diary	Valenciennes 1/100000	11/11/1918	23/11/1918
War Diary	Lens 1/100000	24/11/1918	30/11/1918
Heading	War Diary of 2/6th Battalion Royal Warwickshire Regiment From December 1st 1918 To December 1918 Volume XXXII		
War Diary	Lens 1/100000	01/12/1918	31/12/1918
Heading	2/6th Bn Royal Warwickshire Regiment Copy of War Diary for The Month of January 1919 Volume XXXIII		
War Diary	Yvrench (Lens 1/100000)	01/01/1919	31/01/1919
Heading	War Diary for the month of February 1919 Volume XXXIV		
War Diary	Harfleur	01/02/1919	28/02/1919
Heading	2/6th Battalion The Royal Warwickshire Regiment War Diary for the month of March 1919 Volume XXXV		
War Diary	Harfleur	01/03/1919	02/03/1919
War Diary	Dieppe	03/03/1919	31/03/1919

Heading	2/6th. Battalion The Royal Warwickshire Regiment War Diary for the month of April 1919 Volume XXXVI		
War Diary	Dieppe	01/04/1919	30/04/1919
Heading	2/6th Battalion The Royal Warwickshire Regiment War Diary for the month of May 1919 Volume XXXVII		
War Diary	Dieppe	01/05/1919	31/05/1919
Heading	2/6th Battalion The Royal Warwickshire Regiment War Diary for the month of June 1919 Volume XXXVIII		
War Diary	Dieppe	01/06/1919	30/06/1919
Heading	2/6th Battalion Royal Warwickshire Regiment War Diary for the month of July 1919 Volume XXXIX		
War Diary	Martin Eglise	01/07/1919	01/07/1919
War Diary	Training Coy-'A' Coy	02/07/1919	14/07/1919
War Diary	Training Coy 'C' Coy	15/07/1919	16/07/1919
War Diary	Martin Eglise	17/07/1919	20/07/1919
War Diary	Training Coy-'C'	21/07/1919	27/07/1919
War Diary	Training Coy-'D'	28/07/1919	31/07/1919
Heading	2/6th Battalion Royal Warwickshire Regiment War Diary for the month of August 1919 Volume XL		
War Diary	Martin Eglise	01/08/1919	01/08/1919
War Diary	D Company	02/08/1919	10/08/1919
War Diary	All Un Employed Men	11/08/1919	31/08/1919
Heading	2/6th Battalion The Royal Warwickshire Regiment War Diary for the month of September 1919 Volume XLI		
War Diary	Martin Eglise	01/09/1919	22/09/1919

1002513052194002

61ST DIVISION
182ND INFY BDE

2-6TH BN R. WARWICKS.

~~MAY 1916 — FEB 1919~~

1915 SEP — ~~1916 JAN~~

~~1916 MAY~~ — 1919 FEB

(1916 FEB. MAR. APR. DIARIES MISSING)

SUMMARY OF WAR DIARY

of

2/6th BATTALION ROYAL WARWICKSHIRE REGIMENT.

August 1915.

Unit.	2/6th Batt. R. War. R.
Brigade.	182nd Infantry Brigade.
Division.	61st (South Midland) Division.
Mobilization Centre.	Thorp Street, Birmingham.
Temporary War Station.	Epping., Essex.
Stations since occupied subsequent to concentration:-	Northampton, Kelvedon, Epping, Colchester, Chelmsford, Epping.

(a) MOBILIZATION. Nil.

(b) CONCENTRATION AT WAR STATION. The Battalion remained at Epping during the whole of the month, temporarily moving to Galleywood for two days for the Inspection of the Division by Field Marshall, Earl Kitchener.

(c) ORGANIZATION FOR DEFENCE. Night air picquets have been detailed as usual.

(d) TRAINING. Coys. were taken every day in Physical Training and Bayonet Fighting under Coy. arrangements. The Officers were taken in a special Course of Map Reading.
Brigade and Battalion Tactical schemes for Officers & N.C.O's were also carried out. Battalion continued field training and Battalion and Brigade Field Days were arranged.
Night digging was carried out by the Battalion. The details - Signallers, Machine Guns & Scouts carried out their special work in field training and otherwise continued under selected Officers and N.C.O's.

(e) DISCIPLINE. The discipline of the Battalion continues good, and there is no serious crime.

(f) ADMINISTRATION.

1. Medical Services. General health very good. Inoculation is practically completed, and vaccination in progress. Dental treatment by dentist from Colchester continued.

2. Veterinary Services. Health of horses good.

3. Supply Services. Supply of food good and plentiful.

4. Transport Services. The Battalion is short of its full establishment of waggons and carts. Travelling kitchens are urgently needed.

5. Ordnance Services. All .303 Rifles have now been returned to Ordnance Officer Weedon. Dummy Cartridges for .256 still urgently needed. Also Machine Guns.

6. Billeting & Hutting. Nil.

Summary of War Diary.

(2)

7. Channels of Correspondence. Nil.

8. Range Construction. Nil.

9. Supply of Remounts. 8 more horses have been placed on the strength of the Battalion. 23 are still required.

(g) RE-ORGANIZATION OF T. F. UNITS INTO HOME & IMPERIAL SERVICE UNITS.

All Home Service Officers and men have been transferred to the 81st Provisional Batt. (T.F.)

(h) PREPARATION OF UNITS FOR IMPERIAL SERVICE. Nil. The strength of the Battalion is below 600.

Whitfield

Maldon,
Sept., 4th 1915.

Lieut. & A/Adjt., for
O.C. 2/6th Batt. R. War. R.,

Army Form C. 2118.

WAR DIARY
or
INTELLIGENCE SUMMARY.
(Erase heading not required.)

2/6th Battalion Royal Warwickshire Regt.,

Instructions regarding War Diaries and Intelligence Summaries are contained in F.S. Regs., Part II. and the Staff Manual respectively. Title pages will be prepared in manuscript.

Place	Date	Hour	Summary of Events and Information	Remarks and references to Appendices
Epping.	Sept. 1	1	Programme for the day cancelled in view of Battalion moving to Maldon to-morrow and special work arranged. One man demobilised for munitions work.	
"	"	2	Battalion moved to the Camp, Maldon Wick, marching to Brentwood by night march leaving the Camp Epping, at 1.1. a.m. and arriving at Brentwood 6.15 a.m. The Battalion then entrained and reached Maldon East Station at 8.15 a.m. arriving at the Camp 8.45 a.m.	
Maldon	"	3	7 Men being found medically unfit by Medical Board were transferred to the 61st Provisional Battalion (T.F.) with effect from this day.	
"	"	4	A lecture for all Officers was given by Lieut-Colonel Burrowes on the trenches at Maldon Wick. Lieut-Colonel J.J. Shannessy in command of all troops at Maldon. Eight men proceeded to Goldhanger on a Machine Gun Course. Captain J.A. Fyshe, 1/6th Batt. R. War. R. joined the Battalion. Captain J.A. Fyshe promoted to Major (temp.)	
"	"	5	Camp Church Service. One N.C.O. released for Munitions work.	
"	"	6	The trenches at Maldon Wick were manned by 'A' & 'B' Companies at 8.0 for 24 hours and all routine carried out under strict service conditions. Lieut. J.L. Padmore nominated for Musketry Course at Bisley commencing on the 13th inst.	
"	"	7	A Zeppelin approached within the vicinity of the Camp. All necessary action was taken, but no firing took place as it offered no target. Captain M.C. Wade detailed as Member of Court Martial assembling at Chelmsford on Tuesday the 7th inst.	
"	"	8	'A' & 'B' Companies were relieved in the trenches by 'C' & 'D' Companies who took them over for 24 hours.	
"	"	9	A Brigade Field day was held. The Battalion paraded at 7.30 a.m. and marched to Hatfield Peverel where the Brigade concentrated. In accordance with the special orders issued, the Battalion formed the reserve in the scheme with the 2/5th Batt. R. War. R. prepared to launch a counter attack. "No Parade" was sounded however, before the reserves were put into action.	
"	"	10	The programme of work was cancelled. In accordance with Brigade orders the Battalion continued musketry and arrangements were made for all trained men to pass the elementary preliminary tests. The Battalion was medically examined by the Medical Officer.	
"	"	11	A lecture and practical demonstration of "Trench Warfare" was given by Major J.A. Fyshe to all Officers and N.C.O.'s at the trenches. E.S. Nicholson gazetted 2/Lieut. 2/6th Batt. R. War. R. A Zeppelin passed S.W. of the Camp 11.25 p.m.	as from 16·1·16
"	"	12	Camp Church Service held. First line Transport inspected by O.C. 61st XXXXXXXXXX (S.M.) Divisional Train. Machine Gun Section complete, 24 men 3 N.C.O.'s under 2/Lieut. S. Balcon reported to	
"	"	13	Work as per programme. 2/Lieut. T.E. Price for Refresher Course at Goldhanger.	

Army Form C. 2118.

WAR DIARY
or
~~INTELLIGENCE~~ SUMMARY.xxx

2/6th Battalion Royal Warwickshire Regt.xxx

(Erase heading not required.)

Instructions regarding War Diaries and Intelligence
Summaries are contained in F. S. Regs., Part II.
and the Staff Manual respectively. Title pages
will be prepared in manuscript.

Place	Date	Hour	Summary of Events and Information	Remarks and references to Appendices
Maldon.	Sept. 13		(Continued) - Special Class of 16 men (4 from each Company) instructed under Captain W. Simms for Grenadier work. Available Officers also attend. Lieut. J. L. Pedmore attended Musketry Course at Bisley.	
"	14		Captain N. G. Chamberlain attended District Court Martial assembled at Chelmsford for instruction.	
"	15		Signalling Section and Scout Section parade as sections under Lieut. B. R. Saunders and 2/Lieut. M. K. Jackson respectively. Pte. Bennett No. 3234 gazetted 2/Lieut. S. Staffs. Regt., Sept. 12th discharged from the Battalion. Three bandsmen taken on strength of Battalion.	
"	16		Brigade Field day. Battalion paraded 8 a.m. and marched to Woodham Walter for Brigade training. Retreat onwards sounded at 6 p.m.	
"	17		In view of Brigade Field day route march as per programme cancelled. In place of this the Battalion carried on with Musketry (Standard Tests) and Final Assault practice. 27 Maps ¼" O.S. sheet 30 issued to each Company.	
"	18		Brigade Tactical scheme for Officers who assembled at Russell Green, as per general and special ideas issued. Special Class of prospective N.C.O's dismissed. No.3362.Pte.Jackson gazetted 2/Lieut 14th (Reserve) Cheshire Regt. 17th Sept. 1915 discharged from this Battalion to take up commission. 9 N.C.O's or men attended special class for Barr & Stroud Range finding under Lieut. A. C. Mackenzie for one week.	
"	19		Camp Service. Daily Routine as follows:- Reveille 5.45., Retreat 6. 0 p.m.	
"	20		16 Stretcher bearers brought up to full establishment strength parade under the Medical Officer. 4 N.C.O's report at Terling for Course. New special N.C.O's (Prospective) class started, 6 from each Company under Col: Sergt. Instructor Kirkham. Captain A. D. Willcox transferred to 3/6th Batt. R. War. R.	
"	21		Battalion Field day as per special ideas. Captain T. H. Lawley joined the Battalion from 3/6th Batt. R. War. R. Captain W. Simms detailed as Member of Court Martial assembling at Chelmsford. One N.C.O. attended Course at Military School of Engineering at Ongar. Court Martial on No.3873 Pte. Groves.	
"	21		Capt. H. M. Green 2/6th Batt. R. War. R. attached to Headquarters 61st (S.M.) Division.	
"	22		19 mules taken on strength of Battalion. Captain H. M. Green (gazetted) seconded and vacates appointment as Adjutant. 2/Lieut. D. Gee gazetted a service Battalion of the Regiment to be 2/Lieut. Sept. 19th.	
"	23		Brigade Field day. Battalion paraded at 5 a.m., and marched to Boreham Church, breakfast and dinner being served on the road, when an Advance Guard scheme was carried out. One N.C.O. (Sergt. Harris) retained at Godstone as Instructor for Grenadier Course.	
"	24		Owing to Brigade Field day yesterday, programme was cancelled and Musketry (Miniature Range firing) was continued. Captain W. Simms attended as a Member of Court Martial reassembled	Continued

Army Form C. 2118.

WAR DIARY
or
INTELLIGENCE SUMMARY

2/6th Battalion Royal Warwickshire Regt.

(Erase heading not required.)

Instructions regarding War Diaries and Intelligence Summaries are contained in F.S. Regs., Part II. and the Staff Manual respectively. Title pages will be prepared in manuscript.

Place	Date	Hour	Summary of Events and Information	Remarks and references to Appendices
Maldon.	Sept. 24 1915		(Continued) – at Chelmsford for trial of No.3574 Pte. S. Watts. In accordance with instructions from War Office, poster containing list of trades for munition workers was exhibited and attention of all ranks called to same, and men eligible for those trades called upon to report to the Orderly Room. Lieut. Bushnell A.V.C., attached to this unit for billetting and subsistence. Sergt. Cleaver, No.1898, detained as Instructor for Machine Gun course at Goldhanger.	
"	25		Battalion Tactical scheme for Officers carried out. Standard tests Musketry completed. Special class for backward men under L/Sergt. Kimberley. Sentence of District Court Martial on No.3873 Pte. Groves of 4 months imprisonment without hard labour promulgated.	
"	26		Camp Service held.	
"	27		Parades as per programme. Regimental Court Martial assembled at Maldon for trial of No. 3177 Pte. Yates. H.	
"	28		Programme cancelled. Battalion paraded for Close Order Drill, Musketry, Saluting Drill, Final Assault practice under Regimental. Sergt. Major. Brigade Exercise without troops for all Officers with Coy. Sergt. Majors, Platoon Sergeants, Observers, Scouts, Machine Guns, and Signalling Sections at Woodham Walter Church as per special orders. Certificates from School of Musketry at Bisley issued as follows:- Capt. A. D. Willcox, 1st class; Lieut. A.C. Mackenzie, 1st Class; No.398 Sergt. Davinson, 2nd. Class; No.2960 Coy. Sergt. Major Harper, 1st Class; No.1365 Sergt. Brown; 1st Class. No.3632, Sergt. Stinson; 1st class; No.3041 Coy.Q.M.Sergt.Melville, 1st class; No.1206.Sergt.Lee 2nd class. 90 men vaccinated in Camp. Maldon, Brigade Armourer Sergeant inspected Arms of Battalion. No.3177, Pte. Yates sentenced by Regimental Court Martial to 15 days detention for stealing various articles from comrades. 2/Lieut. F. A. Whitfield obtained 1st class musketry at Bisley and qualified 1st Class Instructor to use one man Range Finder.	
"	29		Wet day; Programme cancelled. Sentence of District Court Martial on No.3574, Pte. S. Watts of two years imprisonment, without hard labour, promulgated by Lieut. J.G. Whitfield A/Adjt.	
"	30		Brigade Training cancelled. Special Programme arranged. Sir George Marks, Representative of Minister of Munitions attended and addressed the Troops on importance of obtaining Skilled Munition Workers; Explained fully the scheme. 1 N.C.O. (Corpl. O.H. Smith) attended School of Cookery, Middlewick.	

For O/C. 2nd/6th. R. War. R.

Army Form C. 2118.

WAR DIARY
or
INTELLIGENCE SUMMARY

2/6th Battalion Royal Warwickshire Regiment.

(Erase heading not required.)

Instructions regarding War Diaries and Intelligence Summaries are contained in F. S. Regs., Part II. and the Staff Manual respectively. Title pages will be prepared in manuscript.

Place	Date	Hour	Summary of Events and Information	Remarks and references to Appendices
Maldon.	Oct. 1st.		Programme cancelled. Brigade Field day was carried out in the neighbourhood of Hatfield Peverel, the troops occuping same position as when "Stand Fast" was sounded for the last Brigade day. Special orders were issued and a further phase of the general idea carried out. Troops returned at three o'clock. Coy. Q. M. Sergt. B. G. Sutters on being gazetted to a commission in the 3/6th Batt. R. War. R. struck off strength of this Battalion.	
"	" 2nd.		Parades as per programme.	
"	" 3rd.		Camp Church Service held.	
"	" 4th.		Programme carried out. No.3800.Pte.Walker.W.proceeded to Leamington for cold shoeing course. No.3262.Sergt.Twelftree proceeded to Bisley for Musketry Course. 2/Lieut. D. Gee proceeded to Woolwich for course in Transport.	
"	" 5th.		Brigade Field day cancelled. Battalion paraded on Battalion Parade Ground.- Skilled Investigator attended and interviewed men who had put down their names for Munitions work. Special aircraft Observation Post mounted daily on Town Hall.	
"	" 6th.		Parades as per programme. 2/Lieut. E. S. Nicholson proceeded to Chelmsford for elementary Course.	
"	" 7th.		Brigade Field training. Special anti-aircraft firing picquet selected to parade daily at Retreat consisting of 10 good shots from each Coy. Special Hostile Aircraft Alarm Orders issued. Special Class in Chiropody under L/Corpl. F. Walker, Battalion Chiropodist. Lieut. E. Osborne, R.A.M.C.(T) promoted to Captain (August 16th)	
"	" 8th.		Parades as per programme. Machine Gun Section complete in personnel moved to Denbury and was brigaded with other sections. Court assembled for report on unserviceable clothing. Four men transferred to 81st Provisional Battalion.	
"	" 9th.		Battalion Exercise for Officers under Major J. A. Fyshe consisting of set of questions on field work.	
"	" 10th.		Camp Church Service.	

WAR DIARY or INTELLIGENCE SUMMARY.

Army Form C. 2118.

2/6th Battalion Royal Warwickshire Regiment.

(Erase heading not required.)

Instructions regarding War Diaries and Intelligence Summaries are contained in F. S. Regs, Part II. and the Staff Manual respectively. Title pages will be prepared in manuscript.

Place	Date	Hour	Summary of Events and Information	Remarks and references to Appendices
Maldon.	Oct. 1915 11th.		Coy.Sergt.Major Turner proceeded to Chelsea for Course at London School of Instruction. Court Martial at Chelmsford on No.3081.Pte.Cooper.H.	
"	12th.		Brigade Training. Battalion marched to Great Totham and occupied section of trenches on Heybridge to Braxted line. Trenches were manned for 24 hours and ordinary routine carried out. Successful communication was maintained. Battalion returned to permanent quarters.	
"	13th.			
"	14th.		No.30.6.Cpl. F. E. Brooks proceeded to Great Dunmow for Signalling Course.	
"	15th.		Foggy day. Brigade tactical exercise cancelled. O.C., A.S.C., inspected 1st Line Transport. 2/Lieut. O. Shenn proceeded to Onger for Engineering Course. Grenadier Specialists selected.	
"	16th.		Battalion Exercise for Officers & N.C.O's carried out as previously embracing an attack. Lieut. J. L. Padmore obtained a "Distinguished" at recent Musketry Course at Bisley.	
"	17th.		Camp Church Service held.	
"	18th. 19th.		Battalion took part in Brigade training in connection with Third Army Exercise, as per scheme and special orders issued. The Battalion marched with rest of the Brigade to Tiptree and occupied a position as per orders. The men were close billeted for the night. Following day Brigade retired from its position and the Battalion formed rear guard and protection while Outpost Line (2/5th Batt. R. War. R.) was withdrawn. The Battalion also formed line of protection while two other Battalions in Brigade occupied an entrenched position, and then took up position in reserve at Great Totham and was billeted there for the night. The following morning (21st) orders were received to return to permanent quarters.	
"	20th. 21st.			
"	22nd.		7, Rifles complete were transferred from the Battalion to the 64th Provisional Batt. Cromer.	
"	23rd.		Battalion Exercise for Officers under Major J. A. Fyshe. Coy. Sergt. Major. H. Harper gazetted to 2/Lieut. R. Warwicks.	
"	24th.		Camp Service.	

Army Form C. 2118.

WAR DIARY
or
~~INTELLIGENCE~~ SUMMARY.

2/6th Battalion Royal Warwickshire Regiment.

(Erase heading not required.)

Instructions regarding War Diaries and Intelligence Summaries are contained in F. S. Regs., Part II and the Staff Manual respectively. Title pages will be prepared in manuscript.

Place	Date	Hour	Summary of Events and Information	Remarks and references to Appendices
Maldon.	Oct. 25th.		Semaphore Course for Junior Officers under Lieut. B. R. Saunders. Special Signalling Class and telephone work at Brigade. A party of 2 Sergeants, 3 Corporals and 3 men (all selected) proceeded to Birmingham in connection with recruiting for the 6th Warwicks.	
"	26th.		Battalion moved into billets at Maldon. 3 men released for Munitions work under authority of War Office letter. Battalion Headquarters moved to "The Gables" High Street, Maldon.	
"	27th.		Address by Lord Salisbury at Chelmsford on "Courts Martial and duties of Officers in connection with the same" for Commanding Officers, Adjutants and Field Officers.	
"	28th.		Wet day. Divisional Tactical exercise previously cancelled. Lectures were given under Coy. arrangements in suitable buildings.	
"	29th.		Battalion Training.	
"	30th.		Two men transferred to Administrative Centre for Munitions work. Tactical questions for Officers under Major J. A. Fyshe.	
"	31st.		Battalion paraded for service at All Saints Church. Anti-aircraft firing picquet discontinued. The following have been received during the month:- 2 Horses. 4 Travelling Kitchens. 1 Maltese Cart. 1 Water Cart. Amongst other stores the undermentioned has been received:- 1 Mounted Tripod Mark IV.	

Mitchell
Lieut. & A/Adjt., for
O.C. 2/6th Batt. R. War. R.

Right Column Order.
No 24.

Copy No

Ref ½" OS.
Sheet 30.

1/6 Royal Warks
182 Infy Bde

10.15
30-10-15

1. Information.

Enemy advanced troops on line GREAT BENTLEY — ARDLEIGH at 5 am this day.

Our own troops will occupy existing entrenchments immediately on the line TOTHAM HILL — WITHAM.

Div Cyclist Co will protect right flank in conjunction with Westminster Dragoons.

2. Detail.

Right column will withdraw in order as per attached march table.

3. Starting Pt.

Road Junction S of O in 180. Head of main body will pass S.P. at 11 am.

4. Outposts

Will be withdrawn immediately Rear Guard are in position.

5. Transport.

First line transport less S A A Tool Carts & mules will be hypassed under B.T.O.

6
Defence.

2/7th & 2/8th R. War. R. will occupy trenches as follows. 2/8th R. War. R. from FABIANS FARM about 650 x E of Road junction point 128 inclusive to Road junction N of G in GREAT TOTHAM (North) Exclusive.

2/7th R. War. R. from road junction N of G in GREAT BRAXTED inclusive to road at G in GREAT BRAXTED inclusive

2/5th & 2/6th R. War R in reserve at WICKHAM BISHOPS

O.C. R.A. will select positions for R.A.

7
Billets.

Billeting parties of 2/5th & 2/6th R. War. R. will meet Staff Capt. at X roads at 2nd S of WICKHAM BISHOPS at noon.

8
Supplies.

Bde issuing Pt X roads at G 2.5 of WICKHAM BISHOPS. Bn Transport Officers will report there at 4 pm.

9
Reports.

To rear of main body during march. After to HIGH HALL WICKHAM BISHOPS

10
Dressing Station.

LANGFORD. Advanced D.S. Schools at WICKHAM BISHOPS.

Time 10.35 am

P. L. Stothyns
Capt & Bde.

March Table.

Adv Gd.   1 Platoon   2/5th Rwn R.

Main Body.   Brigadier 1st line Transport.
Fld Amb less 1 Sec.
Bde Amm Coln.
2/5th Rwn R.
2/7th   "
Bde R.F.A. less 1 Batt.
2/8th Rwn R.
Bde Hdqrs.

Rear Gd.
Comdr Col Shaunessy
2/6th Rwn   1 Batt R.F.A.
2/6th Bn Rwn R.
1 Sec Fld Amb.

Army Form C. 2118.

WAR DIARY
or
INTELLIGENCE SUMMARY

(Erase heading not required.)

2/6th Batt. Royal Warwickshire Regiment.

Instructions regarding War Diaries and Intelligence Summaries are contained in F. S. Regs., Part II. and the Staff Manual respectively. Title pages will be prepared in manuscript.

Place	Date	Hour	Summary of Events and Information	Remarks and references to Appendices
Maldon.	1915 Nov. 1st.		Battalion and Company training was proceeded with. Specialist classes arranged and night bayonet fighting carried out. 2/Lieut. F. A. Whitfield reported at Aldershot for Gymnasia Course. Capt. W. Simms proceeded to Godstone for Grenade Course. Sergt. Crosbee reported for same course. Third Class for prospective N.C.O's commenced, and second class for Backward men commenced under special instructors.	
	" 2nd.			
	" 3rd.			
	" 4th.		Divisional Tactical Exercise was carried out in the neighbourhood of GAY BOWERS. The Battalion was in reserve with 2/8th Batt. R. War. R., the Brigade forming a Flank guard and being attacked by the 183rd Infantry Brigade. The reserves were not called upon. No.3883.Pte.Bartholomew discharged under para.392 (6a) King's Regulations. No.3908.Pte.Hill.A.V. released for Munitions. Inlying Picquet paraded and acts duties of anti-aircraft firing picquet under special instructions – for alternate weeks with 2/8th Batt. R. War. R. Special Observation Post mounted at Town Hall as usual.	
	" 5th.		Lieut-Col. J. J. Shannessy appointed Purchasing Officer of Supplies for the 61st (S.M.)Division.	
	" 6th.		Battalion Exercise for Officers under Major J. A. Fyshe on trench warfare. Individual training during the winter months was entered upon. Programmes arranged in accordance with Divisional Scheme. Special Musketry Classes started, one for Officers under Captain A. E. Whitfield, Sergeants Class under Lieut. J. L. Padmore, and Corporals Class under 2/Lieut. H. Harper. 2/Lieut. R. C. Taylor proceeded to Ongar for Military Engineering Course. No.3285 Pte Spencer and No.3083 Pte.Breeze released for Munitions, and transferred to Administrative Centre.	
	" 7th.			
	" 8th.			
	" 9th.			
	" 10th. " 11th.		Eleven riding horses received for distribution in the Brigade and attached to this Unit.	
	" 12th.		Lecture for Officers by Major Hutchinson, General Staff, Third Army, on "Occupation of Trenches", and Reconnaissance from Trenches".	
	" 13th.		Lieut. B. R. Saunders reported at Brigade Headquarters for signalling course of instruction.	
	" 14th.		Inlying Picquet and anti-aircraft picquet provided by 2/8th Batt. R. War. R. for week ending 20th Nov. Special Observation Post mounted at Town Hall as usual.	

1377 Wt.W10791/1773 500,000 1/15 D. D. & L. A.D.S.S./Forms/C. 2118.

Army Form C. 2118.

WAR DIARY

or

~~INTELLIGENCE~~ SUMMARY~~xxx~~ of 2/6th Battalion Royal Warwickshire Regiment.

(Erase heading not required.)

Instructions regarding War Diaries and Intelligence Summaries are contained in F. S. Regs., Part II. and the Staff Manual respectively. Title pages will be prepared in manuscript.

Place	Date	Hour	Summary of Events and Information	Remarks and references to Appendices
Maldon.	Nov. 15th. 191		Individual Training as per special programmes continued.	
"	16th.		Lecture for Officers by Lieut. A. H. Chovil, B.M.G.O. on the "Machine Gun". No. 2300.Pte. Malcolm.H. and No.1938.Pte.Leonard.H. released for Munitions and transferred to the Administrative Centre. 524 rifles (.305 Lee-Enfield Rifle IX and 220 Lee-Metford IX) received from Ordnance, Devonport.	
"	17th.		Divisional Tactical Exercise arranged but postponed on account of bad weather, and fall of snow. Work carried on as per programme in selected buildings.	
"	18th.		Lecture by Lieut. A. H. Chovil, (B.M.G.O) to N.C.O's on the "Machine Gun".	
"	19th.) 20th.) 21st.)		Routine work was carried on.	
"	22nd.		Brigade Tactical Exercise was carried out in vicinity of LODGE FARM X ROADS. The Battalion with rest of Brigade marched N. to join the 61st (S.M.) Division operating about WITHAM. On receipt of news that enemy was retiring, and small force with guns endeavouring to escape by ULTING WICK the Battalion received orders to take up position in firing line, and successfully caused the Force to retire. Two men transferred to the 81st Provisional Battalion (T.F.)	
"	23rd.		.305 Rifles issued in exchange for .256 Rifles.	
"	24th.		2/Lieut. F. W. Shannessy proceeded to Kelvedon for Trench Fighting Course.	
"	25th.		Lecture to Officers on Machine Gun by Lieut. A. H. Chovil (B.M.G.O)	
"	26th.) 27th.) 28th.) 29th.) 30th.)		Three men released for Munitions work and transferred to the Administrative Centre. (Inlying Picquet & anti aircraft firing picquet provided by the 2/8th Batt. R. War. R. for week (commencing 28th inst.	

Lieut. & Adjt.
Capt. 2/Adjt.
For O/C. 2nd/6th; R. War. R.

1577 Wt. W10791/1773 500,000 1/15 D. D. & L.   A.D.S.S./Forms/C. 2118.

CONFIDENTIAL.

War Diary of

2/6th Battalion Royal Warwickshire Regiment.

from 1st December 1915, to 31st December 1915.

Volume 2.

WAR DIARY

Army Form C. 2118.

INTELLIGENCE SUMMARY. 2/6. R. War. R.

Place	Date	Hour	Summary of Events and Information	Remarks and references to Appendices
Maldon	1.12.15		C.S.M. Rodgewell army gym; diff. units of the Battalion. and both afternoon classes of 10 N.C.Os. in Bayonet fighting & W.O. Letter dated 8 Nov. 1915: ho 9/hf/ two officers transferred to 3/6. R. War. R. viz: W.A. Martin. 2/Lt Campbell. 2/Lt R.C. Taylor. 2 (F.F.3). 2/Lt Morris B.D. 2/Lt W.A. Martin. 2/Lt J.N. Campbell. 2/Lt R.C. Taylor. 2/Lt R.S. Nicholson. Individual training continued. Specialists classes were Specialist officers and Instructors.	[signature]
	2.12.15		C.S.M. Rodgewell took all companies in Physical drill & Bayonet fighting A.M. and officers and N.C.Os in Physical drill P.M. Final stage of musketry Range Competition fired at Woodham Mortimer range for cup presented by G.O.C. Division. Was one of sons of his uncle Observation Post mounted at Town Hall, Maldon daily on hours after sunset manned by the Battalion. Authorities for week ending December 5th inclusive.	[signature]
	3.12.15		[illegible] three officers. i.e. 2/Lt N. Cor Marsden, 2/Lt W. [illegible] for course at female work Lodge Farm, Tubspring Elms - PT 333 - OAK INN - MALDON	[signature]
	4.12.15		and N. Co Sergeant Rochfort Musketry Course at Ongar and two officers transferred to 2/6 R. War. R. viz: 2/Lt J & R.C. Martin, 2/Lt R.C. Baylis. authority	[signature]

WAR DIARY
INTELLIGENCE SUMMARY

2/6. R. War. R.

Army Form C. 2118.

Place	Date	Hour	Summary of Events and Information	Remarks and references to Appendices
Maldon (continued)	5.12.15		W.O. instructed 8 Nov.1915– H.Q. Inf./2 T.F.3). Enemy and anti-aircraft firing Parade mounted by this Battalion for week Dec. 11th inclusive. Church Parade.	M.R.
	6.12.15		Observation Co mounted by 2/8th R. War. R. from 6.12.15 – 15.12.15 inclusive. One Officer (Lt. B.R. Saunders) proceeded to DUNMOW on Shelley guard. One N.Co. proceeded to Brley for musketry course.	M.R. M.R.
	7.12.15	8.12.15	Sig N.Co. Individual training. One officer (Lt. B.F. Hartman) proceeded to R017 FORD to course of instruction Battalion P.S. March MALDON WICK-IMP.DEM.GOS-WHITE ELM-then Company order.	M.R. M.R.
	9.12.15		Range firing was continued, 8 men under Lt J.Gadmore for aerial munition on Book & Stored Range fixed and the performed recorded instructors in charge Rifles examined by Brigade Armourer. Report received Co-Company. As Co a result of a recent examination found by Brigade Armourer the following minor rifles were found in need of examination and repair in addition of accordance with reports were effected. Individual training. Capt. J.H. Godby transferred to 3/6th R.War.R.	M.R.
			Sir N.Co. & men ordered for munitions — W.O. instructed new authority W.O. instructed	M.R.
?	10.12.15		6 Nov.1915 – H.Q. Inf./2. (T.F.3). transferred temporarily and temporarily to admin.	M.R.

Battalion Route march – Route Iveybridge – PL 128 – S of BEACON HILL – Priory Boundary

Army Form C. 2118.

WAR DIARY
or
INTELLIGENCE SUMMARY.
(Erase heading not required.)

2/6. R. War. R

Place	Date	Hour	Summary of Events and Information	Remarks and references to Appendices
	11.12.15.		BLAXTED PARK - Good join W. of school. HEYBRIDGE - Individual training - Church Parade.	Illr.
	12.12.15.		Coll. Halsey cool ord aircraft giving lecture promised by 2/6 R. War. R for next evening Dec. 18th meeting.	Illr.
	13.12.15.		Observation Post of TOWN HALL, MALDON provided by NCO. the battalion for week ending 19.12.15 inclusive. Individual training. 2/Lieut G. S. Willis reported for machine gun course at Bisley. Coy. S. M. Dennison no 398 reported at Chelsea for course qualification.	Illr.
	14.12.15.		On instruction from Bde HdQts in squads of HEYBRIDGE BASIN and MARINE LAKE were taken over from the 8th Prov. Bait. and provided by battalion. Route March, route L of LINGBROOK - T of TYNGDALES - R. of RUSSELL GREEN - M. of MALDON WEST - road training & judging distance practical carried on march. Capt Chamberlain interviewed 6/5/6 R.War.R. temporarily retaining until one Batt. on duty.	Illr.
	15.12.15.		Individual training = 0	
	16.12.15		Individual training	
	17.12.15		official J.P. Campbell transferred to 3/6. R. War. R. Authority W.O. letters quoted above	Illr.

WAR DIARY
or
INTELLIGENCE SUMMARY.
(Erase heading not required.)

2/6. R. War. R.

Army Form C. 2118.

Place	Date	Hour	Summary of Events and Information	Remarks and references to Appendices
Maldon	17.12.15		Batt. Route March. HEYBRIDGE – Rd. HEYBRIDGE – N. of COBBS FARM. – HALL Rd Juncⁿ. S.W. of TOLLESHUNT D'ARCY. – LITTLE RENTERS FARM. –	JW
	18.12.15		Individual training	
	19.12.15		Church Parade.	JW
	20.12.15		All garrison duties company. observation Post. Salving, wire except for Piquet – HEYBRIDGE BASIN Road. HARINE LAKE head. – Patrol – Isolation stores provided by 2/5 R.War.R. For week ending 26.12.15 inclusive. Individual training	JW
	21.12.15		Batt. Route March. HEYBRIDGE – LANGFORD – X roads SMITH – ULTING WICK – MANOR FM –	JW
	22.12.15		2/4 & 2/7 R.Warwick. & 2 U. Coy. reported at Kelvedon for attack. Fighting course. Individual training	JW
	23.12.15		Special lectures given by an officer R.E. Individual training	
	24.12.15		Batt. Route March. X roads SG FM NW. HUNDON WITH PURLEIGH – HAZELEIGH – WOODHAM MORTIMER HALL – DANBURY/HATDON rd.	JW
	25.12.15 9.30 am		Christmas day. Special Church Parade. His Majesty Christmas greeting received and read to the troops –	JW
	26.12.15		Church parade:-	JW
	27.12.15		Garrison duties taken over by the battalion. for week ending 2.1.16. inclusive	JW
	28.12.15		No Parades.	JW
			Batt. Route March. HEYBRIDGE – LANGFORD. BEELEIGH ABBEY. 6 men transferred released for munitions and hanging to Admin. Centre.	JW
	29.12.15		One man reported at Bermondsey Lond. for cookery course. Individual training. Order received to practice march 31:1:15. received from Brigade Headquarters "A" appendix A	JW

WAR DIARY or INTELLIGENCE SUMMARY.

Army Form C. 2118.

2/6. R. War. R.

Place	Date	Hour	Summary of Events and Information	Remarks and references to Appendices
	30.12.15.		Guards at HEYBRIDGE BASIN. and MARINE LAKE withdrawn on instructions from Brigade. Individual training.	JMW.
	31.12.15.		Battalion paraded at 6.30.a.m for Brigade practice march returning to billets - 3.30 p.m. the mounted officers reporting at 11.30 a.m. at Red deer Lodge for a reconnaissance of the position adopted from the orders. Report attached. On march transferred to 8th Gen. Batt. Strength of the Battalion reduced to 31 officers including 5 attached, and 555 other ranks.	appendix "B" JMW.

(signed on Service)

For O/C. 2nd/6th. R. War. R.

Appendix "A".

Practice March 31st December 1915.

182nd Brigade.

OPERATION ORDERS

by

Brigadier General E. K. Daubeney Commanding.

- - - - - - - - - - - - - - - - -

SECRET   Copy No............

2/6th BATTALION ROYAL WARWICK REGIMENT.

OPERATION ORDERS

Ref ½" O.S.
Sheet 30.   31. 12. 15.

1. Information. 'B' Composite Brigade (less Artillery) will assemble at COLD NORTON at 11 a.m. Friday 31st December 1915.

2. Intention. Troops will be prepared to occupy the position ALTHORNE Station – ALTHORNE BARNS, – LAWLING HALL – MARSH HOUSE. Position will not be occupied, but while troops are resting and feeding mounted officers will carry out a reconnaissance of the position, the approaches thereto, and the artillery positions.

3. Detail. The 2/6th Batt. R. War. R. will parade in column of route outside Headquarters, High Street, MALDON at 8.30 a.m.

Starting Point. The head of the column will be at the Railway Bridge W of MALDON at 8.45 a.m.

1st Line Transport. The 1st Line Transport will be in position outside All Saints Church, High Street, MALDON facing N, ready to move off in rear of the Battalion.

4. Protection. O.C.Cyclist Co will be responsible for the protection of the Brigade at point of assembly.

5. Reconnaissce. All Mounted Officers will report to G.O.C. at the RED LION, LATCHINGDON at 11.30 a.m.

6. Reports. Reports to head of column.

7. Routine. O.C.Coys. will strictly adhere to all necessary details and orders contained in the Alarm Orders previously issued with the following exceptions:-

Iron rations, Field dressings, and Operation maps will not be issued, but all arrangements will be made to do so.

O.C.Coys. will render parade state to the Sergeant Major at Headquarters at 7.30 a.m. certain.

Time..5.30.a.m.

Copies as per distribution list.

(Signed) J. G. Whitfield,
Lieut. & A/Adjt.,
2/6th Batt. R. War. R.

SECRET   Copy No. 5

                    182n Inf. Bde Order No 30

Ref ½" O.S.
Sheet 30.   29. 12. 15.

1.   'B' Composite Brigade (less Artillery) will assemble
Information.   at COLD NORTON at 11 a.m. Friday 31st December 1915.

2.   Troops will be prepared to occupy the position
Intention.   ALTHORNE Station - ALTHORNE BARNS, - LAWLING HALL -
                MARSH HOUSE. Position will not be occupied, but
                while troops are resting and feeding mounted officers
                will carry out a reconnaissance of the position,
                the approaches thereto, and the artillery positions.

3.   Troops will assemble in fields immediately E of
Detail.   COLD NORTON Station as follows:-

                Cyclist Co less 2 platoons by route as previously
                            instructed.

                2/2nd R.F.A.Bde (officers only) by route as previously
                            instructed.

                2/2nd Fld Co R.E. by route as previously instructed
                            joining DANBURY column at Rd junc N of
                            1st L in LITTLE GRANGE at 9.30 a.m.

                182nd Inf Bde. Bde Hdqrs, 2/5th & 2/7th Bn. R.War.R.
                            will pass RUNSELL GREEN at 9.7 a.m. in
                            order named. 2/6th and 2/8th Bns. R.War.R.
                            will join the Brigade at X Rds at HAZELEIGH
                            CHURCH at 9.50 a.m. in order named.

                No 2 Fld Amb by route as previously instructed.

4.   O.C.Cyclist Co will be responsible for the protection
Protection.   of the Brigade at point of assembly.

5.   All Mounted Officers will report to G.O.C. at the
Reconnaissce.   RED LION, LATCHINGDON at 11.30 a.m.

6.
Reports.   To head of 182nd Inf. Bde.

Time.. 2.0....

Copies as per distribution list.

                                        (Sgd) O.P.L.Hoskyns, Capt.,
                                              B.M. 182nd Infantry Bde.

INSTRUCTIONS

i. This is a practice march.

ii. Preserved meat and biscuit will be drawn for 31. 12. 15.

iii. Iron rations, Field Dressing and Operation Maps will NOT be issued but all arrangements will be made to do so.

iv. Units will report time taken to turn out to Bde Hdqrs by 6 p.m. 31. 12. 15.

v. Parade States will be handed to Staff Capt 182nd Inf. Bde at point of assembly.

vi. Units will report time of their departure direct to Divisional Headquarters.

Appendix "B".

Practice March, 2/6th Battalion,
Royal Warwickshire Regiment, 31st December 1915.
- - - - - - - - - -

Report by Lieutenant and Acting Adjutant J. G. Whitfield.
- - - - - - - - - -

1. SCHEME. The Battalion took two hours to move off under Alarm Orders and paraded 24 Officers, including attached, and 373 other ranks.

2. General Remarks.

The Battalion halted at COLD NORTON. No man fell out on the march. The Battalion returned to billets at 3.30 p.m.

Mounted Officers met the G.O.C. at the RED LION, LATCHINGDON, at 11.30 a.m. and made a reconnaissance of the position as indicated in the orders.

Lieutenat & Acting Adjutant,
2/6th Battalion
Royal Warwickshire Regiment.

CONFIDENTIAL

War Diary of

2/6th Battalion Royal Warwickshire Regiment.

from 1st January, 1916 to 31st January 1916.

Volume 3.

WAR DIARY

INTELLIGENCE SUMMARY. 2/6. R. War. R.

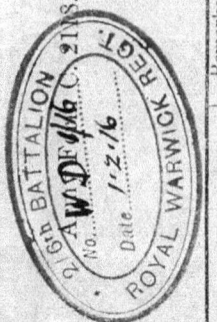

Place	Date	Hour	Summary of Events and Information	Remarks and references to Appendices
MALDON.	1.1.16.		Individual training. Lt. Col. SHANNESSY proceeded on short leave. Major FYSHE assumed command of the Battalion.	Flur.
	2.1.16.	9.45 a.m	Church Parade.	Flur.
	3.1.16.		Lt. Col. SHANNESSY proceeded to FRANCE on a short tour of duty for 4 days at GEN. HEAD QUARTERS. B.E.F. Major FYSHE assumed command of the Battalion. Individual training. 1 man released for munitions, transferred to ADMIN. CENTRE. No 3774 Pte ROBINSON A. proceeded to LEAMINGTON for cadet training course. One officer attended at sections of "tactical training" - 2/Lieut L.T. DAVIES reported at BISLEY for machine gun course. 1 N.C.O reported at BISLEY for musketry course.	Flur.
	4.1.16		Route March. Route. HEYBRIDGE - LANGFORD GROVE. at TOTHAM. TOLLESHUNT MAJOR. LITTLE RENTERS FARM. (Ref. 1/2". O.S. Sheet 30). orders for Brigade tactical exercise 5.1.16 received from O.C. TROOPS. MALDON. 1 man released for munitions and transferred to ADMIN. CENTRE.	appendix (1)
	5.1.16.	12.30 p.m.	Battalion paraded at 9.45a.m for Brigade tactical exercise which consisted of deploying and communication in firing line. N.C.O 182nd Inf.Bde commented on the importance of rapidity in deploying and extensions not being clearly observed by M.G. Colonel.	Flur.
	6.1.16.		2/Lt HARPER reported at ONGAR for military engineering course.	Flur.
	7.1.16		Individual training	Flur.

WAR DIARY
INTELLIGENCE SUMMARY.

Army Form C. 2118.

2/6. R. War. R.

(Erase heading not required.)

Place	Date	Hour	Summary of Events and Information	Remarks and references to Appendices
MALDON (continued)	8.1.16.		Individual training. 1 man. reported at ENFIELD for course on minor repair to small arm. Lt. Col. SHAWNESSY resumed command of the Battalion on his return from four overseas.	
	9.1.16.		Church Parade.	
	10.1.16.		Individual training. Garrison duties provided by the Battalion for week ending 16.1.16. 1 man reported at WOOLWICH for course in repair of service bicycle. Route march on progress. LODGE FARM – RUSSELL GREEN – WIGBOROUGH CHURCH (ref 1/2" O.S sheet 30). 1 man reported at ST. ALBANS for Army course 2 men released for munitions. 1 transferred to ADMIN. CENTRE, Detachment strength 15. 26 Officers retained Saturday on leave, 554 other ranks.	
	11.1.16.			
	12.1.16.		Individual training.	
	13.1.16.		Battalion paraded at 9.30.a.m for Brigade drill at WOODHAM WALTER. GOLF LINKS (Ref 1/2" O.S sheet 30) returning - Shelley - at 1.30. At St.M.Pam. Batt. strength 649 other ranks to ST.P.Pam. Batt. strength 649 other ranks	
	14.1.16.		Route March. Route. HEY BRIDGE. HATFIELD GREEN – WICKHAM BISHOPS. LANG FORD GROVE (ref 1/2" O.S sheet 30). 1 man returned from furlough - Non munition	
	15.1.16.		Individual training.	
	16.1.16.		Church Parade.	
	17.1.16.		Individual training. Diary forwarded by 2/6 R. War R. for week ending 23.1.16.	

Army Form C. 2118.

WAR DIARY
or
INTELLIGENCE SUMMARY. 2/6. R. WAR. R.
(Erase heading not required.)

Instructions regarding War Diaries and Intelligence Summaries are contained in F.S. Regs., Part II. and the Staff Manual respectively. Title pages will be prepared in manuscript.

Place	Date	Hour	Summary of Events and Information	Remarks and references to Appendices
MALDON (continued)	18.1.16		Individual training. 1 N.C.O. reported at GODSTONE for Grenade Course. 1 man released for hairdressing transferred to ADMIN. CENTRE. Draft of 210 men received from 3/6. R. WAR. R.	JW.
	19.1.16		Individual training. The Battalion was inspected at work by Maj. Gen. G.T. DICKSON, Inspector of Infantry. Died B.R. SAUNDERS obtaining 1st cl. certificate at "Entrenched" at III'd ARMY. Signally Course. DUNMOW.	JW.
	20.1.16		Individual training. Battalion joined inspected by Inspector of Physical exercises and Bayonet fighting.	JW.
	21.1.16		Individual training.	JW.
	22.1.16		Battalion drill under Reg. Serj. Major. Officer reconnaissance scheme at QT. TOTHAM. March. C.Q.M.S. MELVILLE posted to communion in the 3/6 S. STAFFS. REGT. return of strengths of the battalion, with effect from 15.1.16. 1 man released for munitions transferred to ADMIN. CENTRE.	JW.
	23.1.16	9.30 am	Church Parade.	JW.
	24.1.16		Individual training. General articles perused by this Battalion for week ending 30.1.16. 2/Lt WILLIS obtained "Order granted" posted in general gun course. BISLEY. 2/Lt STANNESS reported at LONDON DISTRICT SCHOOL of INSTRUCTION CHELSEA for course. 2/Lt. MARTINEAU reported at BISLEY for machine gun course. 1 N.C.O. reported for course of instruction.	JW.

1577 Wt. W10791/1773 500,000 1/15 D.D.&L.   A.D.S.S./Forms/C. 2118.

WAR DIARY
or
INTELLIGENCE SUMMARY.
(Erase heading not required.)

Army Form C. 2118.

2/6. R. War. W.

Place	Date	Hour	Summary of Events and Information	Remarks and references to Appendices
MALDON (cont'd)				
	25.1.16		I.N.C.O. reported at BISLEY for Musketry Course. 100 shot M.L.E. rifle Mk III * received in store.	W.
	26.1.16		Lecture by Lt Col S+HANNESSY on "notes on my visit to the front". Individual training.	W.
	27.1.16		Individual Training.	W.
	28.1.16		Individual Training. Route March. Route thro' N. of MUNDON W+Pit. RD JUNCTION N. of ford N. of LATCHINGTON. Do COLD NORTON (Ref 1/1".O.S. Sheet 30.) Recruits as per special training programme. 2/Lt F.A. WHITFIELD proceed to O.N.G.A.R. for course on Military Engineering	W. W.
	29.1.16		Individual training. I hour released for Munitions throughout 1st/2nd DIV.N. CENTRE. relieved strength of Battalion 28 Officers & 756 other ranks	W.
	30.1.16		Church Parade. Lt Col S+HANNESSY proceeded on leave. Major F/S/1+G assumed command of the Battalion.	W. W.
	31.1.16		Individual training. I hour posted to 21st Gren. Battalion.	W.

W Wylde Major
O/C. 2nd/6th R. War R.

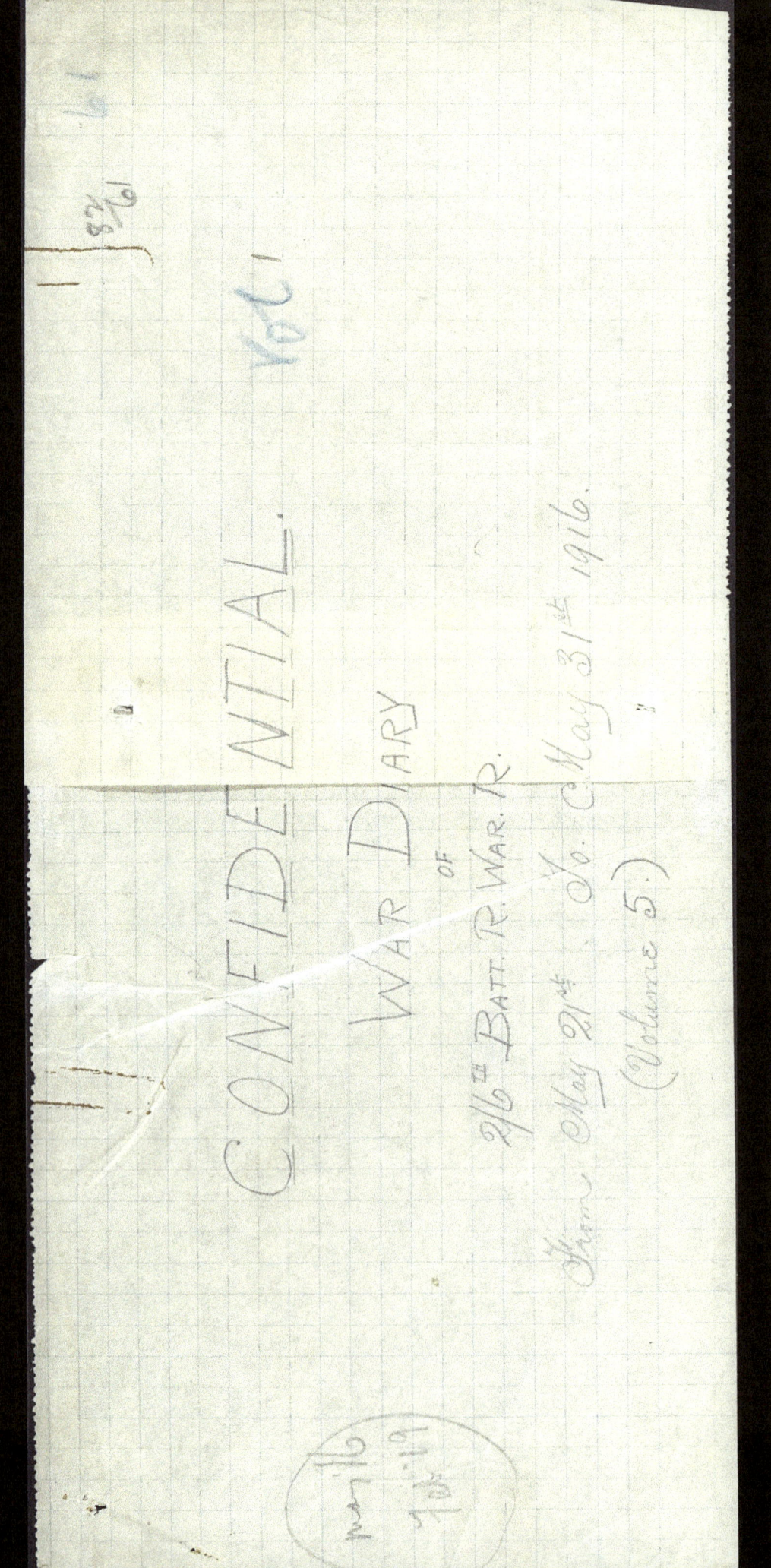

CONFIDENTIAL.   Vol.

WAR DIARY

of

2/6th Batt. R. War. R.

from May 21st to May 31st 1916.

(Volume 5.)

Army Form C. 2118.

WAR DIARY
or
INTELLIGENCE SUMMARY.
(Erase heading not required.)

2/6. R. WAR. R.

Place	Date	Hour	Summary of Events and Information	Remarks and references to Appendices
PERHAM DOWN.	21.5.16		BATTⁿ entraining at LUDGERSHALL for embarkation overseas. STRENGTH :- Officers 33. other ranks 936. Vehicles 21 (including 8 attached from A.S.C.) Bicycles 9. Lewis guns 4. Battⁿ embarked at SOUTHAMPTON & crossed by night disembarking at LE HAVRE 22.5.16	JW
FRANCE. LE HAVRE.	22.5.16		Battⁿ disembarked and marched to No 1. REST CAMP. at H 3 opm orders for entraining received	JW
	23.5.16		Battⁿ paraded at 7.30am and marched to GARE DES MARCHANDISES where it entrained and left 11.30am. O. Room Serjeant (C/Sgt CTRAHAM) reported at H'dqrs: D.A.C. 3rd ECHELON. MONTROLIER-	JW
GONNEHEM.	24.5.16		Battalion detrained at MERVILLE station arriving there via ROUEN. ABBEVILLE. HASBR OOCH. BERGENT at 8.30am and marched to billetting area at GONNEHEM. and companies billetted	JW
	25.5.16		BATT: paraded at 10am for Route march. Route. L'ECLEME-BUSNETTES-LE HAMEL- Inspection men Company commanders. 2/Lt. C. E. J. JUDSON. 4/7 MIDDLESEX reported for duty.	Ref: HASBROUCK 5th corps 2/Lt J. H. STEAD 4/7 MIDDLESEX reported for duty JW
	26.5.16		Batt: paraded at 9.30 am for Route march.	JW
	27.5.16		Battⁿ paraded for Route march. 2/Lt J. H. STEAD 4/7 MIDDLESEX reported for duty	JW

WAR DIARY
or
INTELLIGENCE SUMMARY.   2/6. R WAR R

(Erase heading not required.)

Army Form C. 2118.

Place	Date	Hour	Summary of Events and Information	Remarks and references to Appendices
GONNEHEM	27.5.16 (cont.)		Mr. Gen. Sir R.C.B. HAKING. Commdg. XI Army Corps. addressed all Officers	J/W
	28.5.16		BATTN paraded at 10.45am for Brigade Church Service. 11 am	J/W
	29.5.16		Collective training. Specialists training. SNIPERS fired on Rifle Range	J/W
	30.5.16		Collective training. Specialists training. SNIPERS continued firing practices	J/W
	31.5.16		Collective & Specialist training. Musketry - firing by companies on Rifle Range	J/W
			(W. 21. c. 7.3)	
			2nd Capt. J.J. SHANNESSEY and Capt. A.C. MACKENZIE admitted seriously ill Officers	J/W
			Hospital BETHUNE.	

May 31st/16.

P.C. Mutt
Major
O.C. 2/6th R. War. R.

CONFIDENTIAL

WAR DIARY

of

2/6th Batt: Royal Warwickshire Regt.

From June 1st 1916 - to June 30th 1916.

(Volume 3)

Army Form C. 2118.

2/6 R. WAR. R.

WAR DIARY
or
INTELLIGENCE SUMMARY.
(Erase heading not required.)

Place	Date	Hour	Summary of Events and Information	Remarks and references to Appendices
GONNEHEM	1.6.16		BATT: paraded at 9.30am for ROUTE MARCH. ROUTE. GHOSQUES - VENDIN LE BETHUNE 0m 0 BLINGHEM - firing on Rifle Range continued. (Reg. BETHUNE. Edition 6. 1/40,000.)	flus
	2.6.16.		Attacking and Skirmishing drawing. Musketry on Canal Bank Range	
	3.6.16	9.30am	BATT paraded at 9.30am for ROUTEMARCH. ROUTE - CROSS RDS S.E of Y in LANNOY - Point W14 9.6.2.5 - P36 b.1.1. - GONNEHEM. CAPT and ADJUTANT J.G WHITEFIELD entered hospital with broken leg, caused by horse falling during ROUTE MARCH. He was conveyed to 1st CLEARING STATION CHOCQUES accompanied by an escort at 11.30 a.m. LIEUT J.L PADMORE appointed ACTING ADJUTANT. Musketry on Canal Bank Range.	J.W.P.
		2.30p	Musketry and Bayonet fighting.	
	4.6.16	10.15.	Church parade. LIEUT COL SHANNESSY returned from hospital	J.W.P.
	5.6.16	9.30	Batt: paraded at 9.30 am Musketry, Bayonet fighting, Rifle Exercises, Lecture by Platoon Commanders on "Precautions to be adopted to prevent casualties while clearing rifles". Firing on CANAL BANK RANGE	J.W.P.
	6.6.16		Batt: paraded at 9.30 am for Meets. Back under company arrangements. Firing on CANAL BANK RANGE. Musketry. Bayonet fighting and rifle exercises. Practice in throwing live bombs under BOMBING OFFICER. CAPT MACKENZIE returned from hospital.	J.W.P. J.W.P. J.W.P.

Army Form C. 2118.

WAR DIARY
or
INTELLIGENCE SUMMARY.
(Erase heading not required.)

Instructions regarding War Diaries and Intelligence Summaries are contained in F. S. Regs., Part II. and the Staff Manual respectively. Title pages will be prepared in manuscript.

Place	Date	Hour	Summary of Events and Information	Remarks and references to Appendices
GONNEHEM	7.6.16	6 a.m.	Bath under Company arrangements. COMMANDING OFFICER, ADJUTANT, COMPANY COMMANDERS, SPECIALIST OFFICERS, and C.S.M's visited trenches for instruction.	JLP
BETHUNE	8.6.16	1 p.m.	Batt paraded at 2.15 p.m and marched to BETHUNE. Musketry - close order drill, arms drill, bayonet fighting under Company arrangements. C & D Companies paraded at 2.0 p.m to march to billets at BEUVRY. A & B Companies proceeded to trenches for instruction & were attached to 2nd WORCESTERS and 1st CAMERONIANS respectively.	JLP
BEUVRY	9.6.16		A & B Companies in trenches. C & D Coys. Musketry - Bayonet fighting - close order & arms drill. Practice with gas helmets. C.O and M.O. and 4 SUBALTERNS visited trenches.	JLP
BEUVRY	10.6.16	a.m	A & B Coys: in trenches - C & D Coys - musketry, bayonet fighting - close order & arms drill. 5 Officers & 23 NCOs proceeded to trenches for instruction. C & D Coys paraded at 6.0 p.m & marched to BETHUNE. A & B companies relieved in trenches & marched to BETHUNE.	JLP
BETHUNE	11.6.16		C & D Coys. paraded at 9.15 a.m for CHURCH PARADE.	JLP
	12.6.16		Batt paraded at 10.0 a.m & marched to LAGORGUE arriving at 2.p.m. 2 Lieut FLESHER proceeded to CAMIERS on Course of instruction on MACHINE GUNS. 2/Lieut HUDSON and 31 OTHER RANKS proceeded to LAVENTIE & were attached to PIONEER BATTN 36th DIVISION.	JLP

T2134. Wt. W708—776. 500000. 4/16. Sir J. C. & S.

Army Form C. 2118.

WAR DIARY
or
INTELLIGENCE SUMMARY.
(Erase heading not required.)

Instructions regarding War Diaries and Intelligence Summaries are contained in F. S. Regs., Part II. and the Staff Manual respectively. Title pages will be prepared in manuscript.

Place	Date	Hour	Summary of Events and Information	Remarks and references to Appendices
LAGORGUE	13.6.16	am	Owing to inclement weather work was carried out indoors. 14 OTHER RANKS proceeded to LAVENTIE & were attached to PIONEER BATT.N 35.st DIVISION.	
	14.6.16	a.m	Musketry - rapid loading - Rapid fire - Practice in rapid adjustment of GAS HELMETS. Rifle exercise drill & arms drill. LIEUT SHAWNESSY (+ batman) proceeded to S.t VENANT for STOKES GUN COURSE	
		p.m	Cultivation of spirit of offensive - Bayonet fighting - everything each	
	15.6.16	a.m	Batt.n paraded at 9.30 a.m for Route March. Route L.18.d.5.5.- K.30.d.2.2 - road in K.30.c. - MERVILLE - K.25.c.4.8 LAGORGUE. (Ref: Sheet 36A)	
		p.m	Musketry - rapid loading - rapid fire - firing on range	
	16.6.16	a.m	Musketry - rapid loading - rapid fire - firing on range. Bayonet fighting sprinting short distances in marching Order - assaulting sacks. LIEUT BALCON & 19 OTHER RANKS proceeded to LAVENTIE for attachment to BRIGADE M.G. COMPANY	
	17.6.16	am	Company route marches	
		p.m	Musketry - firing on range - rapid firing - rapid loading. LIEUT JACKSON & party of 6 SNIPERs proceeded to STEENBECQUE for Sniping Course	

Army Form C. 2118.

WAR DIARY
or
INTELLIGENCE SUMMARY.
(Erase heading not required.)

2/6 R. WARWICK REGT.

77½

Place	Date	Hour	Summary of Events and Information	Remarks and references to Appendices
LA GORGUE	18.6.16		Batt. paraded at 4.30 a.m. & proceeded to LAVENTIE, from there carrying parties proceeded to DUMP at M.6.d.5.7 (mg sheet 36) at half hour intervals to carry GAS CYLINDERS to front line trenches.	
	19.6.16			
	20.6.16	a.m.	Batt. paraded at 4.15 a.m. & repeated work done on 18.6.16. LIEUT BALCON + 19 OTHER RANKS returned from BRIGADE M.G. COMPANY. Musketry – rapid loading – rapid firing – fire control – firing on range – practice with GAS HELMETS. Close order drill & arms drill	
		p.m.	Bayonet fighting – Physical drill – sprinting about distance in full marching order with fixed bayonets	
	21.6.16	a.m.	Musketry – rapid loading – rapid firing – firing on range – practice with gas helmets & firing in gas helmets.	
		p.m.	Batt. paraded at 2.0 p.m. & marched to CROIX BARBÉE at M.26.d.5.6 (sheet 36)	
	22.6.16	a.m.	Billets cleaned & improved. Dug-outs in vicinity of billet improved.	
		p.m.	Six WORKING PARTIES (totaling 180 O.R. and 7 Officers) proceeded to various parts of the line for work under R.E.'s from 11 p.m. to 2 a.m. 5 Officers visited 2/7th WARWICKS in trenches. 1 Officer attached to Artillery Battery B.306 and One officer attached to artillery battery D.108 for instruction in requirements of Infantry attacks by Artillery, also taken to O.P.'s	

WAR DIARY or INTELLIGENCE SUMMARY

Army Form C. 2118.

Place	Date	Hour	Summary of Events and Information	Remarks and references to Appendices
CROIX BARBEE	23.6.16	a.m.	Three WORKING PARTIES (totalling 160 OR & 4 Officers) proceeded to trenches for work under R.E.s	773
		p.m.	Six Working parties (totalling 7 Officers & 180 OR) proceeded to trenches for work under R.E's from 11 p.m. to 2.0 a.m. Remainder of Batt" - cleaning billets, equipment etc.	
	24.6.16		Work for 23.6.16 repeated	
In the trenches	25.6.16		At 6.45 a.m. D Coy proceeded to trenches by platoons at 1 hours intervals. Other Companies proceeded in following order at 1 hour intervals. 'C' Coy 'A' Coy and 'B' Coy. Trenches were taken over from 2/7" WARWICKS & relief completed at 3.50 p.m. Line of trenches taken over - M.29.d.9.7. to M.29.d.2.5. (Ref Sheet J) with 2/5" WARWICKS on our right. Enemy artillery showed activity in evening, falling 1 man & wounding one man. Patrols were sent out at night but little information could be obtained owing to marshy condition of ground. At 11.15 p.m. our artillery & 64 machine guns opened fire on enemy & bombarded his trenches. At 11.45 p.m. this was repeated & artillery continued till 1.0 a.m. Enemy artillery retaliated but weakly. Batt" still holding same line of trenches. No activity by day. Our artillery bombarded enemy, commencing at 11.40 p.m. & continued till 2.0 a.m. when enemy retaliated vigorously on our 1st line trenches causing 14 casualties. - An enemy artillery pioneer was seen opposite M.29.4 (Sheet J) & a sniper located & probably hit at M.30.a.2.6. by rifle grenade. LIEUT F.W. SHANNESSY reported at H.Q. 183rd Bde for attachment to Staff.	
	26.6.16			
	27.6.16			

Army Form C. 2118.

WAR DIARY or INTELLIGENCE SUMMARY.
(Erase heading not required.)

Place	Date	Hour	Summary of Events and Information	Remarks and references to Appendices
In the Trenches	27.6.16		Batt" still holds same line. Our artillery & enemy's about all day, except for a little firing at enemy's snipers that appear. There has been but on our right and damaged. Enemy placed about 2 knife rests in gap at N.C.6. Working parties found for R.E's by day & night.	
"	28.6.16		Batt" still holding same line of trenches. Enemy generally quiet. Our artillery fired at intervals at enemy's parapet & caused damage. Rifle grenades fired by us at intervals during night. Enemy is thought to have intended to repair wire at N.C.6, precautions were taken to prevent him & gap still remains. Working parties supplied for R.Es for work in trenches.	
"	29.6.16		CAPT. A.C. MACKENZIE (& 1st man) and Sergt ROBOTHAM proceeded to CONDETTE near BOULOGNE to instruct at 1st Army School. 1 NCO and 3 men attached to DIV: SALVAGE. COY. Sergt SHEPPARD (Coy.png Sergt) reported at DIVISIONAL HEADQUARTERS to proceed to instruct at ARMY SNIPING SCHOOL. Rifle grenades were fired from second front at enemy's trenches with good effect. Enemy retaliated weakly with four rifle grenades at 12 noon. Smoke was then discharged along Brigade front at 2.50 a.m. till 3.2.5 a.m. This was not carried out by the batt owing to unfavourable wind. Bursts of rapid fire by rifles & machine guns & trench guns at enemy's parapet at 2:55 a.m., 3:15 a.m., 3:15 a.m., 4:20 a.m., till 5 a.m. Enemy retaliated by shelling our front line trenches causing damage at places to parapet & causing killing 3 men & wounding MAJOR HUTH DSO.	774
In the TRENCHES	30.6.16		Our artillery bombarded enemy from 2.40 a.m. till 5 a.m. Enemy retaliated by shelling our front line trenches causing damage at places to parapet & causing killing 3 men & wounding MAJOR HUTH DSO.	

WAR DIARY
or
INTELLIGENCE SUMMARY.
Army Form C. 2118.

(Erase heading not required.)

Place	Date	Hour	Summary of Events and Information	Remarks and references to Appendices
Trenches	30.6.16		and 25th R. Twenty five O.R. Enemy artillery was active again at about 8.30 a.m. on M29.4. and 25th R. Twenty five O.R. Enemy artillery replied vigorously on our request + enemy remained silent. At 10.1 p.m. of enemy was to have been exchanged, but owing to unfavourable wind this was cancelled. Our artillery showed activity at this time for about an hour, enemy retaliated with about 20 shrapnel shells. Shell burst near the battery activated at about M22 & y.5.	

L.J. Ramsey Lt Col
Comdg. 2/6. R. War R.

775
VIII

Vol III

Confidential

War Diary of
2/6th Battalion Royal Warwickshire Regiment.
From 1st July, 1916, to July 31st 1916.

Volume 3.

WAR DIARY or INTELLIGENCE SUMMARY

Army Form C. 2118.

(Erase heading not required.)

Instructions regarding War Diaries and Intelligence Summaries are contained in F.S. Regs., Part II. and the Staff Manual respectively. Title pages will be prepared in manuscript.

Place	Date	Hour	Summary of Events and Information	Remarks and references to Appendices
In the Trenches	1.7.16		Battn holding line of trenches from M.24.d.1.6. to M.29.d.9½.7½. with 2/5th WARWICKS on our right and 18th Inf Brigade on our left. Enemy was bombarded at intervals during the day with good results. N.6 was also fired at but little damage appears to have been done. At 9.30 p.m. the enemy suddenly opened a heavy artillery fire on our front line trenches. His range however inaccurate. At 9.45 p.m. our artillery opened a very effective fire on enemy's front trenches & having severely damaged those opened on the 2nd line trenches. The enemy's artillery gradually diminished till at 11 p.m. it was silent. At 11 p.m. we discharged wt complete success smoke, by means of candles & bombs, all along our front. The enemy at once opened rapid fire & Machine Gun fire, & showed nervousness by sending up a number of rockets. The enemy furiously bombarded the Battn on our right & assistance was given them by our right company & Machine guns placed in such a position to get an enflade fire along our wire opposite them :- 1 D.R. proceeded on leave. Machine Gun convoy at CAMIERS. 2/Lt FLESHER returned from leave.	J.P.
In the trenches	2.7.16		Same line of trenches. Message received at 4.12 a.m. from 2/5th WARWICKS asking us to take over 14 June bays as they had been cut off from remainder of battalion. At about 4.30 a.m. there fire-bars (obstacles) at about M.29.d.9½.7½ to M.30.C.1.6) were taken over by this unit. Our artillery fired at N.C 5 at 10.0 p.m. N.C 10.15 p.m. Smoke was discharged at 10.30 p.m. according to instructions, but the wind was unfavorable & blew it into own lines. Enemy artillery opened fire on our parapet but was soon silenced, our artillery opening fire on the enemy	J.P.

Army Form C. 2118.

WAR DIARY
or
INTELLIGENCE SUMMARY.
(Erase heading not required.)

779

Place	Date	Hour	Summary of Events and Information	Remarks and references to Appendices
La Neuvelette	3.7.16	—	Bn still holding same line of trenches. Day quiet except for enemy artillery registering on the left of our line in afternoon. At 10.0 p.m. our artillery opened fire on M 30 a 51 & N.C 5 and N.C.6. The following message of congratulations was received from Lanyard GENERAL MACKENZIE. — "I am desired by the Corps Commander (LT. GEN. SIR R. HAKING, K.C.B.) to convey to you his appreciation of the conduct of the three Battalions of the Brigade holding the line last night, and in particular of that of Lt Colonel Coates and the 5th WARWICKS. I take this opportunity of expressing my own hearty appreciation of the soldierly conduct of all ranks on that occasion." LIEUT. WHITFIELD + 2/LIEUT FLESHER wounded & proceeded to LA GORGUE hospital.	
	4.7.16	—	Day quiet except for a little artillery fire in NC afternoon. At 10.40 p.m. our artillery opened a heavy fire on the enemy. Enemy retaliated especially on our left company. At 10.50 p.m. the 183rd Inf Bde on our left carried out a raid on the enemy remaining in his line till 11.40 pm. During this time we opened bursts of rapid fire at the enemy's trenches.	
	5.7.16	—	At 1.30 am our artillery heavily bombarded the enemy again. He again retaliated on our left particularly, causing heavy casualties (3 killed + 24 wounded). This bombardment continued for about 1½ hours. Our artillery firing continually till the enemy ceased. Day was generally quiet except for a LMG sniping. Artillery fired for about ½ hour from 10 p.m. Orders received to move	

T2134. Wt. W708—776. 500000. 4/15. Sir J. C. & S.

Army Form C.-2118.

WAR DIARY
or
INTELLIGENCE SUMMARY.
(Erase heading not required.)

Instructions regarding War Diaries and Intelligence Summaries are contained in F. S. Regs., Part II. and the Staff Manual respectively. Title pages will be prepared in manuscript.

Place	Date	Hour	Summary of Events and Information	Remarks and references to Appendices
In the trenches	5/7/16		GAS HELMETS in the ALERT from 11 p.m. 5/7/16 to 4.0 a.m. 6/7/16. 250 boxes of 'P' bombs 850 SMOKE CANDLES and 250 boxes of FUZEES taken up to front line trenches, also 500 BROCK LIGHTERS. 4 CADETS attached to Batt. for instruction.	
	6.7.16		Our artillery & enemy's quiet all day, except for a few shells dropped by our communication trenches and Batt Headquarters. SMOKE BOMBS & CANDLES placed in position ready for use. At about 6.30 p.m. and 10.30 p.m. the enemy shelled ERITH POST for about 10 minutes. At 10.15 p.m. the enemy appeared to be attempting to attack our line at M.29.b.9 & 2. Our artillery fired at enemy's lines & he ceased fire. Our patrols reported that there appeared to be no movement on the part of the enemy & that there was better than usual quietly hidden by the long grass. The 4 cadets attached for instruction left for LAGORGUE.	
In the trenches	7.7.16		Batt. still holding same line. Little activity all day. Enemy shelled Batt. Headquarters at 2.30 p.m. and again at 5 p.m. to which our artillery replied. Our artillery again shelled enemy from 10 p.m. to 10.20 p.m. to which he retaliated a little. 2/LIEUT F.A. WHITFIELD returned from hospital	
In the trenches	8.7.16		Our artillery and enemy artillery quiet except for a little registering in the evening. Our artillery bombarded the enemy from 10 p.m. to 10.30 p.m. There was only slight retaliation. 7 OFFICERS reported for attachment = duty with this unit.	

T2134. Wt. W708—776. 500000. 4/15. Sir J.C. & S.

778

WAR DIARY or INTELLIGENCE SUMMARY.

Army Form C. 2118.

Place	Date	Hour	Summary of Events and Information	Remarks and references to Appendices
In trenches	9.7.16		Battn still occupying same line of trenches, but all day. Our artillery bombarded enemy at 11.0 pm till 12.15 am. Bursts of rapid & machine gun fire given by this unit. Also 2/5th WARWICKS made a raid on enemy's trenches on our right. At 11.23 a mine was blown up N. of the BOCAGE. On two guns opened fire immediately after explosion. Surprisingly little retaliation by enemy, pointing to the fact that he had moved some of his artillery.	
RIEZ BAILLEUL	10.7.16		Battalion relieved by 2/5th Warwicks. Relief started at 7.0 am & was completed by 12.30 pm. DREADNOUGHT & TILLELOY POSTS still garrisoned by this unit. MIN, LONELY, LAFLINQUE and several CARETAKERS POSTS garrisoned by this unit. Remainder of day spent in resting and bathing. 2.O.R. proceeded to STEENBECQUE on sniping course. Reorganisation of details.	
	11.7.16		Day spent in Camp bathing etc. & improving billets. Parties supplied for work under R.E's. 3 O.R. reported for LEWIS GUN COURSE at ETAPLES.	
	12.7.16		Day spent in cleaning equipment & wearing new clothes etc. DREADNOUGHT & TILLELOY POSTS relieved. Nothing to report for R.E's. C.O. inspected Battn in morning. 1 Officer attached to this unit for duty (Lieut BENNOY).	
	13.7.16		Continuation of cleaning of billets & general improvement. Fatigue on RIEZ BAILLEUL range. Practice in bombing in bombing pit. All other specialists man their respective offices. Nothing. Parties supplied for R.E's. Dry day.	

780

WAR DIARY
or
INTELLIGENCE SUMMARY.
(Erase heading not required.)

Army Form C. 2118.

783

Place	Date	Hour	Summary of Events and Information	Remarks and references to Appendices
RIEZ BAILLEUL	14.7.16		Large working parties supplied for R.E.'s for carrying. Specialists paraded under specialists officers. CAPT FORBES attacked 'A' Battery B306 at M15 c.2.1. for 24 hours. Additional work of parties as per working a total of 310 O.R. + 8 Officers	
	15.7.16		Large working + carrying parties again supplied at above intervals during the day + night. Totalling 400 OR + 12 Officers.	
	16.7.16		Working parties + carrying parties supplied until sudden orders were received to move into the trenches. Companies moved into trenches independently at very short notice - took over the line of trenches from N13 c32.4.3. to N13 c.9.0. Manβ relieving a party of the 2/7th WARWICKS. Relief was completed by 9.0 p.m. Orders were received to prepare for offensive operations. On arrival the supply of bombs and ammunition in the front line was found to be insufficient. A large party of men had to be organised for carrying loads of bombs, ammunition, water, etc up to the front line. Other carrying parties also were taken to the nearest dumps at HOOGEMONT and the junction of the STRAND TRENCH and the nearer line. The attack was expected to take place early on the morning of the 17th. These parties + all the men had to work at very high pressure, as all the C.O's gold a conference of their company officers, during the night notification was received that grenades + other stores were carried to the dumps. The infantry account being five to start from after zero. Zero hour was fixed for 4 a.m.	

Army Form C. 2118.

WAR DIARY
or
INTELLIGENCE SUMMARY.
(Erase heading not required.)

Place	Date	Hour	Summary of Events and Information	Remarks and references to Appendices
RIEZ BAILLEUL	14.7.16		Large working parties supplied to R.E. Additional working parties supplied making total of 31 OR + 8 Officers. Specialists paraded under their officers. CAPT FORBES attached to Battery B 306 at M.15.6.2.1. for 24 hours.	
	15.7.16		Large working + carrying parties again supplied at 6 hour interval during the day + night. totalling 400 OR and 12 Officers.	
In trenches	16.7.16		Working parties + carrying parties supplied until sudden orders received to move into trenches and take over line from N.13.c.2.4 to N.13.c.9.0. Mostly leaving a part of No 2/7 Warwicks. Relief was completed by 9.0 pm. Orders received to prepare for an offensive on WICK SALIENT. On arrival in trenches supplies + supplies of ammunition bombs etc was found to be insufficient + large working + carrying parties had to be organised to carry same to line also water, sme cutters etc. The reserve dumps at HOUGOUMONT and junction of reserve line + STRAND TRENCH were made up to establishment. As the attack was expected to take place early 17th inst. these parties had to work at high pressure. COMMANDING OFFICER held conference with company commanders + specialist officers. Notification received that zero time was fixed for 4.a.m. 17th inst. Infantry assault being fixed for 7 hours after zero. 2 Lieut MASSEY + Corpl PONZEN wdd. to Physical training school at LA GORGUE.	
	17.7.16	5.a.m.	Zero hour postponed till 11 a.m.	
		10.5 a.m.	Offensive operations cancelled for 17th + 18th owing to muddy weather. Men rested except for	

WAR DIARY or INTELLIGENCE SUMMARY

Army Form C. 2118.

Place	Date	Hour	Summary of Events and Information	Remarks and references to Appendices
Trenches	17.7.16		Company carrying parties for water etc. Notification received that relief would not take place on the 18th & orders received for two companies to return to Billets at RIEZ BAILLEUL. A & C Coys reported that they had left trenches at 4.15 pm.	
	18.7.16		Men rested all day except for small carrying parties for water etc. Telephone communications were improved with front line. — CAPT FORBES admitted to hospital.	
	19.7.16		According to orders received A & C Coys returned to trenches. By 9.30 am companies were disposed as follows. A & C Coys in front line. B Coy in support (reserve line). D Coy in reserve. Commanding Officer held conference with company commanders & specialist officers. Notification received that zero was fixed for 11 am. Officer & 60 OR from each company to be held at Battalion HQ & 6 OR from each company to be held at Battn HQ as working party. At 11 am artillery bombardment started & HQ BSM reported all communications cut up at NOUGOD MONT. At 12 noon companies reported all well. Enemy was retaliating by shelling of 11.0 pm a similar report was received at 1.10 pm. Enemy retaliated most violently with large shells, thought to be	
		4.2	By 2.0 pm shelling by enemy decreased except on the narrow line from the many "duds" were reported.	
		3.0	Company reported enemy trench mortar caused all along their front.	
		4.0	Enemy stopped shelling narrow line but concentrated on the front line using HE & shrapnel.	
		4.30	2nd in command reported that retaliation was slight. Matthews 1st & 2nd O.R. been 8 casualties.	

WAR DIARY or INTELLIGENCE SUMMARY

Army Form C. 2118.

Place	Date	Hour	Summary of Events and Information	Remarks and references to Appendices
In the trenches	19.7.16		At 9.45 pm orders were received that the 2/5th WARWICKS would relieve the Battn and by 1.0 a.m. the relief	
	20.7.16		was complete with the exception of one Coy in the front part of "D" Coy who were unable to bring in so many of the wounded as possible. Eventually all wounded were collected under cover of darkness.	
			The conduct of all ranks throughout the whole action was most excellent, orders being cheerfully carried out without the slightest hesitation under the most trying conditions.	
			Casualties sustained during action fought on 19.7.16 — Officers — Killed CAPT W. SIMMS — missing CAPT A.E. COULTON, CAPT T.S. WATHES, 2 LIEUT H. HARPER, 2 LIEUT BARRON, 2 LIEUT	
			HURDMAN — wounded — CAPT M.C. WADE, LIEUT B.G. MARTINEAU, LIEUT A.S. WILLIS, 2 LIEUT FLESHER, 2 LIEUT BENOY (at duty) — Other ranks killed 9, missing 68, wounded 154. —	
			Other ranks killed 9, Companies paraded & cleaned up generally	
RIFLE BAILLEUL	21.7.16		Battn rested all - day, Companies paraded & cleaned up generally	
			Battn rested with the exception of a short parade of those other ranks Remainder of men rested	
	22.7.16	2.30pm	Battn paraded at 2.15pm for inspection at 2.30 p.m by GENERAL COLLIN MACKENZIE. The following was accepted — "From the General Officer Commanding-in-Chief the British Armies in France"	
			"Please convey to the troops engaged night 19th/20th my appreciation of their gallant effort and though preparation made for it & risk taken to make further enterprise has not been by any means in vain, and	

WAR DIARY or INTELLIGENCE SUMMARY

Army Form C. 2118.

Place	Date	Hour	Summary of Events and Information	Remarks and references to Appendices
In the trenches	19/7/16	5.30pm	The men started to file out through the sally ports to the offensive on WICKSALIENT & formed four lines in NO MANS LAND composed of A & C Companies. Immediately the left Co. was the enemy shelled the sally ports very heavily but not so would Not in a way but him in a crop last him all the officers of A Coy killed & wounded. The lines advanced across NO MANS LAND, then our artillery barrage lifted the enemy line was within 30 yards of WICKSALIENT. Immediately the barrage lifted they were hilled with shrapnel & H.E., & the enemy opened a barrage across NO MANS LAND, at the same time the German trenches became alive with men and a large number of machine guns opened a heavy fire on them moving down the advancing lines. The support Coy being (B) followed at 100 yds distance but was hidden in a similar way. Notwithstanding this, two platoons reached the enemy's parapet but owing to the heavy losses caused in the casualties among the officers, the attack was unable to advance. Meanwhile D Coy in reserve moved 2 platoons up into the front line successfully. The position was reported to Brigade HQ & orders received that the attack would be continued. Telephone communication with the front line was broken but in spite of the heavy fire was quickly restored. Noted that the attack could be pressed till 9.10 & that the various parties of infantry under cover of a barrage by our artillery on the WICK SAL at 9.10 the barrage started and all who could returned to the trenches the attack was now postponed till 9.0 pm & later orders was received that the attack would be abandoned	

784

Place	Date	Hour	Summary of Events and Information	Remarks and references to Appendices
RIEZ BAILLEUL	22.7.16		that the gallantry with which they carried out the attack is fully realised." The following was received from GENERAL MACKENZIE — "Please convey to the following message from the Corps Commander:" — "I wish to convey to all ranks, upon arrival, my appreciation of the gallant attack carried out yesterday by them. Although they were unable to consolidate the ground gained, the spirit in the enemy will be for wanting, will prevent him from making troops easy for our first attack. I wish you all in your next attack a more complete spectacular victory. That you may have the full fruit of the energy & skill displayed by all commands and their staff in the execution of their task". The above act of gallantry devotion but all ranks of every arm & service have carried out in the most exploring & devoted manner, under very trying, on account of labour, situation. I add their endurance & exertion troubles any unqualified praise." Note by BRIG.-GEN GORDON — "Such fine spirit of forwarding the above remarks to all ranks for their gallantry in action, devotion to duty, to express my pride in having such officers, N.C.O.s & men under my command". — Letters & O.R. passed as Physical Training course.	
	23.7.16		Battn paraded at 5.0 p.m. for divine service.	
MERVILLE	24.7.16	12. noon.	Battn & companies marched independently to MERVILLE leaving at intervals from 11 a.m. to 12. noon.	

Army Form C. 2118.

WAR DIARY
or
INTELLIGENCE SUMMARY.
(Erase heading not required.)

Instructions regarding War Diaries and Intelligence Summaries are contained in F. S. Regs., Part II. and the Staff Manual respectively. Title pages will be prepared in manuscript.

Place	Date	Hour	Summary of Events and Information	Remarks and references to Appendices
MERVILLE	25.7.16	am	Musketry, close order drill & arms drill under Company arrangements.	
		pm	Bayonet fighting, Physical drill under company arrangements	
	26.7.16	am	Musketry & close order drill under Coy arrangements	
		pm	Bat.n paraded for arms drill & showed to ceremonial parade to be held on 27.7.16. Batt.n fallout from parade	
	27.7.16		Musketry, close order drill & bayonet fighting under Company arrangements. Bat.n paraded at 11.15 for arms drill.	
		1.15p	Bat.n paraded in Bat.n parade ground for ceremonial parade to form guard of honour to GENERAL SIR CHARLES MUNRO G.C.M.G. K.C.B. Bat.n from up to MERVILLE square & Bde ground salute to Army commander. GEN. SIR C. MUNRO, the inspected the guard. The afternoon was spent after this the General addressed the guard, congratulating all ranks on their behaviour in the field. The guard consisting of 350 O.R. & 15 officers then marched past & returned to billets	
	28.7.16		At bombing field on the range at LE SART. Suppers fuses special course, 2 Companies lakes	
	29.7.16	am	Musketry, Bayonet fighting & close order drill	
		pm	Musketry, Bayonet fighting & close order drill. 2 Companies bathed.	
		pm	Specialists paraded under specialist officers. 9.30 Companies carried out night work till 11 pm	

787.

Army Form C. 2118.

WAR DIARY
or
INTELLIGENCE SUMMARY.
(Erase heading not required.)

Instructions regarding War Diaries and Intelligence Summaries are contained in F. S. Regs., Part II. and the Staff Manual respectively. Title pages will be prepared in manuscript.

Place	Date	Hour	Summary of Events and Information	Remarks and references to Appendices
MERVILLE	29/7/16		in afternoon Auctn. CO. ADJUTANT. + 4 Company Commanders + Bombing Officer went to demonstration given on BANGALOR TORPEDOES. Shewn that one large hut was entirely demolished for a roll of tape.	
	30/7/16		80 O.R. under Bugeon Howie clear held at LABORGUE. Balance were spread 10AM to 10R retired. f.u.P to prepared new town f.u.P	
	31/7/16	am	A Coy upwards were detailed to Laugelew to prepare OK's expl. + safety class in a dug-out trench + coal + bayonet fighting	
		p.m.	Specialists under specialist officers. N.C.O. under newly Tpld Sergts under R.S.M. 1 N.C.O. paraded as Orderly corp. + 1 N.C.O. as Orderly bugler	

T. T. Thames
Lieut-Col.
O.C. 2/6/2/73rd H. L. Nov 12

788
113

Confidential.

War Diary of

2/6th Batt. Royal Warwickshire Regt.

From 1st August 1916, to 31st August 1916.

Volume 3.

WAR DIARY or INTELLIGENCE SUMMARY

Army Form C. 2118.

2/6 Batt R Warwick Regt

190

Place	Date	Hour	Summary of Events and Information	Remarks and references to Appendices
RIEZ BAILLEUL	1.8.16	am	Companies moved independently to RIEZ BAILLEUL from MERVILLE. Move was completed by 9.30 am	
		pm	Companies used rifle range. Bombing used bombing pit. All other specialist paraded under specialist Officers	
	2.8.16	am	Musketry, fire discipline, Bayonet fighting, close order & arms drill, carried out by companies on company parade grounds	
		pm	All specialists under specialist Officers. Bombers in bombing pit. LIEUT BENDY & 4 other ranks reported at STEENBECQUE for sniper course. 1 NCO proceeded to CAMIERS in musketry course. 3 Working parties for R.E. totalling 90 OR & 1 Officer found.	
	3.8.16	am	At B Coy individual instruction – C & D Coys fired on range & carried out bayonet fighting. Close order & Arms drill. 4 Officers & 100 OR held in readiness to move immediately if necessary	
		pm	All specialists under specialist Officers. 1 Officer attached for 24 hours to an army battery for Bayonet fighting, Gas helmet drill, Close order arms drill.	
	4.8.16	am	All specialists under specialist Officers. Working party of 1 Officer & 90 OR found for R.E. work. 1 Officer and 5 O.R. proceeded to LE TOUQUET for Lewis gun course. 1 Officer attached to Battery for 24 hours.	
	5.8.16	8.05–10.25 am	Bayonet fighting, Close order & arms drill	

WAR DIARY or INTELLIGENCE SUMMARY

Army Form C. 2118.

Place	Date	Hour	Summary of Events and Information	Remarks and references to Appendices
RIEZ BAILLEUL	5.8.16	pm	Firing on the range — Specialists under specialist officer. Bombing parties found for R.E. work.	
	6.8.16		By night 1 officer + 90 O.R. — 1 officer attached to Battery for fatigue. Bath parade at 9.50 am for Church parade — 1 officer attached to Battery for 24 hours.	
	7.8.16	Bus. till 10-11.45 a.m.	Bombing parties found 1 Officer + 90 O.R. for R.E. work. 2/Lt DAVIES proceeded on Bayonet fighting Course. Bayonet fighting, Close order drill, Bayonet fighting foot drill still —	
		4 - 6.30	All specialists paraded under the specialist officers — Bombing party of 1 Officer + 90 O.R. found for R.E's. 5 Officers reconnoitred Emergency roads to trenches in morning and 4 in afternoon.	
	8.8.16		1 Company (D' Coy) (left Company) took over the line from M.30.C.0.2. to M.30.C.P.7. relieving one company of the 2/5th WARWICKS. The relief was completed by 12 noon. The company was under the orders of the O.C. 2/7th WARWICKS. Remainder of Battn — Specialists under specialist officers — 4 Officers reconnoitred Emergency roads.	
	9.8.16	9.30-11.0 am	Night work under company arrangements	
		am	Bayonet fighting — firing on the range — remainder of morning under company arrangements	
		pm	Specialists under Specialist officers	
La Flinque	10.8.16 am		Battalion Company (already in trenches) relieved 2/7 Sherwoods in the trenches. Companies moved independently and Lewis + Bomb gunners post over in advance. Relief was made fairly smooth	

Army Form C. 2118.

WAR DIARY or INTELLIGENCE SUMMARY.
(Erase heading not required.)

Place	Date	Hour	Summary of Events and Information	Remarks and references to Appendices
In Trenches	10.8.16	am	occupied by 12 noon. Batt: (including D coy) now hold trenches from M.30.c.1.2. to M.30.a.2.6.½. 2/8" WARWICKS on our right. Night was generally quiet except for a few rifle grenades and about 10 H.E. 6" Hows. fired at about 6pm at M.29.4. These did no damage only one civvie hit being shaken by the enemy. A burial party was sent out during the night & received no proposal, effects of several men in the district of the craters at M.30.c.1.2.4. Being one shot in front of T.C.	
	11.8.16		Short trench mining from M.30.c.0.7 to M.30.a.0.3. Morning quiet. At 5 pm the enemy on trench mortars commenced firing at enemy's front line. Enemy retaliated heavily using H.E. and shrapnel + trench mortars, damaging N.G. line & parapet in places. At 6.45 am a few Germans were seen in No MANS LAND. It was very misty at the time but one is reported to have been killed. It might be owing in front of the front trench was continued. Listening patrols were sent out during the night – No German patrols were seen.	
	12.8.16		Morning quiet. At 2.20 pm our trench mortars bombard the enemy's lines 18/pr batteries & Stokes battery cooperated. Rifle grenades were fired. Enemy retaliated with trench mortars on our front line & came some damage. He also shelled DREADNOUGHT & EARTH POSTS with H.E. At 9.15 pm we exploded a counter-mine in vicinity of HORN TRENCH. At 11.10 pm a german patrol	

792

WAR DIARY or INTELLIGENCE SUMMARY

Army Form C. 2118.

Place	Date	Hour	Summary of Events and Information	Remarks and references to Appendices
In trenches	12.8.16	—	was encountered on the left of the front trench and supposed by Lewis Gun fire. The enemy replied to a small mine at M30.c.5.6.2. Supers claim to mention as a small party of the enemy were seen crawling across NO MANS LAND after the explosion. So.C saw dawn 15 the wire along the stab front. GRANTS POST reported slow damaged.	
	13.8.16		Between 12.30 and 12.50 pm two of our aeroplanes patrolled our front & drew heavy fire from enemy artillery & machine guns. At 4.30 pm re blew up a mine at M36.a.6.b. The enemy did not retaliate at all. At 7.30 pm our Trench Mortars opened fire at enemy's front support lines. Artillery & rifle grenade batteries co-operated. Two dud concentrable retaliation – enemy using M.E. & sp. TMs. Shrapnel & minenwerfers. The Enemy shelled the railway at M24.c.5.1. causing no damage & all grenades were also used by him but about 15% were Blind. Good specimens were obtained. It all. The enemy sent over about 90 minenwerfers & rifle grenades. Aerial torpedoes were also employed. At 9.55pm the enemy sent up a red flare opposite our front. Morning quiet. Between 4.0 pm and 6.0 pm an artillery fired on the enemy's front & support lines. The enemy retaliated slightly bursting about 20 8.5 centimetre shells over the ground between Winchester Post & the Rue BACQUEROT. At 8.10 pm till 8.45pm the enemy shelled our front line & particularly the RAILHEAD with shrapnel & HE. The railway was damaged. At 8.15 pm our Trench guns opened fire	
	14.8.16			

799

WAR DIARY or INTELLIGENCE SUMMARY

Army Form C. 2118.

Place	Date	Hour	Summary of Events and Information	Remarks and references to Appendices
2.16 Trenches	14/8/16	—	opp. on the enemy from M.30.a.7.5 to M.30.c.5.8. At M.30.a.5.5. enemy appeared to be enemy. Owing to slight moon light patrolling was impossible.	
	15.8.16		At 2.26 a.m. our muzzles blew up an enemy sap. Between 9 a.m. and 11 a.m. the enemy dropped about thirty 5.9 shells in the vicinity of SUNKEN ROAD TRENCH. At 12 noon one of our aeroplanes flying too low. Enemy machine gun & artillery fire. At 5 p.m. the Bn of T.C. acted at M.30.c.12.4 xxx blew up by us. The enemy did not fire. From 6 p.m. to 6.30 our artillery bombarded Germa front & support line effectively. The enemy replied with a heavy bombardment on lines between 6 p.m. & 6.45 p.m. So far no casualties. At 11 p.m. enemy used a weak light. Enemy fired several small aerial torpedoes at M.30.d and Sunken Connecter trench. Also a few M.T.M's fell behind our line at M.29.d.2.	
	16.8.16 a.m.		In the morning our 18 pdrs registered on enemy's line. At 12 noon we registered with 4/5 grenades at M.30.b.6.2. He retaliated on both our own left. Enemy shelled TILLELOY SOUTH and BONKER ROAD at 4.45 p.m. and fired rifle grenades on M.30.a.2 later in the evening. A German officer was observed upon a tile behind the enemy front line observing through glasses. A man was seen standing at the station. One of our snipers fired at him & eventually he was seen fall from the tile & 7 men rush there to give	

Army Form C. 2118.

WAR DIARY
or
INTELLIGENCE SUMMARY.
(Erase heading not required.)

Place	Date	Hour	Summary of Events and Information	Remarks and references to Appendices
Laventie	16.8.16		accordance with others. They are fired at & at intervals are uncertain. The men had their previously seen to orob to officer.	JW
	17.8.16		Day generally quiet. A little retaliating to artillery in afternoon - firing on enemys front lines opposed our. During the evening the following NCO's were awarded the MILITARY MEDAL for gallantry & devotion to duty:— 3529 Cpl H.D. BROWN - 3127 L/Cpl C.R. JONES - 3532 Pte OLIVER J.N. - 3147 Pte A.C. WEAVING - 3612 Pte T.R.B. KILNER.	JW
RIEZ BAILLEUL	18.8.16		Battn relieved by 2/7" WARWICKS & moved to billets at RIEZ BAILLEUL - Relief started at 10 am & completed at 11.30 pm. 1 Officer & 50 O.R. left to garrison WINCHESTER POST & hand over wiring party. 1 Off & 50 O.R. proceeded LAVENTIE for work under R.E.s	JW
	19.8.16	am	General cleaning of billets, rifles, equipment etc — firing on range — bayonet fighting. Lewis gun team under L.G.O.	JW
	"	pm	Batt- bathed at LA GORGUE.	JW
	20.8.16	am	Batt- paraded at 9.50 for divine service at 10.0 am. — 90 O.R., unvaccinated. Working party of 2 Off & 50 O.R. provided.	JW
	21.8.16	am	Bayonet fighting on bayonet fighting course — gas helmet drill — close order & arms drill — saluting drill — Lewis gun team under Lewis Gun Officer —	JW

WAR DIARY or INTELLIGENCE SUMMARY

Army Form C. 2118.

Place	Date	Hour	Summary of Events and Information	Remarks and references to Appendices
PLEZ BAILLEUL	21.8.16	pm	Range used by companies & snipers. Bombers in bombing pit under Batt Bombing Officer. Sailing parties totalling 2 Officers & 50 OR found for R.E.s. 1 Officer attached to Battery for 24 hrs.	J.P.
	22.8.16	am	Firing on range – Bayonet fighting on bayonet fighting course – Close order drill stm.- Lewis gun teams under I.C.O.	
		pm	Specialists under respective officers. Lecture by R.S.M. to all N.C.Os newly rank of sergeant. Sailing parties totalling 2 Officers & 50 OR found for R.E.s. Party of 1 Officer & 50 OR at WINCHESTER POST relieved by C Coy. 1 Officer attached to Battery A 205.	J.P.
	23.8.16	Bn 8.45.16 am	Bayonet fighting on bayonet fighting course – Lewis gun team under L.G.O. Remainder of men under Company arrangements.	
		pm	Sports with 2/5" Sanits on rifle range. 4 Officers & 100 OR held in readiness as reserve company.	J.P.
	24.8.16		Sailing parties of 2 Officers & 50 OR found for R.E.s. 1 Officer attached to Battery A 306. Men from HAMPSHIRE REGT transferred to this unit w/c effect from 1.7.16.	J.P.
		8.45 am	LIEUT P.J. JOHNSON awarded MILITARY CROSS for gallantry & devotion to duty.	
			Bayonet fighting – firing on range – remainder of parade under Company arrangements. Specialists under specialist Officers & N.C.Os. Bombers used bombing pit.	J.P.

796

Army Form C. 2118.

WAR DIARY
or
INTELLIGENCE SUMMARY.
(Erase heading not required.)

Place	Date	Hour	Summary of Events and Information	Remarks and references to Appendices
RIEZ BAILLEUL	25.8.16	8.45	Range on .16 range by Companies. - Supins - Bayonet fighting on Bayonet fighting course.	
		12.30	Remainder of morning under company arrangement. - Gas and drill etc.	
		2.30-4.0	Specialists under Specialist Officers. - Bombers on bombing pit.	
			LIEUT P.T. JOHNSON - CORPL N.D. BROWN - 3127 L/Corp. JONES - 3532 Pte OWEN - 3147 Pte WEAVING - 3012 3629	
			Pte KILNER detached to GENERAL HAKING - 1 Officer attached to Artillery for 24 hours.	M.P
LE GRAND PACAUT	26.8.16		Battⁿ moved to billets at LE GRAND PACAUT. - 1 Officer + 50 O.R. at Fort PACAUT - 1 Officer + 10 O.R.	M.P
		8.30 am.	at LAVENTIE and WINCHESTER POST reported Battⁿ	
		2.30-5.0	The parties of 1 Officer + 50 O.R. at LAVENTIE and WINCHESTER POST reported Battⁿ	
			Companies paraded under company arrangements	
	27.8.16		Battⁿ paraded at 9.45 am. for Divine service at 10.30 am in MERVILLE SQUARE.	
	28.8.16	am	Proceeded to LE SART on return. Gas and R. drill.	
			Morning drill. - Bayonet fighting. Gas aide + arms drill. Companies moved across at	
			LE SART commencing at 9.0 am. - Finishing at 5.30 pm. - Sergeant SHEPPARD joined attrd	
			school as temporary instructor. 4 Officers + 4 NCO's reported at MEURILLON for R.E course.	
			10 O.R. reported to O.C 182 T.M.B. for instruction in Bayonet training modern rifle.	
			CAPT A.C. MACKENZIE struck off strength of this unit with effect from 30/8/16 having been	
			permanently attached to 1ˢᵗ Army School of Instruction.	
	29.8.16	8.45	A Coy. - "Field training." - B Coy. Close order drill. Bayonet training. musketry etc - C Coy - Trench attack	
		11.45	4 Officers + 4 NCO's proceeded on R.E course	

Army Form C. 2118.

WAR DIARY
or
INTELLIGENCE SUMMARY.
(Erase heading not required.)

Place	Date	Hour	Summary of Events and Information	Remarks and references to Appendices
LE GRAND PACAUT	29.8.16		D Coy - Bayonet fighting - musketry - close order & arms drill etc	
		11.45	Coy's less specialists under Coy arrangements. Specialists under Specialist Officers. MAJOR BAINES struck off strength of unit wit effect from 28.8.16.	
		1.15		
	30.8.16	am	A Coy - Trench attack practice - B Coy attended gas demonstration by divisional Gas Officer - C Coy Bayonet fighting - musketry - gas helmet drill - etc. D Coy attended course of instruction under R.E.s. Both interrupted by rain.	
		pm	Bombers under Bombing officer in trenches.	
	31.8.16	am	A & B Coys Bayonet fighting - musketry - gas helmet drill etc - Battery C Coy Field training	
		3.4.⁰⁰	D Coy - continued R.E. course under R.E. Officers & N.C.Os	
		pm	Bombers under Batt Bombing Officer.	

J.H. Manning
Lieut-Col.
O.C. 2/6 Y&L Batt. YC & Lak. R.

Vol 5

Confidential.

War Diary of

2/6th Battalion Royal Warwickshire Regiment

From September 1st 1916 to September 30th 1916.

Volume 5.

WAR DIARY or INTELLIGENCE SUMMARY

Army Form C. 2118.

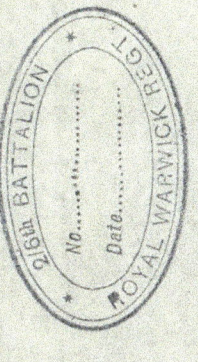

Place	Date	Hour	Summary of Events and Information	Remarks and references to Appendices
LE GRAND PAQUET	1.9.16	6am	The Batt. proceeded in column of route at 6.15 am to moved to L.31.a.6.6. From here two companies deployed at 1000 yards past MAJOR GENERAL COLIN MACKENZIE & then returned to billets. A & B Companies billeting – also musketry, close order drill, bayonet fighting etc. C & D Companies were in position on BEAUPRE – LESTREM Road at 10 am for operations in conjunction with the R.F.C. The companies took up a position which was located by aeroplane by means of firing VERY LIGHTS, ROMAN CANDLES & discharging SMOKE. Messages were also signalled by special signalling apparatus. Medical inspection of all companies.	
		pm	Pte J. WILLIAMSON presented with parchment by G.O.C.	
	2.9.16		Parades. A Coy route march – route Q.5.b.5.5. Q.3.a.2.5.9. Q.28.d.7.0. Q.27.d.3.0. Q.20.c.7.0. Q.15.c.3.9. Q.9.c.5.4. – B Coy Field training – C & D Coy Musketry, Close Order Drill, bayonet fighting, gas helmet drill.	
TRENCHES	3.9.16		Batt. relieved 2/5 GLOSTERS in night on section of FAUQUISSART Sector. Companies moved independently proceeding from LE GRAND PAQUET. Relief was completed by 3.0 p.m. The following posts are also taken over – ROAD BEND – WANGERIE – MAISELOT, FAUQUISSART on our left. 2nd Lt HICKS & 1 N.CO. proceeded on signalling course at LABORSUE	

WAR DIARY or INTELLIGENCE SUMMARY

Army Form C. 2118.

216th BATTALION ROYAL WARWICK REGT.

Place	Date	Hour	Summary of Events and Information	Remarks and references to Appendices
In the trenches	4/9/16	12.30 pm	At 12.30 pm the enemy fired about 20 77 mm shells on ELGIN POST & the C our artillery replied. The remainder of the day was exceedingly quiet, also the night. Enemy patrols were sent out but reported no movement on the part of the enemy. MAJOR G.E. WHITFIELD (MC) reported for duty with Battn.	
	5.9.16	12.30 pm	The enemy again shelled ELGIN POST & our front line. Our artillery replied & the enemy stopped. The enemy's artillery was active throughout the day. At 5.30 pm a bombardment took place as per programme on the WICK SALIENT. During the bombardment 27 duds were noticed. The enemy did not reply on our front line but fired on lines in the rear of WICK SALIENT. As a whole two fires were lit behind our lines. The enemy shelled these for twenty minutes also. Our LTMs and MTMs were active during the day - as a runaway to the enemy's trenches.	
	6.9.16		Our artillery was again active, but enemy retaliated but slightly. A raid was attempted on the enemy's trenches at N.9.a.3.4.2 to N.9.a.8?.6.8. A Bangalore torpedo was placed under the enemy's wire & successfully exploded at 12.10 a.m. The party was however unable to enter the German line owing to a large torous ditch about 15 ft wide & very deep being encountered between the wire & his parapet. The party therefore withdrew returned without loss to our trenches. 5OR speared on 8/gun eamer at LE TOUQUET.	

WAR DIARY or INTELLIGENCE SUMMARY

Army Form C. 2118.

2/6th BATTALION ROYAL WARWICK REGT.

Place	Date	Hour	Summary of Events and Information	Remarks and references to Appendices
S. Kextco	7.9.16		Ration. At 8.45 am 30 aeroplanes were observed passing over our line. Our rifle grenade batteries fired from 9 a.m. to 1 p.m. but drew no retaliation. Throughout the day our 18 pdrs sniped the enemy's line & the Hindjen fired at point blank at the line. — At 5.30 a heavy T.M. was silenced by our artillery party relieves. The enemy's artillery was active during the evening but did little damage.	JMP
	8.9.16 (continued)		2 the early morning must one of our snipers crept out in NO MANS LAND and found a German working party at N.13.c.q.t. At least 4 of the men were killed. Another sniper went out in the evening and found another working party. 3 men were let's seen to fall. Listening patrols were out and a several reconnoitring patrols to find gaps in the enemy's wire.	JMP
	8.9.16		Throughout the day our artillery was very active. In the afternoon our artillery [crossed out: trench] shelled portions of the enemy near man the DISTILLERY, the fire being directed by one of our airplanes. Two large guns taken up a position on a line. In the evening the enemy shelled RUE TILLELOY. Patrols were constantly sent out by all our coys. Patrols were constantly sent out by all coys during the night.	JMP
	9.9.16		Day very quiet both our artillery and the enemy's being inactive. During the night the enemy was very active with M.G. fire — Congratulations received from B.G.C. on raid.	JMP

802

Army Form C. 2118.

WAR DIARY
or
INTELLIGENCE SUMMARY.
(Erase heading not required.)

[Stamp: 2/6th BATTALION ROYAL WARWICK REGT.]

Place	Date	Hour	Summary of Events and Information	Remarks and references to Appendices
2/6 Kemmel	10-9-16		At 3 a.m. a raiding party of 2 Officers (2/Lieut P.J.JOHNSON MC and 2/Lt DUTHIE) and 12 O.R.s raid, attempted to enter the enemy trenches through a gap in the wire at N.19.d.27. However this SHG a BANGALORE TORPEDO was successfully exploded by 2/Lt STEPHENS under the enemy's wire at N.19.a.97.74. to divert his attention. The torpedo was exploded at 3.10 a.m. & the artillery bombarded the enemy's lines. This party returned. 2/Lieut Cox & his men attempted M.G. raiding party had wired a large crater, & shell fire was then opened upon them. Lieut DUTHIE & 6 OR left to try & cut off this M.G. but being subjected to very heavy MG fire had to take cover in a shell hole. One man was severely wounded but was dragged into a SHELL HOLE by 2/Lt DUTHIE & 3 men. During this Cpl fire Lt JOHNSON found it impossible to enter the German trenches & attempted to return, but got to say. At 5.30 am Lt JOHNSON + 3 men returned to our trenches safely. One man (Twomey) been killed & 1 Cpl & further was heard of the remainder of the party, except one man who returned wounded at 4.30 am, & one shine who returned 5am 2/Lt DUTHIE's party bathing. Next they were all a Show very busy Searching a fatigue area and out but were unable to find anyone.	
			The remainder of the day was quiet except for some firing by our LTMS. At night our artillery fired at the WICK SALIENT. At dusk the regimental call was blown as a guide for any men in NO MANS LAND. - NCOs proceeded to advisory trenches at CANTIERS	

803

WAR DIARY or INTELLIGENCE SUMMARY

Army Form C. 2118.

Place	Date	Hour	Summary of Events and Information	Remarks and references to Appendices
Laventie	11.9.16	—	At 4 a.m. LIEUT DUTHIE & Sergt MURRAY returned from NO MANS LAND having remained from 4 am 10th inst. in a shell hole with a wounded man, who however died at 6 am 16th inst. At 8.30 a.m., in broad daylight, 4 men returned from NO MAN'S LAND after the raid carried out in early morning 10th inst. Total casualties as recall of raid:- 8 Killed 1 OR. Missing (believed killed) 1 OR. Missing 2 OR. Wounded 1 OR. 1 OR proceeded to LA GORGUE on sanitary course. 1 Off. + 1 NCO proceeded to LA GORGUE for bayonet. The day was quiet, the enemy hardly replying to our rifle grenades & T.M. fire. In the afternoon we fired a few stokes shell however did no damage. At 9.0 pm our L.T.M's opened rapid fire on the enemy, with great success. Hostiles for stretcher bearers were distinctly heard and cries of "Mercy Camerade"	J.L.
	12.9.16		2 IC moving at about 8.0 am the enemy shelled B EPINNETTE DUMP for a short period. Batn was relieved by 3/17 WARWICKS - relief was completed by 12 noon. Batn billeted at LAVENTIE. 1 Officer & 50 OR reported to OC 3/2nd Field Coy R.E. as permanent working party. 1 Officer & 1 NCO attend DIVISIONAL SCHOOL of Instructors	J.L.
	13.9.16		Bathing parties (totalling 2 Officers & 70 OR) reported to REs at 5.30 am for 6 Framework. Batn bathed & cleaned rifles & equipment. 15 OR reported to 73rd Bombing School for course of instruction. 1 Officer & 5 OR proceeded to LE TOUQUET for Lewis Gun Course.	J.L.

WAR DIARY or INTELLIGENCE SUMMARY

Army Form C. 2118.

Place	Date	Hour	Summary of Events and Information	Remarks and references to Appendices
LAVENTIE	14.9.16	5.0 a.m.	Working party of 2 Officers & 70 OR. supplied for REs.	
		a.m.	Companies not supplying working parties - (A and C) on range - Bayonet-fighting & Physical drill	
		p.m.	Close order drill, gas helmet drill, open order drill, saluting and guard mounting.	
			Specialists under Specialist Officers.	
			1 Officer & 1 NCO per Coy; attended a bombing course under Battn bombing Officer also	
			1 Off. & 1 NCO per coy attend a Lewis gun course under Battn Lewis Gun Officer.	
			LIEUT-COL J.J. SHANNESSY proceed on 1 month's special leave	
			MAJOR A. WHITFIELD (MC) assumes command of Battn.	G.G.
	15.9.16	a.m.	Bayonet fighting, on range - Close order drill & Physical drill (B & D Coys)	
			A & C Coys providing working parties for REs	
		p.m.	Close order drill, gas helmet drill, open order drill saluting & guard mounting.	
			Specialists under Specialist Officers	G.P.
	16.9.16	a.m.	All companies - Bayonet-fighting - Close order drill musketry & saluting drill.	
			A & C Companies - football match.	
		p.m.	B & D Coys - on range. Specialists under specialist officers.	J.W.

WAR DIARY or INTELLIGENCE SUMMARY

Army Form C. 2118.

Place	Date	Hour	Summary of Events and Information	Remarks and references to Appendices
LAVENTIE TRENCHES.	17.9.16		Voluntary Church parade for all denominations	
	18.9.16	am	Working parties totalling 3 Officers and 120 OR found for R.E. Officers and 1 NCO proceeded to 17th Army School. 10% found on account of instruction in A.L. Fuller Phone. Bayonet fighting and Physical drill - Close order drill - Musketry by companies.	
		pm	B + D Coys. football match.	
			A + C Coys firing on range. Specialists under Specialist Officers.	
	19.9.16	5 am	Reserve Company of 5 Officers + 100 OR told in magazine to move up to line at moments notice.	
		2 pm	Large working parties found for R.E. by A + C Coys.	
		am	B + D Coys. Bayonet fighting. Close order drill - musketry.	
		pm	Specialists under Specialist officers. Our NCO pr platoon specially trained in use of SNIPERSCOPE.	
TRENCHES.	20.9.16		Battn relieved 2/ r WARWICKS in the line - taking over from M24.d.5.7. to M13.c.6.8. Relief commenced at 8 am and was completed by 11.15 am. Battn also garrisoned MASSELOT, WANGERIE and ROADBEND POSTS. Our artillery carried out a programme from 10.30 pm to 10.45 p. to which there was no retaliation.	
	21.9.16		At 10.30 am enemy sprinkled with 6 HE and 2 aerial torpedoes in reply to our artillery programme. Our T.M's we thought to have destroyed a dug-out opposite M.24.7. At 4.0 pm an enemy observation balloon was forced to descend hurriedly by our aeroplane. Remainder of day and night quiet.	

WAR DIARY or INTELLIGENCE SUMMARY

Army Form C. 2118.

Place	Date	Hour	Summary of Events and Information	Remarks and references to Appendices
TRENCHES (continued)	21.9.16		1 Officer & 1 NCO proceeded to LA GORGUE on Bayonet fighting course.	JWP
	22.9.16		3 O.R. proceeded to LE TOUQUET on LEWIS GUN COURSE. Our L.T.M's carried out programme at 11 a.m. During the afternoon on Hazebro fired a few rounds on the enemy's back area. The Germans showed greater activity than usual throughout the day with their aeroplanes. During the night the enemy was very active with the M.G.'s	JWP
	23.9.16		Morning very quiet except for a little registration by our artillery. Our snipers shot a German at 6 a.m. Carrier carried out into NO MANS LAND in the morning mist. Our T.M's carried out the programme as normal. The enemy retaliated wit of 7 H.E. shells on N 13.1. A patrol was dispatched to watch a gap in the enemy wire, communication by means of a wire was arranged with the front line & a L.T.M. trained on the gap. The enemy made no attempt however to repair his wire. Our rifle grenade batteries fired at irregular intervals during the night. 2 N.C.Os proceeded to LA GORGUE on Sanitary course.	JWP
	24.9.16		Morning very quiet. In the afternoon the enemy fired 23 77/m H.E. shells at R DE MASSELOT He also fired at our front line obtaining a direct hit on a MTM emplacement but doing no damage. Night quiet except for M.G. fire. — 1 O.R. proceeded to LAVENTIE on cookery course.	JWP

807

WAR DIARY or INTELLIGENCE SUMMARY

Army Form C. 2118.

2/6th Battalion Royal Warwick Regt.

Place	Date	Hour	Summary of Events and Information	Remarks and references to Appendices
TRENCHES	25.9.16	—	Morning quiet, quiet. In the afternoon our artillery did a LITTLE registering on enemy support & front line. Enemy artillery showed more activity than formerly during the day in the trenches. Shelling the TILLELOY with HE during the afternoon. Our trench mortars fired at intervals during the day & at 10 p.m. causing slight retaliation by the enemy. 2/5th WARWICKS took over left subsection from 2/6th WARWICKS.	JW
	26.9.16		Being relieved by 2/7th Warwicks — relief commenced at 5 a.m. and was successfully completed by 11.30 am. Battn proceeded to Billets at LAVENTIE. 1 OR proceeded on cooking course together 50 OR detailed as permanent RE party. 120R proceeded on RE working Party at 7.30 pm Battalion billets remainder of time devoted to cleaning rifles, equipment, clothing etc. and	JW
LAVENTIE	27.9.16		resting in billets. Large Working parties totalling 130 OR & 3 officers found for RE's for not from 5.30 am till 1.30 pm. — 18 OR proceeded on Brigade Bombing Course. 1 OR proceeded on course a "special Sapper".	JW
	28.9.16 am		Working parties found for RE. total 130 OR & 5 Officers. Specialists under Specialist Officers Remainder — Company work — arms drill, bayonet fighting, saluting drill etc.	
	pm		Football match. A Coy v C Coy. D Coy on range & bayonet fighting course.	JW
	29.9.16 am		Usual RE working parties found. Owing to inclement weather coys & specialists worked indoors during the morning.	SOS

Army Form C. 2118.

WAR DIARY
or
INTELLIGENCE SUMMARY.
(Erase heading not required.)

2/6th Battalion Royal Warwick Regt.

Place	Date	Hour	Summary of Events and Information	Remarks and references to Appendices
LAVENTIE	29.9.16	p.m.	Physical training & gathering exercises under Company arrangements.	
		2.30-4.30	5 Officers & 4 N.C.O's instructed in Bayonet fighting by 2.LIEUT E.W. MASSEY	
			2 O.R. proceeded to LA GORGUE on Gas Course. 1 O.R. granted special leave.	A.P.
	30.9.16		R.E. working parties found as usual.	
		9am 10.15	Companies paraded under Company arrangements.	
		10.15	Bath paraded (less R.E. working parties) & marched to M.S.C. 25. to attend demonstration in the FLAMMENWERFER.	
		p.m.	Continuation of Bayonet fighting Course under 2.LIEUT MASSEY.	J.P.
			1 O.R. proceeded on Signalling course on Special "Buzzer" 1 Officer 1 O.R. proceeded on course on LEWIS GUN at LE TOUQUET.	

F.R. West [?]
Major R. War. R.
for O.C. 2/6 R. War. R.

CONFIDENTIAL.

WAR DIARY OF

2/6TH BATTALION ROYAL WARWICKSHIRE REGIMENT.

From 1st October, 1916, to 31st October, 1916.

VOLUME VI.

Army Form C. 2118.

WAR DIARY
or
INTELLIGENCE SUMMARY.
(Erase heading not required.)

Place	Date	Hour	Summary of Events and Information	Remarks and references to Appendices
LAVENTIE	1.10.16	12 noon	Voluntary Church services for all denominations. C.O. held a meeting for all Officers.	JRP
TRENCHES	2.10.16		Bat relieved 2/7th WARWICKS holding over the line from M23.d.4.9. to N.13.C.7.7.2. with 2/6th WARWICKS on our left and 1/8/3rd Inf Bde on our right. Relief commenced at 6 a.m. and was successfully completed by 11.30 a.m. D Coy remained in billets to practice raid. B Coy 2/7th WARWICKS remained in trenches. Morning & afternoon were quiet except for some registration by our artillery. At 5.30 pm our MT.M. & M.T.M's carried out a combined shoot on AC WICK SALIENT. The enemy did not reply to this. At 7.15 pm, 8.50 pm & 12.15 am and 1 a.m. the enemy opened fire on our front & support lines at M.24.5 and M.24.6 with artillery (4.2 & trench mortars) T.M's and Rifle grenades. They also fired heavily with Lewis Machine guns at Aeria Minies. East of these shoots lasted about 15 minutes. Our artillery (18 pounders) replied. These shoots by the enemy were apparently by way of retaliation for the raid carried out by 2/7th WARWICKS the night before. 1 Officer & 1 N.C.O. proceeded to LA GORGUE on 2 days fighting course.	JRP
	3.10.16		The day was quiet. Our T.M's registered at 3.30 pm a between 6.7 pm 16 phos fired on a selected target N. of AC WICK. Enemy showed little activity but appeared nervous during NC	SJ

Army Form C. 2118.

WAR DIARY or INTELLIGENCE SUMMARY.
(Erase heading not required.)

Place	Date	Hour	Summary of Events and Information	Remarks and references to Appendices
TRENCHES	3.10.16	—	Night – Bombing the enemy line on two occasions. A patrol of 1 Officer 2 N.C.O's & 1 man went out to reconnoitre opposite the WICK but were unable to reach the German line as they had to return before 9.0 p.m. owing to raid being carried out on our left by 2/8" WARWICKS. 1 Officer & 1 N.C.O. proceeded on DIVISIONAL COURSE of instruction.	J.P.
	4.10.16		The morning was quiet. The enemy showed some artillery activity during the afternoon. At 6.15 he fired about 45 4.2 shells & some 7.9 on our front line & support trenches. Our snipers observed an enemy working party in the early morning, which was dispersed by our Stokes Guns & the parapet which was being repaired further damaged. Our L.T.M's & M.T.M's fired at 4.30 p.m. according to programme.	J.P.
	5.10.16		The day was generally quiet except for some firing of rifle grenades & L.T.M's by us at irregular intervals. Retaliation was very slight. Night was quiet. Patrols were out but no enemy German seen.	
	6.10.16	—	Day was again quiet except for registration by our L.T.M's at 2.30 a.m. & bombardment on point registered later in day (4 p.m.) Enemy retaliated in afternoon of on ELGIN C.T. at N.19.a.3.3½. A new type of large German Periscope was seen. 1 N.C.O. proceeded on Musketry Course at CAMIERS.	J.M.

Army Form C. 2118.

WAR DIARY
or
INTELLIGENCE SUMMARY.

(Erase heading not required.)

Instructions regarding War Diaries and Intelligence Summaries are contained in F. S. Regs., Part II. and the Staff Manual respectively. Title pages will be prepared in manuscript.

2/6th BATTALION
ROYAL WARWICK REGT.
No............
Date............

Place	Date	Hour	Summary of Events and Information	Remarks and references to Appendices
TRENCHES	7.10.16	—	Day quiet except for a little registration by our 18 pdrs on fronts the German line in preparation for raid. MG carried out on night of 7/6/16. Rifle grenades were dropped on our parapet at 10.50 a.m. A few did little damage. Much carrying of stores & MTM ammunition was done by Companies. German retaliation to our LTM & MTM programme was comparatively scarce. Harrow Man mnel – Night exceptionally quiet.	
	8.10.16	2.45 a.m.	D Company (having remained in billets in LAVENTIE since 2.10.16 to practise) carried out a successful attack raid on the enemy's trenches at N.9.a.6.9. The attacking party consisted of:- LIEUT M.K.JACKSON (in command of party) 2 Lieut L.J. DAVIES, 2 Lieut P.J.W.JOHNSON.M.C. 2 Lieut. D.J. DUTHIE, and 63 O.R. This was subdivided in 4 Bombing parties, 2 Clearing parties and 1 reserve party including runners etc. After a heavy bombardment by the Artillery MTMs & LTM (Stokes shooting was most accurate & excellent) the party entered the enemy's trenches at 3 a.m. The trenches were found to have been very badly damaged & very few of the enemy were encountered. One party of 3 were killed and another party bombed whilst all dug-outs were bombed & it is thought several casualties inflicted. The party withdrew in order covered by Lt JACKSON at 3.20 a.m. bringing with them several identifications such as a greatcoat, cap, pack, rifles, bayonet & papers. 7th Bavarian Regt was identified by means of these. The absence of German M.G. fire was noticeable	J.P.
813

T.J.134. Wt. W708-776. 500000. 4/15. Sir J. C. & S.

Army Form C. 2118.

WAR DIARY
or
INTELLIGENCE SUMMARY.
(Erase heading not required.)

Instructions regarding War Diaries and Intelligence Summaries are contained in F.S. Regs., Part II. and the Staff Manual respectively. Title pages will be prepared in manuscript.

Place	Date	Hour	Summary of Events and Information	Remarks and references to Appendices
TRENCHES	8.10.16		Our casualties were very slight. 1 NCO was killed & 5 OR very slightly wounded. Battn was relieved by 2/7th WARWICKS and proceeded to Billets in LAVENTIE. Relief was successfully completed by 11.30 a.m. Working party supplied for R.E's. 50 OR. 1 Off detailed for permanent R.E work.	JWP
LAVENTIE.	9.10.16 (cont)	—	1 top R.E working party supplied. 2 OR proceeded to LA GORGUE on signalling course.	
	9.10.16		5 OR proceeded to LE TOUQUET on Lewis Gun course. 4 Officers & 105 OR detailed as wiring project. Large R.E working parties provided by day & night. Remainder of Battn bathed & spent time cleaning equipment etc.	
	10.10.16	a.m.	1 Officer & 1 NCO proceeded to LA GORGUE on bayonet-fighting course. 1 Officer & 10 O.R. commenced Divisional bombing course. Brigade Bombing course commenced for staff. 2 Officers & 18 OR were detailed. 8 OR proceeded on Lewis Gun Course at LAVENTIE. 4 OR proceeded to CLARQUES on LTM course. Large R.E working parties provided by day & night.	JWP
		a.m.	Remainder of Battn. – Bayonet fighting – musketry – close order drill etc under Company arrangements. Specialists under specialist Officers (except bombers)	
	11.10.16	a.m.	Medical inspection of Companies – 4 Officers & 100 OR detailed as wiring project. Large working parties provided for R.E's. Remainder of Battn – under Company arrangements – specialists under specialist officers (except bombers)	JWP

Army Form C. 2118.

WAR DIARY
or
INTELLIGENCE SUMMARY.
(Erase heading not required.)

Instructions regarding War Diaries and Intelligence Summaries are contained in F. S. Regs., Part II. and the Staff Manual respectively. Title pages will be prepared in manuscript.

Place	Date	Hour	Summary of Events and Information	Remarks and references to Appendices
LAVENTIE	11.10.16	pm	C.O. M.O. and 1 Officer per Company also 2 NCO's per Company attended demonstration in use of the small BOX RESPIRATOR.	J.P.
	12.10.16	am	Usual working parties detailed for R.E. work. Remainder of Coys under Coy arrangements — including Bayonet fighting. Specialists of C.B. & D. Coys under Specialist Officers. 4 Officers & 100 O.R. detailed as working fatigue.	J.P.
	13.10.16		R.E. working parties detailed as usual.	
		9.30 am	Voluntary Holy Communion Service held.	
		10.15	Coy inspected B Coy.	
		10.45 – 12.30	B. Coy Company Route march. — Remainder on working parties. OC Companies visited trenches prior to taking over from 2/7th WARWICKS also CO. & ADJUTANT. Lieut Berry proceeded to XI Corps Supply School as instructor.	J.P.
TRENCHES	14.10.16		Batt relieved 2/7th WARWICKS in the line taking over from ERITH STREET (exclusive) to FLEET ST (inclusive). Relief successfully completed by 11.30 am. 2/6" WARWICKS on left.	J.P.
	15.10.16		Remainder of day & night quiet except for M.G. fire. Lieut OUTHIE & 40 O.R. proceeded to STEENBECQUE on Sniping Course. — Draft of 62 O.R. received. (all WARWICKS) Everything quiet as normal. L.T.M's carried out programme between 1.15 to 1.45 pm. Every was action with M.T.M's occasionally. Nine action with M.G.s. Rain usual at night. He also showed activity with aircraft.	J.P.

T2134. Wt. W708—776. 500000. 4/15. Sir J. C. & S.

Army Form C. 2118.

WAR DIARY
or
INTELLIGENCE SUMMARY.
(Erase heading not required.)

Instructions regarding War Diaries and Intelligence Summaries are contained in F. S. Regs., Part II. and the Staff Manual respectively. Title pages will be prepared in manuscript.

Place	Date	Hour	Summary of Events and Information	Remarks and references to Appendices
LAVENTIE	15.10.16		Draft of 91 OR received	
	16.		Day exceedingly quiet. Our LTM's fired between 7 and 7.30 am and the enemy fired some 25 shells in our area during the day doing no damage. During the afternoon he shelled LAVENTIE. Our artillery shelled AUBERS. Enemy aircraft active in afternoon. 3 OR proceeded on H.G. Course. 1 Officer & 1 NCO proceeded on Bayonet Fighting Course at LAGORGUE.	J.P.
	17		Our LTM's fired at 7.30 am. Enemy retaliated with a few aerial torpedoes. Our artillery (18 pdrs and How.) immediately opened fire great activity shown by an Inny rifle grenades. Usual work was carried on in front line.	J.P.
	18.		Many rifle grenades fired during day & night. Our MTM's and LTM's fired at 6.45 am on enemy's front line. Aventin. Enemy retaliated with 8 shells on RUE TILLELOY. Our Lewis guns fired 3000 rounds during the night dispersing working parties. Draft of 10 received. Following awarded military medal for gallantry & devotion to duty, particularly on 8th.10.16 during raid. No 2040 Coy. F. HUDSON, 2967 Pte E A WOODS - 6260 Pte J. PARHAM. 6320 Pte E. PATTENDEN. 6319 Pte G J PALMER	J.P.
	19.10.16	-	Everything was quiet & normal during the day. MTM's & LTM's fired according to programme on enemy's front support lines. Enemy replied with rifle grenades. Night quiet. Draft of 62 OR received.	J.P.

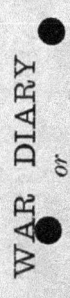

WAR DIARY or INTELLIGENCE SUMMARY

Army Form C. 2118.

2/6th BATTALION ROYAL WARWICK REGT.

Place	Date	Hour	Summary of Events and Information	Remarks and references to Appendices
LAVENTIE	20.10.16	a.m.	Morning quiet	
		p.m.	Battalion relieved by 2/7th WARWICKS. Proceeded to Billets at LAVENTIE. Relief successfully completed by 5 p.m. Working party of 16 O.R. supplied for R.E. Permanent working party of 1 Off. & 50 OR reported to OC 1/3rd Field Coy. R.E. Flying piquet detailed 4 Officers & 100 OR.	J.P.
	21.10.16		Battn bathed. RE working parties supplied for R.E. 204 Coy. HUDSON, 2987 Pte EAWOODS 6260 Pte J PARNUM, 6320 Pte E PATTENDEN 6319 G J PALMER decorated by Militia at LA GORGUE	J.P.
	22.10.16		2/Lieut J FORSYTH reported for duty with battn. Neural working parties supplied for R.E. Voluntary Church service. 1 Officer & NCO proceeded to LA GORGUE for Bay-Fighting course. 1 Off. proceeded on L.T.M course.	J.P.
	23.10.16		Flying Piquet (4 Officers & 100 OR) detailed Battn inspected by BRIGADIER GENERAL BURNELL NUGENT. 2/Lieut DAWSON and 10 OR proceeded on divisional bombing course.	J.P.
	24.10.16		Battn relieved 2/7th WARWICKS in the line taking over the line from ERITH ST (exclusive) to FLEET ST (inclusive). Relief completed by 11:30 a.m. Day and night quiet	J.P.
	25.10.16		Morning quiet. One trench mortars carried out normal programme during the afternoon. Exceptionally little M.G. fire at night. Our artillery registered during the day.	J.P.

Army Form C. 2118.

WAR DIARY or INTELLIGENCE SUMMARY.
(Erase heading not required.)

Instructions regarding War Diaries and Intelligence Summaries are contained in F.S. Regs., Part II. and the Staff Manual respectively. Title pages will be prepared in manuscript.

Place	Date	Hour	Summary of Events and Information	Remarks and references to Appendices
TRENCHES	26.10.16	—	Day again quiet except for intermittent shelling on front line and some aerial torpedoes. Reconnoitring patrols active out by night. Our wire strengthened.	J.P.
	27.10.16		Enemy artillery more active than usual. Our 6TMs had a shoot in retaliation. Enemy shelled communication trenches and RUE TILELOY. O.C. 1/4th LONDONS & 1/13th KENSINGTONS and Company commanders reconnoitred to line & posts prior to taking over.	J.P.
	28.10.16		Battn relieved by 1/14th LONDONS. Relief was successfully completed in spite of heavy shelling of track area by enemy at 12 noon. Battn proceeded to billets at LAVENTIE.	J.P.
LAVENTIE				
MERVILLE	29.10.16	a.m.	Battn marched to the billets at MERVILLE arriving at 12.10 p.m.	
	30.10.16		Being to inclement weather outdoor work was impossible till 11.0 a.m.	J.P.
		11.0 a.m.	Musketry, Physical drill - bayonet fighting etc under Company arrangement.	
		p.m.	Football match (inter-company)	J.P.
	31.10.16	9.30 a.m.	Battn tactical route march including artillery formations & extensions.	
		p.m.	Specialist under specialist officers	

A.B. Whitfield Capt
O.C. 2/6th R. Lancashire Regt

CONFIDENTIAL.

WAR DIARY OF

2/6th BATTALION ROYAL WARWICKSHIRE REGIMENT.

From 1st November to 30th November 1916.

VOLUME VII.

Army Form C. 2118.

WAR DIARY
or
INTELLIGENCE SUMMARY.
(Erase heading not required.)

Instructions regarding War Diaries and Intelligence Summaries are contained in F.S. Regs., Part II. and the Staff Manual respectively. Title pages will be prepared in manuscript.

Place	Date	Hour	Summary of Events and Information	Remarks and references to Appendices
MERVILLE	1/11/16	9.30	Company training including - Close order drill, Musketry, Bayonet fighting	
		12.30	Entered on air drill and Physical training.	
		1.30	Junior Officers paraded under CAPT G L BODDINGTON for Communicating drill - 20 each	
			Shot from each Company fired on range at LE SART	
			Specialists paraded under specialists officers.	
BUSNES	2.11.16		Battn paraded at 9.30 am and marched to BUSNES where it was billeted for the night	
AUCHEL	3.11.16		Battn paraded at 9.25 am and marched to AUCHEL where it was billeted.	
MAGNICOURT	4.11.16		Battn marched to MAGNICOURT where it remained during the night	
HOUVIN	5.11.16		Battn marched to HOUVIN where it remained for the night	
BONNIÈRES	6.11.16		Battn marched to BONNIÈRES. Congratulatory note received from BRIG-GEN BURNE LL NUGENT on march.	
	7.11.16	am	Complete inspection of all kit and equipment. Musketry, Bayonet fighting and Arms drill. Lewis Gunners paraded under Battn L.G.O. Signallers & range finder paraded	
		pm	Bathing of men.	
			Congratulations received from G.O.C. 6th DIVISION on the result of the march, and march discipline and arrangements	

WAR DIARY
or
INTELLIGENCE SUMMARY.
(Erase heading not required.)

Army Form C. 2118.

Place	Date	Hour	Summary of Events and Information	Remarks and references to Appendices
BONNIERES	8.11.16	am	Drive drill, box respirator drill, Musketry, Extended order work, Bayonet fighting. Lewis Gunners (no 3 and 4 teams) paraded also Company Bombers.	JL
		pm	Close order drill including "marching past" & saluting	
			Lewis Gunners (no 3 and 4 teams)	
BONNIERES	9.11.16	7.15 am	Bash Gymnastic Batt.	
		9.30	Box respirator drill – Bayonet fighting – Close order drill – Open order work continuing	
		& 12.45 pm	Musketry and extended order	
			Lewis Gunners, Bombers, Snipers cont. & paraded as specialists	
		2.30 & 3.30	Practice in setting out working parties & allotting tasks	
		10 am	C.O. Company commanders & 5 NCOs per Coy attended demonstration on setting out working parties	
	10.11.16	am	Battn paraded at 9.30 am for practice in the attack. Specialists under Specialist officers.	JL
		6 pm to 7 pm	Practice in setting out roads & tasks	
	11.11.16	am	Close order drill, musketry under Coy arrangements. Practice in Company in attack. Snipers, Bombers & Lewis Gunners under Specialist Officers	

WAR DIARY
or
INTELLIGENCE SUMMARY.
(Erase heading not required.)

Army Form C. 2118.

Place	Date	Hour	Summary of Events and Information	Remarks and references to Appendices
BONNIERES	11/11/16	pm	Bayonet fighting & Physical training	JR
	12/11/16		Junior Officers paraded under the Adjutant	
		12.0	Battn paraded for Church parade	JR
		pm	Tactical scheme for Platoon officers & senior NCOs	
	13/11/16	9.30 am	Battn paraded for practice in the attack	
		2.30 - 3.30 pm	Specialists under Specialist Officers	
			Companies. Close Order drill - to expand to all Coy.	
	14.11.16	5.10 pm	32 O.R. for fog. and 1 Officer per Coy. dug strong point for further purposes.	JR
		9.0 PM	Close order drill - musketry - Bayonet drill - Company in attack under Coy. arrangements	
		am	Specialists under Specialist Officers	
		2.30 pm	Bayonet fighting and Physical drill - Specialists under specialist officers	JR
BERNAVILLE	15.11.16	8.30	Battn marched to BERNAVILLE when it was billeted	JR
BERTAUCOURT	16.11.16		Battn marched to billets at BERTAUCOURT	JR
RUBEMPRÉ	17.11.16		Battn marched to billets at RUBEMPRÉ	JR
WARLOY	18.11.16		Battn marched to billets at WARLOY. 1 NCO proceeded on 5th ARMY SCHOOL OF INSTRUCTION	JR
BOUZINCOURT	19.11.16		Battn marched to BOUZINCOURT	JR

Army Form C. 2118.

WAR DIARY
or
INTELLIGENCE SUMMARY.
(Erase heading not required.)

Instructions regarding War Diaries and Intelligence Summaries are contained in F. S. Regs., Part II. and the Staff Manual respectively. Title pages will be prepared in manuscript.

Place	Date	Hour	Summary of Events and Information	Remarks and references to Appendices
WARLOY	19.11.16	am	Brigadier under Company arrangements, of all R.E. & Equipment. Working party of 5 Officers & 200 O.R. provided for work at AVELUY SIDING. 2 Officers and 2 (Coy) Sergeant Officers and 108 proceed on 10 days leave	JW?
	20.11.16	am	Specialists under Specialist Officers. Companies Musketry. Close Order drill and practice in attack	
			Draft of 44 O.R. received	JW?
BOUZINCOURT	21.11.16	—	Batt. marched to Billets at BOUZINCOURT	JW?
	22.11.16	am	Working party of 11 Officers and 400 O.R. provided for work at AVELUY SIDING. Remainder of Batt. employed in improving Billets. CSM GEORGE reported to give Report which...	JW?
	23.11.16	am	Bayonet fighting - Extensive Musketry - close order drill - practice in rapid deployment. Specialists under Specialist Officers	
		pm	Arms drill & inspection. 6 Officers & 8 NCO's under CSM GEORGE for bayonet fighting instruction. 2 O.R. proceeded on 10 days leave.	JW?
	24.11.16	am	Arms drill, Musketry, & bayonet fighting - practice in attack formation. Specialists under Specialist Officers	
		pm	Close order drill & inspection. 6 Officers & 8 NCO's under CSM GEORGE for bayonet instruction	

Army Form C. 2118.

WAR DIARY
or
INTELLIGENCE SUMMARY.
(Erase heading not required.)

Instructions regarding War Diaries and Intelligence Summaries are contained in F. S. Regs. Part II. and the Staff Manual respectively. Title pages will be prepared in manuscript.

Place	Date	Hour	Summary of Events and Information	Remarks and references to Appendices
BOUZINCOURT	25.11.8	10.30	Batt paraded in above mil. during parade	
		12.30	Indoor work owing to inclement weather	
		4pm	Training of Coy Commanders - Owing to inclement weather indoor work was carried out	
			3 OR proceed on leave	
	26.11.16	10.15am	Company Church Service. Two Officers and 9 OR present on leave	
	27.11.16	11.0am	Batt went from billets to trenches	
	28.11.16	9.0-11.0am	Batt paraded the attack from trenches	
HERCAMP(?)	29.11.16	2-4 pm	Arms drill — company — bayonet fighting. Specialist parades under specialist officers	
		5.30pm-7pm	Practice in night patrolling	
	29.11.16	9.30am	Practice in extending and shooting parties. Specialist under specialist officers	
		2pm	Bat. working out manoeuvre entry for given exercises under Coy arrangements	
		4pm	Specialist under specialist officers	
		6.30-7.30pm	Practice in night patrolling	
	30.11.16	10am	Batt parades arms from trenches	
		1-4pm	Arms drill - bayonet fighting - musketry. Specialist parades under specialist officers	
		5.30-7pm	Practice in night patrolling	

Boustifield
Major
O/C. 2nd/6th D War R.

CONFIDENTIAL

Vol 8

2/6TH BATTALION R. WARWICKSHIRE REGT.
-o-o-o-o-o-o-o-o-o-oo-o-

W A R D I A R Y

DECEMBER 1ST 1916 to DECEMBER 31ST 1916.

(VOLUME 8)

WAR DIARY
or
INTELLIGENCE SUMMARY.
(Erase heading not required.)

Army Form C. 2118.

Place	Date	Hour	Summary of Events and Information	Remarks and references to Appendices
HEDAUVILLE	1/12/16	9.30-11.30am	Close and extended order drill, musketry cum bayonet fighting — working parties of 6 officers and 300 O.R. reporter to R.E.s	
		2-3.30pm	Musketry and interrogating for Officers and NCO's	LJD
MARTINSART	2/12/16	am	The Batt marched to the Support Area at MARTINSART and were billeted in huts.	CJD
	3/11/16	am	Fatigue parties of 12 officers and 450 O.R. were found for R.E.s	CJD
	4/12/16	9.30-10.10am	Close order drill, musketry, physical drill and games	
		10.10-10.50	Practice in moving through woods	
		9.30-9.00	Bombers and snipers under respective officers	CJD
		2.30-3.30	Bayonet fighting & lectures on attack from trench	CJD
		6.30	Practice in night patrolling	
	5		Draft of 28 O.R. reported	
	5/11/16	am	Fatigue parties of 10 officers and 300 O.R. reported to R.E.s	
		9.30-10.10	Close order drill, musketry	
		10.30-11	Practice in the attack from trench	
		11.30-12.30	Bayonet fighting, box respirator drill – lecture on patrolling	
		5.30-6.30	Instruction of NCO's in use of magnetic compass	CJD

Army Form C. 2118.

WAR DIARY
or
INTELLIGENCE SUMMARY.
(Erase heading not required.)

Place	Date	Hour	Summary of Events and Information	Remarks and references to Appendices
MARTINSART	6/12/16	a.m.	Working parties of 129 officers and 1300 O.R. found for R.E.s	GJR
	7/12/16		One officer and 3 O.R. returned from leave	GJR
	8/12/16	9:30-10:30	Photo. Working parties of 12 officers and 400 O.R. found for R.E.s. Arms drill - Lewis gun drill - musketry	GJR
		p.m.	Inspection of men by C.O.	GJR
	9/12/16	a.m.	Working parties of 15 officers and 400 O.R. found for R.E.s. Company commanders and one other officer per coy reconnoitred the trenches	GJR
	10/12/16	a.m.	The Bn. relieved the 2/4th Gloucesters in the trenches. Two officers and 10 O.R. reported from leave. Capt. & a/adj. PADMORE returned from leave	GJR
WELLINGTON HUTS	11.12.16.		Two companies (A & D) relieved in the line - A Coy by 2/5 WARWICKS - D Coy by 2/5/1st WARWICKS. B Coy under orders of O.C. 2/5 WARWICKS & Coy under orders of 1/8 & 2/5 Bdes. A & D Coy returned to WELLINGTON HUTS. HQ moved to WELLINGTON HUTS	JW
	12.12.16		2/Lieut L.J. DAVIES proceeded on leave. also 3 O.R.	
	13.12.16.		A & D Coys proceeded to line for wiring under O.C. 2/5 WARWICKS	GJR
			B Coy proceeded to line for wiring under O.C. 2/5 WARWICKS	
	14.12.16	—	A & D Coy proceeded to line to wire. 2795 RQMS JEROMES C.L. appointed Quartermaster with honorary rank of LIEUT.	

WAR DIARY
or
INTELLIGENCE SUMMARY.

Army Form C. 2118.

(Erase heading not required.)

Place	Date	Hour	Summary of Events and Information	Remarks and references to Appendices
In the line	15th		Batt relieved 2/5th WARWICKS in the line during night of 15/16th. Batt held line from SIXTEEN Rd to B.G.1. — 2/8th WARWICKS on right — 11th DIVISION on left. Relief completed at 3.15 am — Artillery active during the day.	J.P.
	16.12.16		Enemy artillery activity rather below normal. Snug was done during the early hours of morning. — Patrols sent out by both Coys in front line. — Patrol from night Coy got into touch with the Batt on our right. All available men employed in driving	J.P.
	17.12.16		Snug continued all day-break. — Enemy very normal during the day. Patrols sent out at night — Enemy reported to be holding trench in R.16.a. — Snug continued.	J.P.
	18.12.16		Our artillery active especially during the morning. Enemy retaliated—chiefly on HESSIAN and FIELD TRENCHES. — Large working parties continued to use the front. Patrols again sent out by both Coys in front line. — patrol from left Coy encountered enemy	J.P.
	19.12.16		2/4th R. BERKS. R. relief completed by 8.30 p.m. Batt proceeded to	J.P.
MARTINSART	20.12.16		enemy Lt NICHOLSON and 9 OR proceeded on leave. Batt relieved by 2/4 R. BERKS. R.	J.P.
	21.12.16		huts at MARTINSART Batt rested	
HEDAUVILLE	22.12.16		Batt moved to HEDAUVILLE.	J.P.

Army Form C. 2118.

WAR DIARY
or
INTELLIGENCE SUMMARY.
(Erase heading not required.)

Instructions regarding War Diaries and Intelligence Summaries are contained in F.S. Regs., Part II. and the Staff Manual respectively. Title pages will be prepared in manuscript.

Place	Date	Hour	Summary of Events and Information	Remarks and references to Appendices
HEOUDVILLE	23.12.16		Whole day devoted to cleaning, reorganising & bathing	J.P.
	24.12.16		Spent in cleaning and reorganising	J.P.
	25.12.16		Inspection of Coys by Coy Commanders — 3 O.R. proceeded on leave.	J.P.
	26.12.16	am	Close order drill, arms drill and saluting — Bayonet fighting quickening exercises etc	J.P.
		pm	Company drill — Box respirator drill — and lecture by M.O.	
	27.12.16	9.45-11.45 am	Close order & arms drill — Batt" drill — and Relay —	J.P.
		2.15-4.15 pm	Specialists under specialist Officers. 10 O.R. proceeded on leave.	J.P.
	28.12.16		Fatigue party of 6 Officers and 200 O.R. proceeded for O.C. 9" Labour Corps BOUZINCOURT	J.P.
		am	D Coy Close order drill and arms drill — Bayonet fighting musketry	
		pm	Rapid wiring practice.	
	29.12.16	9.45 -11.45	Owing to inclement weather Batt" carried out work in camp under company arangments	J.P.
		pm	Specialists under specialist Officers — Map reading for Officers & NCOs.	J.P.
	30.12.16	—	Batt" marched to huttments at MARTINSART (support area) C.O. proceeded CAPT J. PADMORE assumed command during absence. 3 O.R. proceeded on leave.	J.P.
	31.12.16		Working party of 270 O.R. proceeded and 5 Officers.	J.P.

G.W. Johnson Major
O.C. /B RWarR.

CONFIDENTIAL

WAR DIARY OF

2/6th BATTALION ROYAL WARWICKSHIRE REGIMENT.

From 1st January 1917 to 31st January 1917.

VOLUME IX.

Army Form C. 2118.

WAR DIARY
or
INTELLIGENCE SUMMARY.
(Erase heading not required.)

Instructions regarding War Diaries and Intelligence Summaries are contained in F. S. Regs., Part II. and the Staff Manual respectively. Title pages will be prepared in manuscript.

Place	Date	Hour	Summary of Events and Information	Remarks and references to Appendices
MARTINSART	1.1.17		Working parties totalling 270 O.R. and 5 Officers detailed.	J.P.
	2.1.17		6 Officers attended lecture by G Staff Officer. Working parties totalling 5 Officers on working parties.	J.P.
	3.1.17		Working parties found as for 2nd inst. 1 NCO proceeded on Gas Course.	J.P.
	4.1.17		Working parties totalling 270 O.R., 5 Officers found. 2 O.R. proceeded on Lewis Gun Course at ETAPLES. 3 Coy. 1 Platoon of C Coy quartered at WELLINGTON HUTS.	J.P.
	5.1.17		Normal working parties detailed	J.P.
WARWICK HUTS	6.1.17		Batt. moved to quarters at WARWICK HUTS. Working parties of 200 O.R. + 6 Officers detailed. 1 Coy proceeded to dug-outs at XIII. 1 Coy to dug-outs in RIBON S.	J.P.
	7.1.17		Batt. employed in improving quarters, collecting salvage etc. burying dead bodies	J.P.
	8.1.17		Working parties detailed for carrying duck-boards up to the Line. Salvage collected. LIEUT M.K. JACKSON attached to Battery for 4 days. 2 NCO's proceeded on bayonet fighting course. 1 O.R. proceeded on engineering course.	J.P.
	9.1.17		Large working parties (for carrying duck-boards) detailed. MAJOR G.E. WHITFIELD gazetted Lt.Col. CAPT A.B. WHITFIELD gazetted Major, CAPT M.C. WADE gazetted Major. LIEUT. M.K. JACKSON + B.R. SAUNDERS gazetted CAPTⁿˢ. 2/Lt. JOHNSON (P.J.W.) 2/Lt. MASSEY and 2/Lt L.T. DAVIES gazetted Lieuts. All above with effect from 29 Oct 1916. LT. D. GEE gazetted Lieut. from 26ᵗʰ Sept	J.P.

WAR DIARY
or
INTELLIGENCE SUMMARY.

(Erase heading not required.)

Army Form C. 2118.

Place	Date	Hour	Summary of Events and Information	Remarks and references to Appendices
WARWICK HUTS	10.1.17		Working parties found. LIEUT F.P. STEPHENS & one Platoon of D Coy proceeded to trenches to carry out raid on early morning of 11th	J.P.
	11.1.17		After bombardment of 48 tons LIEUT STEPHENS and party of 34 O.R. assembled in no-mans land at R.16.a.7.0 to carry out raid on FOLLY TRENCH in conjunction with a large raid to be carried out by one company of 2/8th R.War.R. Owing to short shooting by our own artillery 2/8th R.War.R were compelled to withdraw, while the party of two units were obliged to halt in own Jog 15 minutes under heavy fire. When barrage had lifted Lieut STEPHENS and 4 NCOs and 2 men then went forward and carried out the task allotted to them and entered FOLLY TRENCH finding no enemy there however. The whole party returned safely and without casualties at 7.15 am bringing useful information. Battn relieved 2/5th R.War.R in the line, relief commenced at 4.30 pm and was successfully carried out without casualties. Battn got into touch with 2/8th R.War.R on right + 11th D.L.I. on left.	
	12.1.17		Everything normal. LIEUT STEPHENS and a small party went out on patrol. They found that the enemy wire commencing post at LONE TREE and blown which had not been there on the previous night was found. Other valuable information was obtained. Other patrols sent out to get into touch with battns on our left & right.	J.P.

Army Form C. 2118.

WAR DIARY
or
INTELLIGENCE SUMMARY.
(Erase heading not required.)

Instructions regarding War Diaries and Intelligence Summaries are contained in F. S. Regs., Part II. and the Staff Manual respectively. Title pages will be prepared in manuscript.

Place	Date	Hour	Summary of Events and Information	Remarks and references to Appendices
St Martin	13.1.17		Everything normal. Enemy artillery quiet an artillery quiet all day. Patrols sent out by night. LONE TREE kept under intermittent artillery fire during the night to prevent enemy working.	J.P.
	14.1.17		Everything normal. Artillery inactive. Patrols sent out by night but nothing special to report.	J.P.
	15.1.17		At 12.30 am an enemy shelled ZOLLERN REDOUBT but gas-shells. Day quiet. Batt relieved in the line by 7th BEDFORDS. No casualties during relief. Batt' to RUBEMPRE in motor busses. – Lieut HICKS + 20R proceeded on bayonet fighting course.	J.P. J.P.
RUBEMPRE	16.1.17		Batt rested all day in billets	J.P.
CANDAS	17.1.17		Batt marched to billets at CANDAS	J.P.
DOMLEGER	18.1.17		Batt marched to billets at DOMLEGER.	J.P.
CANCHY	19.1.17		Batt marched to billets at CANCHY. Capt M.K. JACKSON and 5 OR proceeded on Lewis Gun Course.	J.P.
"	20.1.17	10:am	Muster parade of Batt. C.O. addressed batt on parade. Remainder of day spent in cleaning up.	J.P.
	21.1.17		Whole day spent in cleaning up and reorganising companies in new organisation of 1 hosting + 1 Lewis Gun section per platoon.	J.P.

Army Form C. 2118.

WAR DIARY
or
INTELLIGENCE SUMMARY.
(Erase heading not required.)

Instructions regarding War Diaries and Intelligence Summaries are contained in F. S. Regs., Part II. and the Staff Manual respectively. Title pages will be prepared in manuscript.

Place	Date	Hour	Summary of Events and Information	Remarks and references to Appendices
CANCHY	22.1.17	9.0 am	Bath parade by companies.	
		10.0 am	Remainder of morning, cleaning equipment etc and organising.	J.P.
	23.1.17	9.0 am	Company Commanders meeting to discuss training. 1 OR proceeded to ST RIQUIER on field engineering course.	
		1.0 pm	Close order drill - saluting drill - Extended order drill - Bayonet fighting - Musketry - Lectures by Company Commanders to NCO's -	
		4 pm	Company commanders meeting to arrange training.	N.P.
	24.1.17	9.0 am	Football matches (inter-platoon) — 1 Officer proceeded on signalling course.	
		10 pm	Training as for 23rd.	
		4 pm	Football	J.P.
	25.1.17	9.0 am	Meeting for all officers.	
		10 pm	Training as for 23rd inst.	J.P.
		4 pm	Football and Lewis Gun throwing competition. Bayonet fighting competition between Coys	
	26.1.17	9.0 am	Officers meeting. 1 OR proceeded on musketry course	J.P.
		10 pm	Parade as for 24th inst. Officers meeting in evening. Football in afternoon.	J.P.
	27.1.17	"	Training as on 26th inst. Football in afternoon. Meeting for all officers in evening.	J.P.

Army Form C. 2118.

WAR DIARY
or
INTELLIGENCE SUMMARY.
(Erase heading not required.)

Instructions regarding War Diaries and Intelligence Summaries are contained in F. S. Regs., Part II. and the Staff Manual respectively. Title pages will be prepared in manuscript.

Place	Date	Hour	Summary of Events and Information	Remarks and references to Appendices
CANCHY	28.1.17	10.0	Church parade for 200 O.R.	J.P.
			CAPT SAUNDERS and 1 N.C.O. proceeded on 5th ARMY Course.	
			Officers meeting held in evening. 1 Officer & 11 O.R. proceeded on G/S Course at ETAPLES.	
	29.1.17	9.0 am	Close order drill – company in attack – Bayonet fighting – musketry – Lecture by Company commander	J.P.
		2.0 pm	Afternoon – football – Officers meeting to discuss training	
		7 pm		
	30.1.17	9.0 am	Training as for 29th inst.	J.P.
		2.0 pm		
		7 pm	Football – Meeting of Company Officers	
			1 N.C.O. proceeded on Cookery Course.	
	31.1.17	9.0 am	Training as for 30th inst.	J.P.
		1.0 pm		
		7 pm	Football – Meeting of Officers.	

B. Mitchell
Lt. Col.
O.C. 2/6 L. Batt. 42. War MR.

Vol 10

CONFIDENTIAL

WAR DIARY OF

2/6TH BATTALION ROYAL WARWICKSHIRE REGIMENT.

From February 1st 1917 to February 28th 1917.

VOLUME X

Army Form C. 2118.

WAR DIARY
or
INTELLIGENCE SUMMARY.
(Erase heading not required.)

Instructions regarding War Diaries and Intelligence Summaries are contained in F. S. Regs., Part II. and the Staff Manual respectively. Title pages will be prepared in manuscript.

Place	Date	Hour	Summary of Events and Information	Remarks and references to Appendices
CANCHY	1.2.17	9 a.m / 2 p.m	Close order drill - Coy in attack - Bayonet fighting Musketry - Range practice - Training of Bombers & Lewis Gunners.	JP.
"	2.2.17	9 a.m / 1 p.m	Bayonet fighting - Musketry - Physical training and Bayonet fighting - Close order drill. Specialist training.	JP.
"	3.2.17	"	Company and specialist training as for 1st inst. - Officers meeting in evening.	JP.
"	4.2.17	10 a.m	Church parade for 100 O.R. - Medical inspection - 1 Officer & 2 O.R. proceeded on course.	JP.
YAUCOURT BUSSUS	5.2.17	a.m.	Batn moved to YAUCOURT BUSSUS. - 2 O.R. proceeded on Lewis gun course.	JP.
"	6.2.17	9 a.m / 1.30 p.m	Company training and specialist training - Specialist training in afternoon.	JP.
"	7.2.17	9 a.m / 1.0 p.m	Company training including attack practice & trench digging - Specialists training.	JP.
"	8.2.17	6 - 7.0	NCO's under Coy Commander - 2 NCO's proceeded on Gas course.	JP.
"	8.2.17	9 - 1 - 2	Company training "Specialist training"	JP.
"	"	3 - 0 - 5.0	Specialist training - remainder Route march.	JP.
"	"	6 - 0 - 7.0	NCO's under Coy Commander. 1 Off & 24 O.R. proceeded to Brigade bombing course.	JP.
"	9.2.17		Training as for 8th. Class of 40 NCO's under Musketry instructor 11 - 12.0 Bat drill 12 - 1.0	JP.
"	10.2.17	9 - 0 - 10	As for 8th inst. - Musketry practice to fit up artillery formation.	JP.
"	11.2.17	10.30	Batn paraded for Church Service. - 1 Officer & 3 O.R. proceeded on Divisional Course.	JP.
"	12.2.17	9.10 12.30 / 1.30 - 3.30	Battn in attack Physical training & Bayonet fighting - Specialist training	JP.

Army Form C. 2118.

WAR DIARY
or
INTELLIGENCE SUMMARY.
(Erase heading not required.)

Instructions regarding War Diaries and Intelligence Summaries are contained in F. S. Regs., Part II. and the Staff Manual respectively. Title pages will be prepared in manuscript.

Place	Date	Hour	Summary of Events and Information	Remarks and references to Appendices
CANCHY	13.2.17		Transport section moved to ST SAVEUR.	
		8.10·45	Bayonet fighting – close order drill – Physical drill.	
		11.120	Batn drill	
		12.10	Practice in recpt clothing out into artillery formation for relieve of cooks	JP.
	14.2.17		Kit inspection of all Coys by C.O. Medical inspection of Batn. Transport moved to MARCELCAVE	JP.
MARCELCAVE	15.2.17		Batn entrained at PONT REMY and moved to MARCELCAVE	JP.
	16.2.17	9.30 am 12.50	Bayonet fighting – close order drill – Musketry. Training of Specialists – S.6 O.R. proceeded on 2nd Brigade bombing course.	JP.
	17.2.17	9.30	As for 16th inst. for training.	JP.
	18.2.17	9.30 - 12.20	Company and Specialist training. C.O. and 2 Coy Commanders proceeded to front line. Batn marched to HARBONNIERES	JP.
HARBONNIERES	19.2.17			JP.
	20.2.17	2.30 - 3.50	Specialist training – Remainder of Batn – cleaning billets.	JP.
		9.30 - 12.30	Specialist training Remainder cleaning & improving billets.	JP.
	21.2.17	"	Under Coy arrangements for training – Specialist training for Lewis Gunners & 1 O.R. proceeded to 1/5 School	JP.
	22.2.17	"	Bayonet fighting, Musketry – Close order drill – Box respirator drill – Specialist training	JP.
	23.2.17	2.30 - 4.0	Specialist training – Remainder cleaning & repairs in billeting area.	JP.

Army Form C. 2118.

WAR DIARY
or
INTELLIGENCE SUMMARY.
(Erase heading not required.)

Instructions regarding War Diaries and Intelligence Summaries are contained in F. S. Regs., Part II. and the Staff Manual respectively. Title pages will be prepared in manuscript.

Place	Date	Hour	Summary of Events and Information	Remarks and references to Appendices
KRAWNIERS	23.2.17		Training as for 22nd inst - including box respirator drill. 2 Coy Commrs proceeded to Elm.	J.P.
	24.2.17	9.12am	Musketry. Bny out fighting- close order drill. Box respirator drill.	J.P.
		2.30	Reading of Divisional Tunnel standing orders.	J.P.
IN SUBPART	25.2.17		Battn moved into Brigade support in dug-outs. Relief completed by 5.30pm.	J.P.
	26.2.17		Working party of 100 OR found for R.E.	
	27		Working parties found of 150 OR each, for work on communication trenches. 3 casualties.	
	28.		Working parties found of 150 OR each, for work on communication trenches.	

Birmingham
Lt. Col.
Comdg. 2/6 R.Warw.R.

Vol XI

CONFIDENTIAL

WAR DIARY OF

2/6th BATTALION ROYAL WARWICKSHIRE REGIMENT.

From March 1st 1917 to March 31st 1917.

VOLUME XI.

Army Form C. 2118.

WAR DIARY
or
INTELLIGENCE SUMMARY.
(Erase heading not required.)

Instructions regarding War Diaries and Intelligence Summaries are contained in F. S. Regs., Part II. and the Staff Manual respectively. Title pages will be prepared in manuscript.

Place	Date	Hour	Summary of Events and Information	Remarks and references to Appendices
Support Trenches VERMAND OVILLERS	1.3.17		Nothing Factice totalling 6 officers and 300 OR found for work on communication trenches. Officers reconnaître route to front line &c.	J.P.
"	2.3.17		Nothing Factice found as for 1st inst	J.P.
"	3.3.17		Batt relieved 2/5th R.WARWICKS in the line during night 3/4th - One patrol sent out. Enemy reported holding his front line. - 2/6th WARWICKS on our left	J.P.
FRONT LINE.	4.3.17		Everything normal during daytime. Left front coy withdrawn before dawn for artillery shoot on salient opposite KRATZ WOOD. Two patrols sent out at night - enemy reported working on salient after shoot.	J.P.
"	5.3.17		Everything normal during day and night. Parties under R.E. worked on construction of posts. 2 Patrols sent out by night. 1 Officer & 10 R to bayonet fighting course.	J.P.
"	6.3.17		Everything normal. Inter - company relief at night. 2 Patrols sent out after completion of the relief. Work under R.E.'s continued.	J.P.
"	7.3.17		Artillery slightly more active than usual. Nothing unusual. 2 Patrols out at night - Enemy report holding line by posts. 1 Officer & 1 O.R. to musketry course.	J.P.
	8.3.17		Batt relieved by 2/1st WORCESTERS and 2/4th GLOSTERS. - relief successfully completed without casualties - Batt billeted at VAUVILLERS.	J.P.

Army Form C. 2118.

WAR DIARY
or
INTELLIGENCE SUMMARY.
(Erase heading not required.)

Instructions regarding War Diaries and Intelligence Summaries are contained in F. S. Regs., Part II. and the Staff Manual respectively. Title pages will be prepared in manuscript.

Place	Date	Hour	Summary of Events and Information	Remarks and references to Appendices
VAUVILLERS	9.3.17		Day spent resting & cleaning up.	AP
	10.3.17		Whole day spent in general cleaning up. M.O. inspected Battn.	AP
	11th	9.30-12.30	Training - including Platoon training for raids - close order drill, bomb throwing.	AP
		2.30-4.30	Musketry & trench raids. - Battn. bathed - 1 O.R. + 6 Offr. to bayonet fighting course.	
	12.3.17		Training as for 11th inst.	AP
	13.3.17		Training as for 12th inst. 1 Officer and 16 O.R. to signalling course.	AP
	14.3.17		Whole Battn. bathed and commenced new treatment for prevention of "trench foot".	AP
			Advanced party proceeded to trenches.	
TRENCHES	15.3.17		Battn. relieved 4 OXFORDS in the line (ABLAINCOURT left subsection) Relief completed at	AP
		3.15 am	without casualties. Front line posts withdrawn for artillery shoot.	
	16.3.17		Day and night normal - No decrease in artillery fire observed - 2 Patrols sent out reported enemy holding his front line with posts, shots fired upon our	AP
			patrols. 1 Officer and 16 O.R. to Lewis Gun course.	
	17.3.17		Enemy reported to have retired from his front line system. Information concerning this was obtained from the 39th Division on our left & found to be correct. Line of	AP

Army Form C. 2118.

WAR DIARY
or
INTELLIGENCE SUMMARY.
(Erase heading not required.)

Instructions regarding War Diaries and Intelligence Summaries are contained in F.S. Regs., Part II. and the Staff Manual respectively. Title pages will be prepared in manuscript.

Place	Date	Hour	Summary of Events and Information	Remarks and references to Appendices
TRENCHES	17.3.17		Outposts established along railway line W of MARCHELEPOT - Posts established in enemy 2nd line. Coy HQ in Bush front line. - Patrol pushed out to E boundary of MARCHELEPOT.	JP
LICOURT	18.3.17		Line of outposts established in line LICOURT - PERTAIN. Posts established along railway W of MARCHELEPOT. Battn HQ moved to German old 2nd line. No enemy encountered.	JP
"	19.3.17		Outpost line established 700 yds E of LICOURT running N and South. Touch maintained with 2/8 WARWICKS on right and 5/9th Durhams on left. Post established on E boundary of EPERANCOURT. Battn HQ at LICOURT.	JP
"	20.3.17		Same outpost line held by Battn - Support Coys employed in road clearing & repairing.	JP
"	21.3.17		Battn outpost line taken over by 2/7th WARWICKS - 3 Coys remain in LICOURT one company at EPERANCOURT - Batt employed in road repairing & clearing.	JP
"	22.3.17		Batt employed in road clearing all day & in repairing the village - Bathing & clothing.	JP
"	23.3.17		As for 22nd inst.	JP
"	24.3.17	9.0 am 4.30 pm	R.S.G. Batt employed in trench digging & in salvage work - consolidating position W of R.SOMME.	JP
"	25.3.17	9.0 am 4.0 pm	Whole Batt employed in road repairing and clearing, & consolidating position W of R SOMME.	JP
"	26.3.17	9.0 am 4.30 pm	Batt employed on road repairing & on salvaging, & bridge building & bridge building under RE	JP

Army Form C. 2118.

WAR DIARY
or
INTELLIGENCE SUMMARY.
(Erase heading not required.)

Instructions regarding War Diaries and Intelligence Summaries are contained in F. S. Regs., Part II. and the Staff Manual respectively. Title pages will be prepared in manuscript.

Place	Date	Hour	Summary of Events and Information	Remarks and references to Appendices
LICOURT	27.3.17		Battn rested all day	J.P.
DEVISE	28.3.17	2. am	Battn marched to DEVISE arriving 5·15 am	
		8 pm	Battn marched to dig trenches in W 34 b and d (62 c S.E). Battn worked at the support line of trenches till 5 am then it returned to TERTRY and was billeted.	J.P.
	29.3.17		Remainder of day spent in resting.	
TERTRY	30.3.17	12·15 am	Battn relieved 2/7th WARWICKS in the line - Battn HQ remained at TERTRY	J.P.
	31.3.17		Battn still draws from the line - Battns on right and left having advanced.	J.P.

Justin Hill
Lieut Col
O.C. 2/6 R. Warwick.

2353 Wt. W2544/1454 700,000 5/15 D. D. & L. A.D.S.S./Forms/C. 2118.

C O N F I D E N T I A L.

WAR DIARY OF

2/6TH BATTALION ROYAL WARWICKSHIRE REGIMENT.

From April 1st, 1917, to April 30th, 1917.

VOLUME XII.

WAR DIARY
or
INTELLIGENCE SUMMARY.
(Erase heading not required.)

Army Form C. 2118.

Place	Date	Hour	Summary of Events and Information	Remarks and references to Appendices
TERTRY	1.4.17	9 a.m. to 4.0 p.m.	Whole battn employed in clearing and repairing roads and in filling large crates in TERTRY	
"	2.4.17		Battn employed for 6 hours in clearing out repairing roads & filling craters	
"	3.4.17		Battn employed all day in clearing and repairing roads & filling craters.	
"	4.4.17		Battn employed in road clearing and repair – 2 Coys filling craters in TERTRY	
"	5.4.17		As for 4.4.17 – Complimentary order received from GENERAL RAWLINSON.	
VILLEVEQUE	6.4.17		Battn marched to VILLEVEQUE. Battn under orders of G.O.C. 183 Inf. Bde and in support	
K.No.line	7.4.17		Battn relieved 2/8 WORCESTERS in line – 2/7" WARWICKS on our right – 184 Inf Bde on left, Southern boundary – R. OMIGNON – north boundary road about 4 miles N of FRESNOY-LE-PETIT.	
"	8.4.17		Preparations made and reconnaissances carried out for attack to be made on morning of 9th. All quiet in the line.	
"	9.4.17		After intense bombardment of enemy trenches for ½ hour by divisional artillery, two companies (C, D) closely supported by one Coy of two 2nd (A) and one of 2/8 WARWICKS attacked HILL C on HILL 120. The hostile wire gave sufficient opposition. Burning candles in the shelters and other signs, pointed to a hurried retreat by enemy very shortly before the attack was achieved. B' Coy held posts on line of resistance – 1 Coy 2/8" WARWICKS in reserve at MAISSEMY.	

Army Form C. 2118.

WAR DIARY
or
INTELLIGENCE SUMMARY.
(Erase heading not required.)

Instructions regarding War Diaries and Intelligence Summaries are contained in F. S. Regs., Part II. and the Staff Manual respectively. Title pages will be prepared in manuscript.

Place	Date	Hour	Summary of Events and Information	Remarks and references to Appendices
In the line	9.4.17	—	The Captured lines of trenches were consolidated & two posts pushed forward and established. 3 patrols were sent out – BERTHENCOURT reported held by enemy. Casualties – 1 O.R. Killed 8 O.R. wounded.	J.P.
VILLECHOLLES	10.4.17		Batt. relieved by 2/8 WARWICKS – Batt. moved to VILLECHOLLES	J.P.
UGNY	11.4.17		Batt. moved to UGNY and LANCHY – HQ. Transport & QM stores at UGNY – 2 Coys at LANCHY Batt. rested all day.	J.P.
"	12.4.17	9.30 a.m.	Day spent in cleaning and refitting and bathing	
"	13.4.17	12.30 p.m.	Also rifle - gun and saluting drill - Bayonet fighting, Musketry, Platoon in attack – Lewis gun class under L.G.O. – signallers under Signalling Officer.	J.P.
"	14.4.17	8 a.m. – 12 noon	Two Coys employed in filling crater at W.9.a.o.9. (66.D.) & clearing TERTRY – BEAUVOIS Road.	J.P.
		12 n. – 4 p.m.	Two Coys attached other two on road clearing. – Specialists under specialist officers.	J.P.
"	15.4.17		As for 14th inst. – road repairing	J.P.
"	16.4.17	8 a.m. – 12 noon	A & C Coys road clearing and repairing	
		12 noon – 4 pm	B & D Coys relieved A & C Coys.	J.P.
"	17.4.17	8 a.m. – 12 noon	B & D Coys road repairing & filling craters	J.P.

Army Form C. 2118.

WAR DIARY
or
INTELLIGENCE SUMMARY.
(Erase heading not required.)

Instructions regarding War Diaries and Intelligence Summaries are contained in F. S. Regs., Part II. and the Staff Manual respectively. Title pages will be prepared in manuscript.

Place	Date	Hour	Summary of Events and Information	Remarks and references to Appendices
UGNY	17.4.17	12 noon	A + C Coys working on water & road repairing	J.P.
		4 p.m.	Batt" noted	J.P.
18.4.17			Batt" noted on road clearing and repairing do 17.4.17.	
	19.4.17	9.30-1.0	Batt" trained. — Attacked guard scheme, close order drill — practice in patrolling by day and by night	J.P.
		2.30-4.0	Cleaning and repairing billets.	
SAVY	20.4.17		Batt" marched to SAVY and became reserve Batt" to 14th Inf Bde. 1 O.R. sent to hospital sick. CO & Company commanders reconnoitred line	J.P.
	21.4.17		Batt" noted and CO and Company commanders noted line again	J.P. Inf Map A7.13.S.W.
	22.4.17		Batt" relieved 2nd Batt" MANCHESTER Reg" taking over the line from S.27 central to S.15.d.1.5 (62 B.S.W.) — 184th Inf Bde on our left.	J.P.
BROWN LINE S.2 Section	23.4.17		Everything normal during the day — enemy shelled back areas. Batt" relieved of part of the line — now holding line from S.21.f.5.0 to S.15.d.15. — 2/7 R.WAR.R. relieved Batt".	Ref map 62 B.S.W.
	24.4.17			J.P.
Outpost Line	24.4.17		Batt" relieved 2/8th Batt" R.WAR.R. in outpost line taking over from S.6 central to S.23.6.9.5. French army on our right and 184 Inf Bde on our left	J.P. (62.S3 S.W)
	25.4.17		Left company relieved by 184 Inf Bde — Batt" returned now holds from S.23.b.9.5. to S.12.a.7.6.	62 B.S.W map.

Army Form C. 2118.

WAR DIARY
or
INTELLIGENCE SUMMARY.
(Erase heading not required.)

Instructions regarding War Diaries and Intelligence Summaries are contained in F. S. Regs., Part II. and the Staff Manual respectively. Title pages will be prepared in manuscript.

Place	Date	Hour	Summary of Events and Information	Remarks and references to Appendices
Outpost line S.28.c.5.5 S.21.a.7.6	26.4.17		Batt holding line. Everything normal during the day. At 7.30 pm SOS signal was fired by company on right of 164 & 7 Bde. No action was necessary by this Batt. Batt relieved by 2/7th Batt R.WAR.R. Batt proceeded to SAVY becoming reserve Batt.	J.P.
"	27.4.17			J.P.
SAVY	28.4.17		Batt found working party of 20 OR for work on craters. Carrying party no also provided.	J.P.
	29.4.17		Working and carrying parties totalling 120 O.R. provided	J.P.
BROWN LINE S.14.6.5.5. S.15.d.1.0	30.4.17		Working party of 30 OR provided in morning. Batt relieved 2/5th Batt R.WAR.R. in the BROWN LINE holding line from S.14 & 5.5. to S.15.d.1.0.	Relief S.14.b.5.5 to S.15.d.1.0

Justin Field
Lieut. Colonel
O.C. 2/6 R.War.R.

2353 Wt. W.2344/1454 700,000 5/15 D. D. & L. A.D.S.S./Forms/C. 2118.

C O N F I D E N T I A L.

WAR DIARY OF

2/6TH BATTALION ROYAL WARWICKSHIRE REGIMENT.

From May 1st to May 31st, 1917.

VOLUME XL11.

Army Form C. 2118.

WAR DIARY
or
INTELLIGENCE SUMMARY.
(Erase heading not required.)

Instructions regarding War Diaries and Intelligence Summaries are contained in F. S. Regs., Part II and the Staff Manual respectively. Title pages will be prepared in manuscript.

Place	Date	Hour	Summary of Events and Information	Remarks and references to Appendices
S 14 d.5.5 S 15 d.1.0 BROWN LINE	1.5.17	—	Battn holding left subsection of BROWN LINE. Whole Battn engaged during hours of darkness in digging and carrying and during the day. Battn rested by day.	Ref Map 62 B.S.W. JC
"	2.5.17	9.15 pm 4 a.m.	Battn employed in digging, wiring and carrying. The six instructors of HQ dug out. Situation quiet by day.	JC
"	3.5.17	9.15 pm 4 a.m.	Battn employed in completing continuous line of trenches. For S 14 & 5.5 to S 15.d.1.0. Construction of HQ. Situation quiet all day and night. Tactical belt of wire commenced.	JC
"	4.5.17		Battn rested in morning.	
		3p-6pm	2 Companies employed in improving existing trenches.	
		9.15-4.0am	Digging and wiring. Continuous line of trenches from S.14.&.5.5 to S.15 d.1.0. Battr on left and Battn on right (2/7th K.L.R.L) completed. Trenches joined up with Bdes on left and right (Standard type) continued. 4 inboard dragons disposed of firing. Bell of coils (4th Army Standard type) to BROWN LINE in carrying material up to BROWN LINE. Battn rested. Afternoon - 2 Coys employed in improving trenches, latrine mending fire steps etc	62 B.S.W. JC
	5.5.17			

Army Form C. 2118.

WAR DIARY
or
INTELLIGENCE SUMMARY.
(Erase heading not required.)

Instructions regarding War Diaries and Intelligence Summaries are contained in F. S. Regs., Part II and the Staff Manual respectively. Title pages will be prepared in manuscript.

Place	Date	Hour	Summary of Events and Information	Remarks and references to Appendices
BROWN LINE S.14.b.5.5 S.15.d.1.a.	5.6.17	9.15–4.0am	Continuation of tactical role. Baturnous belt completed from S.14.b.5.5. to S.15.d.1.a. Situation quiet all day, incl. night.	J.P.
Outpost line S.21.b.9.3. b. S.12.a.7.6	6.5.17		Battn relieved 2/8th R.War.R. in outpost-line. 184 Inf Bde on our left. Trench dug during on our right. Relief successfully completed without casualties. Two patrols sent out. Day very quiet.	J.P. 6.2.13. 8v) J.P.
"	7.5.17		After dusk wiring material was carried up to the piquets. Wire erected and strengthened. Piquet posts improved. Night quiet. No casualties. Patrols sent out. Day quiet.	J.P.
"	8.5.17		Wiring was carried on after dusk. Wiring in front of piquets continued. Enemy showed considerable activity with M.G.s and artillery during the evening and night, apparently suspecting a relief. No casualties. Day as usual, very quiet.	J.P.
"	9.5.17	9.30pm	The Battn was relieved by 2/7th Battn R.War.R. and proceeded to quarters at SAVY. Relief successfully completed without casualties.	J.P.
SAVY	10.5.17		Battn rested during the day, except for about 70 O.R. who were detailed as working parties & carrying parties up to the line. Battn in support.	J.P.

WAR DIARY
or
INTELLIGENCE SUMMARY.
(Erase heading not required.)

Army Form C. 2118.

Place	Date	Hour	Summary of Events and Information	Remarks and references to Appendices
SAVY	11.5.17		Bathing and carrying parties totalling 2 Officers and 120 OR detailed. 1 Batt bathed and received pick clean clothing.	J.P.
"	12.5.17		Bathing parties of 2 Officers and 130 OR detailed. Remaining half of Battalion bathed & issued with clean clothing.	J.P.
"	13.5.17		Bathing parties detailed as for 12.6.17.	J.P.
BEAUVOIS	14.5.17		Batt. was relief returned in support area by 1st Batt 121st FRENCH REGt and proceeded to BEAUVOIS.	J.P.
HERLEY	15.5.17		The Battn marched to HERLEY (near NESLE) and billeted there.	J.P.
	16.5.17		The Battn rested during the day.	J.P.
LONGEAU	17.5.17		The Battn marched to NESLE where it entrained and proceeded to LONGEAU.	J.P.
			Thence it marched to FLESSELLES	
FLESSELLES	18.5.17	9.45	Battn trained - Musketry - Bayonet fighting - Close order drill - Lecture and practice	J.P.
		12.45	in outpost work.	
	19.5.17	9.45	Battn training - Every Officer NCO & man tested box respirator tested in	J.P.
		12.45	Gas chamber 900.	
		2.30	Practice in Company in attack.	
		3.30		

Army Form C. 2118.

WAR DIARY
or
INTELLIGENCE SUMMARY.
(Erase heading not required.)

Instructions regarding War Diaries and Intelligence Summaries are contained in F. S. Regs., Part II. and the Staff Manual respectively. Title pages will be prepared in manuscript.

Place	Date	Hour	Summary of Events and Information	Remarks and references to Appendices
FLESSELLES	20.5.17	9.30 am	Batt. trained. Musketry - Close order drill - Company in attack.	
		12.45 pm	Brigade paraded to presentation of decorations by G.O.C. 61st Div: After the ceremony a Church service was held.	W.P. G.P.
GEZINCOURT	21.5.17		The Batt. marched to GEZINCOURT. N° 241757 SERGt WILLIS mentioned in despatches.	
	22.5.17	9.30 am	The Batt. paraded for inspection by BRIG-GEN SACVILLE-WEST.	
		4.0 pm	CO, 2nd in Command, Adjutant and Coy Commanders attended STOKES MORTAR demonstration.	G.P.
IVERGNY	23.6.17		The Batt. marched to IVERGNY.	
BERNEVILLE	24.5.17		Batt. proceed by motor lorries to point on ARRAS-DOULLENS main road & then marched to BERNEVILLE	W.P. G.P.
	25.5.17		Cos. inspected kit & equipment etc of all Companies.	
	26.5.17	7.30/11.0	Batt. trained. - Musketry - Close order drill - Company in attack, SCR. per Coy attended Batt. L.G. Class.	
		5.7	(Extra class) Snipers, Lewis Gunners, squadrons, unit rapetive Officers also rifle grenadiers Lewis Gunners, Scouts, training under Coy arrangements	G.P.
	27.5.17	7.45 am	Musketry - Bayonet fighting - Bomb throwing - Close order drill -	
		10.30 am	Church parade.	

WAR DIARY
or
INTELLIGENCE SUMMARY.
(Erase heading not required.)

Army Form C. 2118.

Place	Date	Hour	Summary of Events and Information	Remarks and references to Appendices
BERNEVILLERS	5.17	7.30–11.0	Battn. trained. Practice in Battn. in attack	
		5.30 p.m	Battn. parade for inspection by C.O. and Battn. drill	
	29.5.17	7.30 p.m	Battn. trained – Bayonet fighting – musketry – close order drill – Bett classes for Scouts and Snipers, Stokes – Bearers.	g.P.
		5–7 p.m	Battery Action and S/S Sections training in their particular work under Company arrangements. 4 min. per Coy training on sure 5T rifle grenade.	g.P.
	30.5.17		All Companies used the range during the day. Owing to inclement weather, other training carried out in doors.	g.P.
	31.5.17	8.15 a.m	Battn. marched to & from training ground and took part in Brigade practice attack	g.P.
		5 p.m	After attack Battn. put through smoke & gas cloud	
		4 p.m	B.G.C. 182 Bde inspected transport and billets	g.P.
			Strength of Battn. 36 Officers and 644 O.R. (fighting strength)	

Signed
Lieut-Colonel.
OC 2/6 R.Sus.R.

CONFIDENTIAL.

WAR DIARY OF

2/6TH BATTALION ROYAL WARWICKSHIRE REGIMENT.

From June 1st, 1917, to June 30th, 1917.

VOLUME XIV.

Army Form C. 2118.

WAR DIARY
of
INTELLIGENCE SUMMARY.
(Erase heading not required.)

Instructions regarding War Diaries and Intelligence Summaries are contained in F. S. Regs., Part II. and the Staff Manual respectively. Title pages will be prepared in manuscript.

Place	Date	Hour	Summary of Events and Information	Remarks and references to Appendices
BERNAVILLE	1.6.17	9.30am	The Battalion marched to billets at AGENICOURT	
	2.6.17	9-11am	Physical & bayonet fighting, musketry, close order drill. One subaltern trained on an the specialist officers	
		2-4pm	Co-operation of arms for bn & higher. Bayonet drill bn musketry course	
	3.6.17	10am	The Battalion paraded for inspection by the Commander-in-Chief and Church parade	
	4.6.17	9am	The Battalion paraded for inspection by CO	
		9.30-11am	Company training	
		5pm	All officers and sergeants of C.D. Coy paraded under the CO for a Tactical Scheme	
	5.6.17	7am-11am	Captain & platoon commanders of two companies—class order drill bayonet fighting, musketry, hyperocle	
		5pm	All officers and sergeants of A & B Coy paraded under the CO for a Tactical Scheme	
	6.6.17	8am-11am	A&B Coys—(under a Range). C&D Coys—close order drill, bayonet fighting, musketry, practice & construction of figure, objective and turning of hostile line	
		5-7pm	C Coy on Range. A & D Coys on Tactical Platoons in attack (open warfare)	
	7.6.17	7.30-11am	D Coy only on Range. (The other Coys having the command) Physical drill close order drill & bayonet fighting. All companies drill musketry.	
			Lectures and organisation of offense & a demonstration in field communication & bivouac & overhead cover & working.	
	8.6.17	8am-11am	Company training	
		7.30-11am		
		6-6:30pm	All specialists paraded under Specialist officers.	
	9.6.17	8am-11am	The Battalion less D Coy worked on constructing a range and bayonet fighting course	

Army Form C. 2118.

WAR DIARY
or
INTELLIGENCE SUMMARY.
(Erase heading not required.)

Instructions regarding War Diaries and Intelligence Summaries are contained in F. S. Regs., Part II and the Staff Manual respectively. Title pages will be prepared in manuscript.

Place	Date	Hour	Summary of Events and Information	Remarks and references to Appendices
BERNEVILLE	10.6.17	10 am	The Batt paraded for Church of England Service	AR
		9 am	Service for No Conformists and Roman Catholics	AR
		4pm-6.30p	The Batt bathed	
"	11.6.17	5.30 am	Batt marched to billets at DAINVILLE	
DAINVILLE	12.6.17	9 am	Battalion paraded for inspection by BRIGADIER GENERAL THE HON. SACKVILLE WEST	AR
		5-7 pm	Company drill, Saluting drill, physical training, extra training in particular weapons	
"	13.6.17	7-9 am	Musketry, physical training, close order drill, bayonet fighting. Specialists paraded under their respective officers	
		9.30-11 am	Company training in advance guard. Lieut Col C.V. Rowbotham assumed command of the Batt vice Lt Col A E Hopkins AR	
"	14.6.17	6 am-10 am	Battn (less B Coy) paraded for a route march	
			B Coy worked on ammunition range and bayonet fighting Course	
		1.30-4 pm	Route marches	
"	15.6.17	7-11 am	Company training - musketry, bayonet fighting. The training of section leaders commenced. The on the range	
			Specialists paraded under their respective officers	AR
"	16.6.17	7-9 am	Company training - close order drill, musketry, running drill. Specialists under specialist officers	
		9-11 am	Company in attack	AR
			"C" Coy relieved a company of the 7/6 Cheshires on "D" ammunition dump Guard	AR

Army Form C. 2118.

WAR DIARY
or
INTELLIGENCE SUMMARY.
(Erase heading not required.)

Instructions regarding War Diaries and Intelligence Summaries are contained in F. S. Regs., Part II. and the Staff Manual respectively. Title pages will be prepared in manuscript.

Place	Date	Hour	Summary of Events and Information	Remarks and references to Appendices
DAINVILLE	17.6.17	9.30 a.m	The Batt (less C Coy) paraded for Church of England Service. Capt T Cliff H Reaver admitted to Corps Rest Station.	GR
"	18.6.17	6.30-10.30a	The Batt (less C Coy) practiced advance guard and open warfare tactics.	GR
		5-6.30pm	Reconnaissance Training.	GR
	19.6.17		No training. 2Lt. 18 hf. Cole Hone Shea and Smith were killed at 2pm	
	20.6.17	6.30-9.30a	Company training. Specialists however were then respective officers	
		9.30-10.30a	Battalion drill under the Commanding Officer	
		4p-5p	Reconnaissance training	GR
	21.6.17	7-11am	Company training and firing on the range	GR
		5-6.30pm	Recreational Training	
	22.6.17	4-10am	Company Training – The Regtl. hamper marched to BOBREUVRETTE. 'C' Coy was relieved from '9' Dump	GR
	23.6.17	9.00am	The Batt. marched by Bde. to ST GEORGES and billet.	GR
ST GEORGES	24.6.17	11.15a	A voluntary Church of England Service was held.	GR
	25.6.17	7-9am	Company training. Specialists however under their respective officers	
		9-12noon		
		5-4.30p	Recreational Training	
	26.6.17	7-8	Company training. Specialists however under their respective officers	GR
		9-12		
		5-6.30p	Recreational Training.	
	27.6.17	10.—	Tactical exercise without troops for all officers under the Commanding Officer	GR
		9-12	Company recreational training	
		5-6.30	Reconnaissance Training	

Army Form C. 2118.

WAR DIARY
or
INTELLIGENCE SUMMARY.
(Erase heading not required.)

Place	Date	Hour	Summary of Events and Information	Remarks and references to Appendices
ST. GEORGES	28.6.17	7-8am	Company Training	
		5-6.30	Recreational Training.	
	29.6.17	2/Lieut A.H.R Rumsby was accidentally killed during bombing practice and 2 O.R. wounded. Draft of 13 O.R. reported.	AJR
		6.15-1pm	2Lt Beresford Peirse was wounded fighting in the BOIS au HESDIN	AJR
		4pm	4112 Pte QUMILLY was buried in the churchyard ST GEORGES	AJR
	30.6.17	8.15-1pm	Companies practised woods fighting in the BOIS au HESDIN	AJR

R. Dunlop Lieut. Col.
Commanding 1/6 R War R

CONFIDENTIAL.

WAR DIARY OF

2/6TH BATTALION ROYAL WARWICKSHIRE REGIMENT.

From July 1st, 1917, to July 31st, 1917.

VOLUME XV.

Army Form C. 2118.

WAR DIARY
or
INTELLIGENCE SUMMARY.
(Erase heading not required.)

Instructions regarding War Diaries and Intelligence Summaries are contained in F. S. Regs., Part II. and the Staff Manual respectively. Title pages will be prepared in manuscript.

Place	Date	Hour	Summary of Events and Information	Remarks and references to Appendices
ST. GEORGES	1/7/17	11 am	Voluntary service for all denominations.	RJP.
"	2/7/17	9-1 pm	Battalion practiced wood fighting	RJP
		5-6.30 pm	Recreational training	
"	3/7/17	7-8 am	Company and Platoon training. A+B Coy fired on the range	RJP.
		9-12 noon		
		5-6.30 pm	Recreational training	
"	4/7/17	7-9 am	Company & platoon training. C+D Coy fired on the range	RJP.
		9-12 noon		
		5-6.30 pm	Recreational training.	
"	5/7/17	6.30-1 pm	Finals of Inter-Platoon Competition. Lieut & Adjt J.F. Ardman returned from leave	RJP.
"	6/7/17	7-8 am	Company and platoon training	RJP
		9-12 noon		
"	7/7/17	7-8 a-	Battalion dies	RJP
		9-11 am	Company and Platoon training	
		11 am	Bn Lecturer gave a demonstration to the reserves of the Batt in the Platoon in attack on acting enemy	
"	8/7/17	11 -	The Brigade practised for Church of England service - During the afternoon the following Brigade finals were arm finals were tied:- Semi final of water of water polo between tug of war, final of platoon relay race, final of features for Brigade Football tournament Draw 1.70 B/R Whites	RJP

Instructions regarding War Diaries and Intelligence Summaries are contained in F. S. Regs., Part II. and the Staff Manual respectively. Title pages will be prepared in manuscript.

WAR DIARY
or
INTELLIGENCE SUMMARY.
(Erase heading not required.)

Army Form C. 2118.

Place	Date	Hour	Summary of Events and Information	Remarks and references to Appendices
ST GEORGES	17/7/17	5.45am	The Battalion practiced a trench to trench attack	
			C Coy represented the Battalion in the final of the Divisional – inter-coy open fighting competition	GJD
	18/7/17	7-8	Company training	
		9am-4pm	Every coy fired on the range for 3 hours	GJD
	19/7/17	8.15-1pm	The Battalion practiced a trench to trench attack	
			Lewis gun class of 8 OR per coy paraded under the LGO	GJD
	20/7/17	10.30am	The Brigadier General Commanding inspected the Battalion less transport	
		4-9pm	Route March – route :- FRESNOY – INCOURT – BLINGEL – BEALENCOURT – cross roads ½ mile W of BEALENCOURT CHURCH – AUCHY-LES-HESDIN – cross roads ¼ mile SSW of HLn HERAUVILLE – ST GEORGES	Ref map Lens 11 1/100,000
		7-8am 9-1pm 5-7pm	Lewis gun class of 8 OR per coy paraded under LGO. and Bombing class under Bombing officer	GJD
	21/7/17	am	The hours practice in trench to trench attack under coy arrangements.	
			The Battalion bathed.	
		5pm	A Battalion boxing tournament was carried out	
			A draft of 83 O.R reported to the Battalion	GJD
	22/7/17	am	Voluntary services for all denominations	GJD
			Capt H.N. DAVENPORT. 1/4 Bn. Oxford & Bucks Light Infantry reported for duty and assumed the position of 2nd in Command of the Battn	GJD

A7092. Wt. W1239/M1293. 750,000. 1/17. D. D & L., Ltd. Forms/C2118/14.

Army Form C. 2118.

WAR DIARY
or
INTELLIGENCE SUMMARY.
(Erase heading not required.)

Instructions regarding War Diaries and Intelligence Summaries are contained in F. S. Regs., Part II. and the Staff Manual respectively. Title pages will be prepared in manuscript.

Place	Date	Hour	Summary of Events and Information	Remarks and references to Appendices
ST GEORGES	9/7/17	7-8 a. 9-1 p.	3 Company and Platoon training. A & D Coys fired on the range from 9-1 pm	GJP
	10/7/17	10 a.m.	The Regiment had little holiday! Divisional Sports were held at WILLEMAN	GJP
	11/7/17	7-8 a. 9-1 p.	Battalion drill Company and Platoon training	GJP
	12/7/17	7-8 9-1 9-1	Company and Platoon training. B & C Coys fired on the range Lewis gun teams of B & D Coys and bombing class of 9 or Co fired Coy musketry operational officers	GJP
	13/7/17	7-8 9-1	Company and Platoon training Lewis gun and bombing classes were their respective officers	GJP
	14/7/17	7.30 a. 9-1	The Batt.n practised an open warfare attack Lewis gun classes of B & D formed under L.A.O.	GJP
	15/7/17	11.30 a. 9.30 -	Voluntary services for Church of England and Roman Catholics Voluntary service for Non Conformists. Draft of 96 OR reported to the Batt.n	GJP
	16/7/17	11.30 p 1st - 4 am 5 - 8 pm	Batt.n practised night marching and assembling for an attack at daybreak down Route march	GJP

Army Form C. 2118.

WAR DIARY
or
INTELLIGENCE SUMMARY.
(Erase heading not required.)

Instructions regarding War Diaries and Intelligence Summaries are contained in F. S. Regs., Part II. and the Staff Manual respectively. Title pages will be prepared in manuscript.

Place	Date	Hour	Summary of Events and Information	Remarks and references to Appendices
ST GEORGES	22/7/17	8.30 am	The Battalion practiced attack to Trench attack	JR
		9-1/5-7	3 hours gun drill for LG for personnel under LGO	JR
LIGNY-SUR-CANCHE	24/7/17	am	The Battalion marched to billets at LIGNY-SUR-CANCHE	JR
	25/7/17	8 am	A Coy reported to the R.T.O. FREVENT for entraining duties the Bde. Capt. L.L. GREENER reported as Bde Entraining officer	JR
			2 hours route march was carried out under Coy arrangement	
ROUBROUCK	26/7/17		The Battalion entrained at FREVENT station and proceeded to CASSEL where it marched to billets in the ROUBROUCK area	JR
	27/7/17		No Battalion parades. The company commanders to company research	JR
	28/7/17	8-12 noon	The following were carried out under Coy arrangement :- Bomb and Lewis Gun drill, musketry, section lead, a practice in flanking and digging trenches for a harassed trench	JR
	29/7/17	am	Voluntary services were held for all denominations	JR
	30/7/17	9-12 am	A draft of 1 Offr. 40 OR. reported to the Battalion	
			Musketry and platoon drill under Coy arrangement. Lewis Gun class practice under LGO	
		3.30-7.30	Musketry. "A" Coy fired full range. Lewis Gun class practice under L.G.O.	JR
			The Regular Junior Commanding inspected the draft which arrived on 29/7/17	
	31/7/17	11.30	The Battalion practiced attack to trench attack	JR
			Fighting strength of the Battalion 40 officers and 915 O.R.	

J. Brickman
Lieut-Colonel
O.C. 2/6th R. Sussex Regt.

CONFIDENTIAL

WAR DIARY OF

2/6th Battalion Royal Warwickshire Regiment.

From August 1st, 1917 to August 31st, 1917.

@@@@@@@@@@
@
@VOLUME XVI@
@@@@@@@@@@

Army Form C. 2118.

WAR DIARY
or
INTELLIGENCE SUMMARY.
(Erase heading not required.)

Instructions regarding War Diaries and Intelligence Summaries are contained in F. S. Regs., Part II. and the Staff Manual respectively. Title pages will be prepared in manuscript.

Place	Date	Hour	Summary of Events and Information	Remarks and references to Appendices
ROUBROUCK	1.8.17 to 15.8.17		Battalion trained.	JP
	16.8.17		Battalion entrained at ARNEKE & moved by rail to HOPOUTRE and thence marched to the BRANDHOEK No 1 area.	Rz maps 27 NW and sheet 28. J & J-
BRANDHOEK AREA (Dirrensaal house)	17.8.17 to 24.8.17		The Battalion trained	JP
	25.8.17		The Battalion marched to Dirrensaal support at YPRES NORTH area	JP
YPRES NORTH	26.8.17 to 29.8.17		The Battalion provides working parties for the transport areas	JP
	30.8.17	pm.	The Battalion relieves the 2/4 Batt Worcestershire Regt as the right support Battalion	JP
	31.8.17		The Battalion was in line as right support Coy. Fighting strength 39 officers 953 O.R.	JP

W. W. Drumhele
Major
for O. C. 1/6 Cheshire

Vol 17

CONFIDENTIAL

WAR DIARY OF

2/6th Battalion Royal Warwickshire Regiment.

From September 1st,1917 to September 30th,1917

VOLUME XVII

Army Form C. 2118.

WAR DIARY
or
INTELLIGENCE SUMMARY.
(Erase heading not required.)

Instructions regarding War Diaries and Intelligence Summaries are contained in F.S. Regs., Part II. and the Staff Manual respectively. Title pages will be prepared in manuscript.

Place	Date	Hour	Summary of Events and Information	Remarks and references to Appendices
Field	1.9.17.		Right Support Battalion of 182 Infantry Brigade. A large amount of salvage collected and work done in improving accommodation in old British front lines. Area slightly shelled at times. Casualties:- Officer wounded, Capt. A.L. ANTHONY, R.A.M.C. (attached) O.R. 2 killed: 2 wounded.	
	2.9.17.		Commencing at about 8.30 p.m. the relief of 2/5th R.War.R. in right sub-sector of front line, was carried out. The relief was completed by 12.15.a.m. 3.9.17. The 42nd Division was on the right of the Battalion, and the 2/8th R.War.R. on the left. Dispositions were as follows from right to left:- 'A' Coy. in POMMERN CASTLE and in shell-holes to the EAST of it. 'C' Coy. in Trenches and shell-holes on NORTH and NORTH WEST slopes of HILL 35. 'D' Coy. holding SOMME and DONT TRENCH with 1 Platoon at BANK FARM. 'B' Coy. in support having one Platoon at PLUM FARM and the remaining 2 Platoons round JASPER and UHLAN FARMS. Battalion H.Q. were in a dug-out near BANK FARM. Capt. P.M. PRIDMORE, M.C., was killed by a shell as he was leading his Company in. Other casualties were O.R. Killed 2, wounded 1 and 2 Missing. Except for intermittent shelling of the line POMMERN CASTLE - BANK FARM and SPREE FARM, the night 2nd/3rd Sept. was uneventful. 3 days rations were carried by all ranks.	
	3.9.17.		Orders had been received the previous day to capture the hostile position on HILL 35 on the night 3rd/4th September. This hostile position was a strong one consisting of 4 gun pits connected by a Trench with 2 concrete and steel M.G. emplacements immediately in rear - the whole being connected with IBERIAN (in front of 42nd Division) from which locality strong cross fire could be brought to bear. In addition cross fire could be brought to bear from enemy trenches about D.13.Central, and further fire from the neighbourhood of GALLIPOLI. The strength of the garrison was estimated at about 40 men with numerous Machine Guns.	

Army Form C. 2118.

WAR DIARY
or
INTELLIGENCE SUMMARY.
(Erase heading not required.)

Place	Date	Hour	Summary of Events and Information	Remarks and references to Appendices
Field	3.9.17. (contd)		The plan of attack was as follows:- ZERO was to be at 10.0.p.m. At ZERO - 2 an intense Lewis Gun and Rifle grenade fire was to be opened on the Western face of the position from POMMERN REDOUBT. At ZERO the 18 pr. protective barrage was to open on a line behind the position (to the EAST and N.E.) with a box barrage on IBERIAN. This barrage was to consist of shrapnel, H.E. and Smoke shells. At the same time a feint attack by 1 platoon of 'A' Coy. under 2/Lieut. I. SOWERBY, was to be made on the Western face of the position from POMMERN CASTLE. At ZERO + 2 'C' Coy. (2/Lieut. J. FORSYTH) in column of platoons at 15 paces distance, was to rush the position from the Northern flank, having previously moved to a convenient assembly position. The operation commenced punctually, but the assault was a failure, owing to the intense machine gun fire brought to bear on the Assaulting Troops from 3 sides. At about mid-night we re-occupied our original line. Our casualties were:- Officers: Killed 2/Lt. I. SOWERBY. Wounded 2/Lt. J. FORSYTH. 2/Lt. W.A. ASSINDER. 2/Lt. G.H. SWANN. 2/Lt. A.J. LAW. O.R. Killed 3. Wounded 37. Missing 10.	
Trenches	4.9.17.		A quiet day except for occasional heavy shelling of line POMMERN CASTLE - BANK FARM. During the night 'B' Coy. moved up and relieved 'A' Coy. in POMMERN CASTLE. 'C' Coy. moved back into Support and 'A' Coy. remained in the neighbourhood of BANK FARM, our most forward Coy, having to be evacuated before dawn to allow the heavies to bombard HILL 35. 2/Lieut. A.W. JOHNSON was slightly wounded, but remained at duty.	

Army Form C. 2118.

WAR DIARY
or
INTELLIGENCE SUMMARY.
(Erase heading not required.)

Place	Date	Hour	Summary of Events and Information	Remarks and references to Appendices

Field	5.9.17.		6" and 8" howitzers shelled HILL 35 all day and harrassing fire was brought to bear on the gun emplacements by 18 prs. It was determined to make another attempt to capture the gun emplacements on HILL 35 shortly after dark.
			A creeping 18 pr. barrage was to be employed this time.
			ZERO was at 8.45 p.m.
			Before ZERO, 'B' Company (Capt. B.R. SAUNDERS) deployed into assault formation to the EAST of POMMERN CASTLE.
			At ZERO the 18 pr. barrage opened on a line roughly half way between POMMERN CASTLE and the gun emplacements.
			At ZERO + 5 the barrage lifted on to the emplacements and 'B' Company followed it.
			At ZERO + 10 the barrage lifted off the objective and remained on its protective line till ZERO + 2 hours.
			On the barrage lifting off the objective, 'B' Coy. assaulted. The assault was much broken up by machine gun fire, but some portions of the 2nd and 3rd waves actually reached the emplacements. Severe fighting ensued which lasted an hour, when, in response to a second S.O.S. sent up by the enemy, a heavy barrage was put round the Northern and Western sides of the emplacements and about 50 yards from them. This barrage was additional to the one invariably put down on the line POMMERN CASTLE - BANK FARM, and made the sending up of assistance to 'B' Coy. extremely difficult.
			Small parties of 'B' Coy. still persisted in trying to effect an entrance into the emplacements and "pill-boxes" in rear, but the machine gun fire of the enemy prevented this.
			'B' Coy. was eventually withdrawn to POMMERN CASTLE about 11.30 p.m.
			Our casualties were:-
			              Other ranks Killed 13.
			                          Wounded. 56.
			                          Missing. 7.	

	6.9.17.		Commencing about 1.0.a.m. relief by 2/5th R.War.R. was carried out. Relief was complete about 4.0.a.m. Battalion moved back to Right support.	

Army Form C. 2118.

WAR DIARY
or
INTELLIGENCE SUMMARY.
(Erase heading not required.)

Instructions regarding War Diaries and Intelligence Summaries are contained in F. S. Regs., Part II. and the Staff Manual respectively. Title pages will be prepared in manuscript.

Place	Date	Hour	Summary of Events and Information	Remarks and references to Appendices
FIELD	7.9.17		The Battalion was in Right Support and was relieved by the 2/4th Oxford & Bucks on the night of 7/8th. Relief was complete at midnight and the Battalion proceeded by train from ST. JEAN to QUERY CAMP (VLAMERTINGHE).	
QUERY CAMP	8.9.17 - 11.9.17.		The Battalion remained at QUERY CAMP and re-fitted.	
	12.9.17.	8.a.m.	The Battalion moved to RIDGE CAMP at G.11.c.4.8. (Map Sheet 28).	
RIDGE CAMP	12.9.17 - 13.9.17.		The Battalion trained.	
	14.9.17.		The Battalion marched to CLYDE CAMP at L.9.b.5.6. (Map Sheet 27).	
CLYDE CAMP.	15.9.17. 16.9.17.	11.30.a.m.	The Battalion trained under Company arrangements. A Voluntary C. of E. Service was held in the Camp.	
	17.9.17.	7.30.a.m.	The Battalion marched to billets in the ECKE Area.	
	18.9.17.	9.30.p.m.	The Battalion marched to CAESTRE STATION and entrained there, detraining at ARRAS No. 1 Station at 8.a.m. and marched to billets at DAINVILLE.	
	19.9.17 - 21.9.17		The Battalion trained at DAINVILLE.	
	22.9.17.		The Battalion marched to GRIMSBY CAMP (ST. NICHOLAS) and relieved the 12th MANCHESTER REGT.	
	23.9.17.		The Battalion relieved the 10th Battalion SHERWOOD FORESTERS as right Battalion in the CHEMICAL WORKS SECTOR. (Ref. Map PLOUVAIN). Relief was successfully completed at 10.p.m.	
	24.9.17.		At 4.30 a.m. the enemy attempted a raid on the trenches of our centre Company. An intense barrage composed of T.M. Shells of various calibres 77 mm. 4.5 cm and 5.9 cm was put down on line CORFU AVENUE and thence along COLUMBO SWITCH	

Army Form C. 2118.

WAR DIARY
or
INTELLIGENCE SUMMARY.
(Erase heading not required.)

Instructions regarding War Diaries and Intelligence Summaries are contained in F. S. Regs., Part II. and the Staff Manual respectively. Title pages will be prepared in manuscript.

Place	Date	Hour	Summary of Events and Information	Remarks and references to Appendices
FIELD	24.9.17	4.32am	An S.O.S. signal, which appeared to have been fired from our extreme right flank, was observed. The Artillery were informed and promptly fired on their S.O.S. lines. At the same time, movement was observed in front of our own wire at I.14.c.6.9., and rifle and Lewis Gun fire was opened. One of the enemy who succeeded in crawling through a recognised gap in our wire was hit by Lewis Gun fire and taken prisoner. Nothing more was seen of the enemy and no attack developed. The barrage continued with intensity till 5.15 a.m., at which time it commenced to diminish slightly. At 7 a.m. all was reported quiet. A patrol was sent out at dusk the same day, to the supposed place of assembly of the enemy raiding party, but no wounded or further identifications could be found. Our casualties 8 other ranks killed, Capt.B.R.Saunders and 3 other ranks wounded.	
	25.9.17		The day was quiet except for occasional shelling by enemy T.M's. All available men worked in improving and revetting the trenches.	
	26.9.17		With the exception of occasional shelling of our front and support lines by enemy T.M's, the day was quiet.	
	27.9.17		During the morning the enemy bombarded our front line from 8 a.m. to 9.30 a.m. with T.M's of all calibres. The trenches were blown in, in several places but no casualties inflicted.	
	28.9.17		Our Artillery fired on enemy T.M's with 6" hows. in retaliation for his activity the previous day. The enemy did not retaliate.	
	29.9.17		The Battalion was relieved by the 2/5th Royal Warwickshire Regiment and withdrew to right support. Relief was complete at 9.50 p.m.	
	30.9.17		During our tour a large amount of work had been done in revetting and improving the trenches. The Battalion was in right support and found working parties of 5 Officers and 320 O.R. for front line system with R.Es.	

FIGHTING STRENGTH 790. ALL RANKS.

W.L.O'Connell Major.
O.C.2/6th Batt.K.War.R.

CONFIDENTIAL

WAR DIARY OF

2/6th Battalion Royal Warwickshire Regiment

From October 1st 1917 -to- October 31st 1917.

VOLUME XVIII.

Army Form C. 2118.

WAR DIARY
or
INTELLIGENCE SUMMARY.
(Erase heading not required.)

Instructions regarding War Diaries and Intelligence Summaries are contained in F.S. Regs., Part II. and the Staff Manual respectively. Title pages will be prepared in manuscript.

Place	Date	Hour	Summary of Events and Information	Remarks and references to Appendices
Field	1 – 4.10.17.		The Battalion was Right Support Battalion in the CHEMICAL WORKS Sector. All available men were employed on work in front line system under the R.E's, and in carrying trench mortar ammunition up to the line.	
	5.10.17.		The Battalion relieved 2/5th R.War.R. in the Right Battalion sub-sector of the CHEMICAL WORKS Sector. The extent of the front held was from T.14.c.5.1. to T.14.a.6.5. With 75th Division on the right and 2/5th R.War.R. on the left. Relief successfully completed by 10.50.p.m. without casualties. Disposition: 'A', 'C' and 'D' Companies in front line, and 'B' Company in Support in GORDON RESERVE.	Ref Map. GRENAY 1:10000 TRENCH MAP.
	6.10.17.		The day was exceptionally quiet. By night, the enemy fired the usual bursts of machine gun fire. Patrols were sent out during the night, one of which observed and dispersed an enemy working party with Lewis gun fire. All available men worked in improving "Posts" and constructing shelters in the front line.	
	7.10.17.		Day quiet, except for a few trench mortars on Support line. Patrols were sent out by night. All available men employed on improving front line and constructing shelters in the front line under R.E. supervision.	
	8.10.17.		Day quiet, except for intermittent shelling on GORGIA SUPPORT and C.T. Patrols were sent out during the night. There was no enemy wiring parties and encountered no enemy patrols. 'B' Coy. (Support) was relieved by 1st Coy. 2/5th R.War.R. and withdrew to PENNIN TRENCH. (Ref. map VERMOUX French Map).	
	9.10.17.		Intermittent shelling by 77 mm guns during the day. A destructive shoot was carried out by our artillery and trench mortars between 2.0.p.m. and 8.0.p.m. The enemy retaliated with a few rifle grenades. Patrols were sent out at night.	

Army Form C. 2118.

WAR DIARY
or
INTELLIGENCE SUMMARY.
(Erase heading not required.)

Instructions regarding War Diaries and Intelligence Summaries are contained in F. S. Regs., Part II. and the Staff Manual respectively. Title pages will be prepared in manuscript.

Place	Date	Hour	Summary of Events and Information	Remarks and references to Appendices
FICHEUX	10.10.17.		In order to simulate a raid, an 18-pdr. barrage was put down on the enemy front line from 1.11.b.00.00. to 1.14.b.00.60 from 9.0.a.m. to 9.5.a.m. Smoke candles were lighted simultaneously from our front trenches and an excellent smoke barrage produced. At 9.5.a.m. an intense rifle grenade and L.T.M. barrage was opened on the same part of the enemy's line, in order to cause casualties and to wound his parapet. There was no retaliation by the enemy. Patrols were sent out by night to prevent the enemy raiding. All available men were employed in improving the front line posts and in constructing shelters in the front line.	Reference Map. GREENLAND HILL TRENCH MAP
	11.10.17.		A gas bombardment was carried out by the M.T.M's between 1.0.a.m and 1.15.a.m. L.T.M's and M.G's co-operated. The enemy did not retaliate. The Battalion (less 'D' Coy.) was relieved by 2/5th R.War.R., and withdrew to Support. The relief was complete by 10.45.p.m. The Battalion was disposed as follows :- Batt. H.Q. and 'D' Coy. in PUDDING TRENCH. 'A' Company in cellars in FAMPOUX. 'B' Coy. (under orders of O.C. 2/5th R.War.R.) Support Coy. to 2/5th R.War.R. in CORDITE TRENCH. 'C' Company in GATTE TRENCH with one Platoon in close Support to 2/5th R.War.R. in CORDITE RESERVE. Total Casualties during tour in the Front line - 3 O.R. wounded.	Ref. Map. FAMPOUX Trench Map.
	12.10.17. 13.10.17.		Battalion was in Right Support. All available men were employed in carrying trench mortar ammunition and on working parties under R.E. supervision.	
	14.10.17.		Battalion was in Right Support. All available men were employed in carrying and working parties. 'A' Company relieved 'B' Company and 1 Platoon of 'C' Coy. in CORDITE RESERVE, and came under the orders of O.C. 2/5th R.War.R. 'B' Company withdrew to FAMPOUX and the platoon of 'C' Company to GATTE TRENCH.	
	15.10.17.		Battalion in Right Support. All available men employed in carrying and working parties. 'A' Company was relieved by 'D' Company 2/5th R.War.R. and withdrew to PUDDING TRENCH.	

Army Form C. 2118.

WAR DIARY
or
INTELLIGENCE SUMMARY.

(Erase heading not required.)

Instructions regarding War Diaries and Intelligence Summaries are contained in F. S. Regs., Part II. and the Staff Manual respectively. Title pages will be prepared in manuscript.

Place	Date	Hour	Summary of Events and Information	Remarks and references to Appendices
Field	16.10.17.		The Battalion was relieved by 2/7th WORCESTERSHIRE Regt. 'A' and 'D' Companies - PUDDING TRENCH - were relieved by day, the relief being complete by 8.0.a.m. The relief of 'B' & 'C' Companies was complete by 8.45 p.m. The Battalion withdrew to quarters in ARRAS.	
	17.10.17 to 27.10.17.		Battalion was in Divisional Reserve at ARRAS and trained. Working parties totalling 70 O.R. per day, were found.	
	28.10.17.		The Battalion relieved 2/4th Battalion R. BERKS in the left sub-sector of the GAVRELLE HILL Left Sector. The Relief was successfully completed by 11.5.p.m. Dispositions were as follows: 'A' Company, Right Coy., 'B' Company, Centre Front Coy., 'D' Coy. Left Front Coy., 'C' Coy. in Support from I.l.b.60.35. to I.l.b.10.30., 7th 2/6th R.War.R. on Right and 47th Division on our left.	Power. COMMAND USLB Trench Map.
	29.10.17.		A quiet day. One trench mortar bombarded the enemy's front line at intervals during the day. Two patrols were sent out by night to examine the enemy's wire. 1 gap was located at T.7.C.10.70. In addition, fighting patrols, consisting of 1 N.C.O. and 10 men each, patrolled the battalion front during the hours of darkness. No enemy patrols were seen. All available men were employed in improving and revetting the front line.	Ref. Map. Ditto. -do-
	30.10.17.		Our artillery and Trench Mortars were active during the day. The enemy retaliated on COY. SUPPORT and CHICKEN RESERVE with 4.2. c.m. shells. Fighting Patrols of 1 N.C.O. and 10 men patrolled the battalion front during the night but encountered no enemy. A patrol sent out to locate enemy M.G.'s reported Machine Gun posts at T.I.H.35.3., T.I.b.83.4 T.I.b.55.85., and a rifle post at T.I.b.68.60.	

Army Form C. 2118.

WAR DIARY
or
INTELLIGENCE SUMMARY.
(Erase heading not required.)

Place	Date	Hour	Summary of Events and Information	Remarks and references to Appendices
Fauq.	31.10.17		The enemy's artillery was unusually active during the day. This was probably in retaliation to a bombardment of the enemy's lines at 6.25.4.45.05. (Opposite 47th Division's Front).	Ref. Maps
			In reply to SOS shells on BAHA COPSE (G.27.2) the enemy fired 20 gas shells at CORNET during the afternoon.	57 B. N.E and GREENLAND
			No Aviation report was received throughout the hour of darkness & nothing was heard of 1 I.C.O. and 10 men each. No enemy patrols or working parties were seen.	VILLE 3? Trench Maps.
			Work was carried out in improving and rewetting the front line.	
			Fighting Strength. 24 Officers & 750 O.R.	

R. Davidson
Lieut-Colonel,
Commanding 2/6th B.W.R.

CONFIDENTIAL

WAR DIARY OF

2/6th Battalion The Royal Warwickshire Regiment.

From November 1st 1917 to November 30th 1917.

@@@@@@@@@@@@
@----------@
@ VOLUME XIX. @
@----------@
@@@@@@@@@@@@

Army Form C. 2118.

WAR DIARY
or
INTELLIGENCE SUMMARY.
(Erase heading not required.)

Instructions regarding War Diaries and Intelligence Summaries are contained in F. S. Regs., Part II. and the Staff Manual respectively. Title pages will be prepared in manuscript.

Place	Date	Hour	Summary of Events and Information	Remarks and references to Appendices
Field	1.11.17		In reply to a bombardment of his front line trenches at C.25.d.5.0 (opposite 47th Divl. front) and to a bombardment of his front line from I.d.95.45 to I.2c.02.27, the enemy's artillery was very active during the afternoon. CORK SUPPORT was heavily shelled with 4.2's and 5.9's. CHICAGO RESERVE, CALEDONIAN AVENUE and CIVIL AVENUE were also shelled. There was a very noticeable increase in the amount of hostile artillery. Patrols were sent out by night to obtain information about enemy posts between I.2.c.05.65 and I.2.a.05.00. Fighting patrols of 1 N.C.O. and 10 men each patrolled "NO M N'S L ND", throughout the night. One enemy working party was seen and dispersed with Lewis gun fire.	Map:- GREENLAND HILL TRENCH MAP
Field	2.11.17		The increased hostile artillery activity shown on the 1st inst., was maintained. Systematic shelling of CORK SUPPORT, CHICAGO RESERVE, CIVIL AVENUE, CORK D, CORK SUPPORT and CALEDONIAN was carried out from 10.0 a.m. till dusk. Our T.M's carried out several shoots during the day on the enemy's wire and front line. Fighting patrols of 1 N.C.O. and 10 men each patrolled "NO M N'S L ND" continually throughout the night. A small gap in the enemy's wire was located at I.1.b.60.55.	J.P. Map:- GREENLAND H TRENCH MAP
Field	3.11.17		Hostile artillery was far less active during the day.	J.P.

Army Form C. 2118.

WAR DIARY
or
INTELLIGENCE SUMMARY.
(Erase heading not required.)

Place	Date	Hour	Summary of Events and Information	Remarks and references to Appendices
Field	3.11.17		The Battalion was relieved by the 2/5th R.W.S.R. and withdrew to left support, in HARRY and HUMID TRENCH. Relief was successfully completed by 8.45 p.m. Total casualties during the tour in the trenches, killed 1 O.R. Wounded 4 O.Rs.	
Field	4.11.17		Battalion was in Left support. Working parties of 9 Officers and 250 O.R. were found. In retaliation to raid by 47th Division on our left at 4.30 p.m., there was a considerable amount of hostile shelling in the neighbourhood of HUMIB TRENCH, T N. LUMP and C N VALLEY.	
Field	5.11.17 to 8.11.17		Battalion was in Left Support. Working parties of 9 Officer and 250 O.Rs. provided daily.	

Army Form C. 2118.

WAR DIARY
or
INTELLIGENCE SUMMARY.
(Erase heading not required.)

Instructions regarding War Diaries and Intelligence Summaries are contained in F. S. Regs., Part II. and the Staff Manual respectively. Title pages will be prepared in manuscript.

Place	Date	Hour	Summary of Events and Information	Remarks and references to Appendices
In the Field.	9. 11. 17.		The Battalion relieved the 2/5th R.War R. in the left Sub-sector of the GREENLAND Hill Sector Relief was complete at 7.25.p.m. The 2/8th Battn. R.War.R. were on the right and the 1/7th Battn. The London Regt. on the left. Fighting Patrols were out throughout the night, but no enemy patrols were encountered. A patrol went out to ascertain the state of the enemy's wire at the junction of WIT and WANT trenches. A gap 7 or 8 yards wide was found. Enemy artillery and trench mortars were very quiet during the night.	Ref.Map GREENLAND HILL Trench Map.
	10. 11. 17.		The enemy artillery and trench mortars were exceptionally quiet during the day. Patrols were out throughout the night but did not encounter any enemy patrols. Lewis guns were fired at intervals during the night to keep the gap at the junction of WIT and WANT TRENCHES open.	
	11. 11. 17.		The enemy artillery was more active during the day and fired intermittently on CORK and CURSE SUPPORT and CHICKEN Reserve with 4.2's and on CIVIL AVENUE with 77 mms. Patrols were out through the night but did not encounter any enemy patrols.	
	12. 11. 17.		The enemy shelled CORK Support intermittently throughout the day. Our artillery and trench mortars carried out a destructive bombardment of the enemy trenches opposite the Battalion Front from 12 noon to 2.p.m. There was slight retaliation on CURSE SUPPORT and CONRAD trench. Fighting patrols were out throughout the night and a reconnoitring patrol reported that the gap in the wire at the junction of WIT AND WANT trenches was still open. The 24th Battn. The London Regt. relieved the 1/7th Battn. The London Regt. on our left.	
	13. 11. 17.		At intervals during the day the enemy shelled CURSE and CONRAD Support and CIVIL AV with 4.2s His trench mortars during the day were exceptionally quiet. Fighting patrols were out throughout the night, but did not encounter any of the enemy	

Army Form C. 2118.

WAR DIARY
or
INTELLIGENCE SUMMARY.
(Erase heading not required.)

Instructions regarding War Diaries and Intelligence Summaries are contained in F. S. Regs., Part II. and the Staff Manual respectively. Title pages will be prepared in manuscript.

Place	Date	Hour	Summary of Events and Information	Remarks and references to Appendices
In the Field.	14.11.17.		Enemy artillery was quiet during the morning. Between 1.p.m. and 7.p.m. he shelled CIVIL AV. and CORK SUPPORT with about sixteen 80 4.2's. Fighting patrols were out throughout the night, but did not come into contact with the enemy	Ref. Map. GREENLAND HILL Trench Map
	15.11.17.		A bombardment of enemy trench system opposite the Battalion was carried out by 6" and 4.5" Hows 18 Pdrs., and trench mortars between 1.30 p.m. and 4.p.m. The enemy retaliated with about 100 4.2's on CIVIL AVENUE, CONRAD and CURSE 2/Lt. T.J. POOLE and 34 O.R. of 'D' Coy. were sent out of the trenches to practice for a raid to be made on the enemy trenches on the night of 20th Novr.	
	16.11.17.		A bombardment of the enemy trenches in I.14.b. & c and I.15.c was carried out with chemical shell at 7.p.m. The Battalion was relieved by the 2/5th Battn. R.War.R. and withdrew to left support in Harry Trench and HUMID Trench. Relief was complete at 6.30.p.m.	Ref. Map. FAMPOUX TRENCH Map.
	17 - 20. 11.17.		The Battalion was in left Support. All available men were employed on working parties under the R.E. and in carrying trench mortar ammunition to the front line. N.C.O's from the the raiding party proceeded to the trenches every night to patrol "NO MAN'S LAND" and find out if the gap in the enemy wire at junction of WIT and WANT Trenches was still open. On the night of the 20th 'D' Company relieved the left Coy. of 2/5th Warwicks in the line. Relief was complete by 5.30.p.m. A patrol consisting of C.S.M. MURRAY and 1 Sergt. went out from our line at 6.p.m. to ascertain if the gap was still open and to lay a guiding wire from the gap in the enemy's for the raiders our wire to the gap in the enemy's for the raiders. When within 20 yards of the enemy wire C.S.M. W.W. MURRAY was hit and as the Sergt. was unable to bring him in he returned for assistance. Patrols were sent to the place where the C.S.M. was hit but he could not be found and it was believed that he was taken prisoner. Owing to this, and the fact that the gap had not been found, the Raid was cancelled.	
	21.11.17.		The Battalion was relieved by the 2/6th Gloucesters and proceeded to LEWIS BARRACKS, ARRAS	
	21 - 27. 11.17.		The Battalion was in Divisional Reserve in ARRAS and trained. Working parties of 2 officers and 100 men were found daily for work on new ranges.	

Army Form C. 2118.

WAR DIARY
or
INTELLIGENCE SUMMARY.
(Erase heading not required.)

Place	Date	Hour	Summary of Events and Information	Remarks and references to Appendices
In the Field.	28.11.17.		The Battalion marched to billets at DAINVILLE.	Ref Map Sheet 57c
	29.11.17.		The Battalion trained.	
	30.11.17.		The Battalion marched to BEAUMETZ where it entrained for BAPAUME. Whilst marching from detraining station to quarters at BEAISTRE orders were received for the Battalion to proceed towards the line immediately and Battalion was conveyed in motor busses with all possible speed, from a point on the BAPAUME - BANCOURT road to ROYAULCOURT whence it marched to METZ arriving at 5.p.m. where it was accommodated as well as circumstances permitted. The regimental transport proceeded by road from DAINVILLE to ROYAULCOURT ~~whica had~~ and after a halt of 3 hours, continued to HEUDICOURT arriving at 9.0.a.m. 1st December.	
			Strength 30.11.17 - 38 Officers : 740 O.R.	

W.L. Campbell
Major for
O.C., 2/6th R.War.R.

CONFIDENTIAL.

WAR DIARY OF

2/6th Battalion The Royal Warwickshire Regiment.

From December 1st 1917 to Decr. 31st 1917

VOLUME XX.

Army Form C. 2118.

WAR DIARY
or
INTELLIGENCE SUMMARY.
(Erase heading not required.)

Place	Date	Hour	Summary of Events and Information	Remarks and references to Appendices
Field.	1. 12. 17.		In accordance with orders received during the night, the Battalion left METZ at about 3.0.a.m. on the morning of the 1st Decr. 1917, and moved into position about W.14.d. West of HEUDECOURT by 7.0.a.m. where it remained all day, and night of 1st/2nd.	Ref. Map. 57c.S.E. 1/20,000.
	2. 12. 17.		Orders having been received during the night, that the Batt. was to relieve the 20th Division in the line on the night of 2nd/3rd inst., the Batt. moved at 9.0.a.m. via FINS and METZ to GOUZEAUCOURT WOOD, and marching where rations and Lewis Guns were issued. At 4.15.p.m. the Batt. left GOUZEAUCOURT WOOD, and marching via BEAUCAMP and VILLERS PLOUICH relieved certain Companies of the 2/6th Sherwood Foresters and 9th Durham Light Infantry. From verbal orders received from the Brigadier, 'B' Company was sent to support 2/8th R.War.R. in the line on the left and 'D' Company to support 2/7th R.War.R. in the line in the centre. 'A' and 'C' Coys. and Batt. H.Q. took up their positions in the trench running South of the HINDENBERG Front Line at R.9.d.70.75. in Brigade Support. The night was quiet.	
	3. 12. 17.		About 7.20.a.m. an intense barrage was put down by the enemy on HINDENBERG TRENCH, LA VACQUERIE and the Trench occupied by 'A' and 'C' Companies. LA VACQUERIE was attacked and taken by the enemy. The Batt. Right was extended as far as possible towards CORNER SUPPORT. During the morning, several parties of the 2/4th and 2/6th Glos. Regt. and 2/5th R.War.R. reported for instructions. These parties were sent to prolong the Right down CORNER Support and CORNER Trench, where they got into touch with the 2/5th R.War.R. and the 183rd Infantry Brigade. Bombing blocks were ordered to be made in the HINDENBERG Line in WOOD Trench and EMDEN Trench. Later in the day, 'G' Company, 2/4th O. & B.L.I. was placed under my orders, and this Coy. was placed on the right of 'A' Coy. to prolong the Right towards FARM Trench. The situation now was that the Battalion - less 'B' and 'D' Companies - plus 'G' Coy. 2/4th O.B.L.I. and various parties of the Units previously mentioned, was holding what was now the Front line in this particular Sector. Later at night, 'D' Coy. - which had been occupying EMDEN Trench in Support to the 2/7th R.War.R. - was ordered to vacate its position and came under my Command. I placed this Coy. between 'C' and 'A' Coys. to strengthen the line, the garrison of which had been considerably weakened owing to casualties. The Batt. line then ran from R.9.d.70.75. to junction of FARM Trench and CORNER Trench as follows:-	Ref. Map. GOUZEAU- COURT Trench Map. 1/20,000.

Army Form C. 2118.

WAR DIARY
or
INTELLIGENCE SUMMARY.
(Erase heading not required.)

Instructions regarding War Diaries and Intelligence Summaries are contained in F.S. Regs., Part II. and the Staff Manual respectively. Title pages will be prepared in manuscript.

Place	Date	Hour	Summary of Events and Information	Remarks and references to Appendices
Field.	3.12.17 (contd).		'C' Coy. on the left, 'D' Company, 'A' Company, 'C' Coy. 2/4th O.B.L.I. with the parties of 183rd Inf. Bde. and 2/5th R.War.R. (who had placed themselves under my orders) holding CORNER Trench and CORNER Support.	Ref.Map. BOUZEAU-COURT Trench Map 1/20,000.
	4. 12. 17.		Except for occasional heavy shelling - a quiet day. In the evening, Batt. H.Q. moved back to a dug-out at R.9.b.15.25 in the HINDENBERG Line, WOOD Trench and 'B' Coy. (which had been supporting 2/8th R.War.R.) was again placed under my command and occupied a trench running South from WOOD Trench to junction of CORNER Trench and FARM Trench in Support.	
	5. 12. 17.		Occasional heavy shelling of our Front and Support lines and repeated enemy bombing attacks down EMDEN Trench, EMDEN Support and to our left. All these attacks down EMDEN Trench were successfully stopped. All spare bombers were sent to reinforce 'C' Company who were holding a block in EMDEN Trench. At 12.46 p.m. I placed 2 complete Bombing Sections of 'B' Company at the disposal of Major LEFROY, 2/7th R.War.R. to assist him in driving back the enemy, who had penetrated a portion of his Front. In the meantime, a Company of the 2/5th Glos. Regt. had also been sent to occupy the trench occupied by 'B' Coy. to reinforce our Support line. During the night, the 9th Inniskilling Fusiliers relieved the 2/7th R.War.R. on our left and took over a portion of our front, which included the junction of our Front line and EMDEN trench. The night was quiet. During the night, 2 Companies (4 Platoons) of the 2/8th R.War.R. were placed at my disposal and relieved Companies of 2/5th Gloucester Regt. in my Support line, 1 Platoon of which I sent up to the right of my Front line. I also sent 4 Lewis guns from these two Companies to take up positions in the Front line, as so many of my own had been knocked out.	
	6. 12. 17.		During the morning, strong enemy attacks against the Battalion on our left. At one time during the morning, his bombers were seen about R.9.b.65.65. bombing down towards WOOD Support. I brought one Company of 2/8th R.War.R. from my Support line to a position of readiness about R.9.b.0.3½, but as the attack was successfully stopped by the 9th Inniskillings, I sent them back to the Support Line. During the night, I handed over my front and Support line partly to the 11th Inniskilling Fusiliers - who had relieved the 9th Inniskilling Fusiliers - and partly to the 3 Companies 2/8th R.War.R. The Battalion then withdrew to HAVRINCOURT WOOD, which it reached about 8.30.a.m. on the morning of the 7th inst.	Ref.Map. 57c.S.E. 1/20,000.

For Casualties, see Appendix 'A' attached.

Army Form C. 2118.

WAR DIARY
or
INTELLIGENCE SUMMARY.
(Erase heading not required.)

Instructions regarding War Diaries and Intelligence Summaries are contained in F.S. Regs., Part II and the Staff Manual respectively. Title pages will be prepared in manuscript.

Place	Date	Hour	Summary of Events and Information	Remarks and references to Appendices
Field.	7.12.17.		Bivouacs - HAVRINCOURT WOOD.	
	8th		-ditto-	
	9th		-ditto-	
	10th		-ditto- The Battalion was inspected and addressed by Major-General COLIN MACKENZIE, Commanding Division. Relieved 2/5th Glos. in Left Sub-Sector of LA VACQUERIE.	
	11th		In trenches. Quiet day.	
	12th		-ditto- RHONDDA Night of the 12/13th Relieved by 2/8th R.War.R. Moved back into Brigade Support in RONDDA and MERTHYR Trenches.	
	13th		In Support.	
	14th		ditto.	
	15th		ditto.	
	16th		Night of the 15/16th, Relieved 2/8th R.War.R. in Left Sub-Sector of LA VACQUERIE. In trenches. Quiet Day.	
	17th		Night of the 16/17th Relieved by 2/4th O.B.L.I. Moved into Divisional Reserve in HAVRINCOURT WOOD.	
	18th		Reserve in HAVRINCOURT WOOD. Moved by March Route to Huts and Tents at MANANCOURT.	
	19th to 22nd.		In Divisional Reserve at MANANCOURT. Time occupied in re-fitting and inspection of Companies.	Ref. Map. AMIENS. 1/100,000
	23rd.		Battalion transferred to XVIIIth Corps, Fifth Army. Entrained at ETRICOURT - Detrained at CORBIE - marched to SAILLY-le-SEC.	
	24th		Rested.	
	25th		Divine Service. Christmas Dinners in the afternoon.	
	26th		Occupied in road-clearing.	
	27th - 29th.		Training and Road clearing.	
	30th.		Battalion marched to CAIX. Billetted the night.	
	31st.		Battalion marched to HANGEST. In Billets. Fighting Strength - 26 Officers - 653 O.R.	

Lieut.-Colonel,
Comdg., 2/6th R.War.R.

APPENDIX 'A' to WAR DIARY for December 1917.

Date	Officers			Other Ranks		
	Killed.	Wounded.	Missing.	Killed.	Wounded.	Missing.
3.12.17.	3	6	-	14	31	-
4.12.17.	-	-	-	2	9	-
5.12.17.	1	4 (includes 1 'At Duty')	-	12	52	2 (includes 1 believed P.O.W.)
6.12.17.	-	-	-	1	9	-
7.12.17.	-	1	-	-	-	-

CONFIDENTIAL.

WAR DIARY
of
2/6th Battalion Royal Warwickshire Regiment.
From January 1st to January 31st, 1918.

VOLUME XXI.

Army Form C. 2118.

WAR DIARY
or
INTELLIGENCE SUMMARY.
(Erase heading not required.)

Instructions regarding War Diaries and Intelligence Summaries are contained in F.S. Regs., Part II. and the Staff Manual respectively. Title pages will be prepared in manuscript.

Place	Date	Hour	Summary of Events and Information	Remarks and references to Appendices
In the Field	1 to 6.1.18		Billets, HANGEST: Training.	Ref: Map AMIENS 1/100,000
	7		Moved by march route to billets at NESLE.	
	8		Rested.	Ref: Map 66D 1/20,000
	9		Moved by march route to billets at GERMAINE.	
	10		Resting.	Ref: Map 62C S.E. 1/20,000
	11		Relieved a Battalion of the 5th French Division in Support in HOLNON WOOD.	
	12/13		In support in HOLNON WOOD.	
	14		Re-distribution of Battalion, 3 Companies moving to SAVY WOOD.	
	15		In Support.	
	16 to 18		Night of 15/16th relieved 2/7 R.War.R. in Right Sub-sector of ST.QUENTIN. In trenches: Quiet	Ref: Map 62B S.W. 1/20,000 Ref: Map 62C S.W. 1/20,000
	19th to 24th		Night of 18th/19th, relieved by 2/7th Worcester Regt. and withdrew to Brigade Reserve in HOLNON WOOD. Organisation of Companies, Training and work on defences of Battle Zone.	Ref: Map 66D 1/40,000
	25th		Presentation of ribons and parchments by G.O.C. Division. Moved by march route to GERMAINE.	
	26th		Rested. Night of 26/27th relieved 2/1st Bucks.Batt.O.B.L.I. in Support at MAISSEMY.	Ref: Map 66C S.E. 1/20,000
	27th to 30th		Left Support. Work on defences of forward Zone.	

Army Form C. 2118.

WAR DIARY
or
INTELLIGENCE SUMMARY.
(Erase heading not required.)

Instructions regarding War Diaries and Intelligence Summaries are contained in F. S. Regs., Part II. and the Staff Manual respectively. Title pages will be prepared in manuscript.

Place	Date	Hour	Summary of Events and Information	Remarks and references to Appendices
In the Field			Night of 30/31st, relieved 2/7 R.War.R. in Left Sub-sector.	Ref: Map 62B S.W 1/20,000
	31		In trenches. Quiet day.	
			Fighting Strength - Officers 41, other ranks 694.	

[signature]

Major
Comdg. 2/6th Batt. R. War. R.

Army Form C. 2118.

2/6 R Warwick

WAR DIARY
or
INTELLIGENCE SUMMARY.
(Erase heading not required.)

Instructions regarding War Diaries and Intelligence Summaries are contained in F.S. Regs., Part II. and the Staff Manual respectively. Title pages will be prepared in manuscript.

Place	Date.	Hour	Summary of Events and Information	Remarks and references to Appendices
Field	Feby. 1st-3rd		Front Line trenches in Left Sub-sector of Left Sector of Divisional Front. Quiet Tour. Active patrolling done every night. Night of 3rd/4th Relieved by 2/7th R.War.R. and withdrew to Support in M.ISSEMY.	62.b.S.W. 1/20,000.
	4th		In Support. Work on Redoubt Line. Night of 4th/5th Raided Wood in M.17.c. Found to be unoccupied by enemy.	62.b. S.E. 1/20,000. 62.b. S.W. 1/20,000.
	5th - 7th		In Support. Work on ESSLING REDOUBT. Night of 7th/8th Relieved 2/7th R.War.R. in Front Line.	62.b. S.W. 1/20,000.
	8th - 11th		Front line trenches. Enemy inactive. Fighting Patrols occupied NO MAN'S LAND nightly, but did not encounter enemy. Night of 11/12th Relieved by 1/8th Argyll & Sutherland Highlanders 183rd Infantry Brigade. Moved by march route to billets at VAUX.	
	12th		In billets at VAUX - rested.	66.D. 1/40,000.
	13th - 18th		Work on improving Defences of Battle Zone. Draft of 17 Officers and 350 O.R. transferred to this Unit. 15th. 2/5th R.War.R. disbanded.	
	19th		Prepared for trenches. Night of 19/20th Relieved 2/4th O.B.L.I. 184th Infantry Brigade.in Support of Right Sector of Divisional Front. in Dug-outs HOLNON and SAVY WOODS.	62.c. S.E. 1/20,000.
	20th & 21st		Work on burying cable to Front Line Battalion H.Q.	
	22nd		Moved to Dug-out M.D.E. HOLNON WOOD.	
	23rd - 26th		Work on improving defences of the Battle Zone.	
	27th		Prepared for Front line trenches. Night of 27/28th Relieved 2/8th Worcs. in Right Sector of Divisional Front.	62.b.S.W. 1/20,000.
	28th		In front line trenches. Work on improvements of Defences.	

Fighting Strength - Officers 55. O.R. 1044.

R. Winder
Lieut.-Colonel,
Commanding 2/6th R.War.R.

2/6 R.War.R.

Army Form C. 2118.

WAR DIARY
or
INTELLIGENCE SUMMARY.
(Erase heading not required.)

Instructions regarding War Diaries and Intelligence
Summaries are contained in F. S. Regs., Part II.
and the Staff Manual respectively. Title pages
will be prepared in manuscript.

Place	Date	Hour	Summary of Events and Information	Remarks and references to Appendices
Field	1918 Feby. 1st-3rd		Front Line trenches in Left Sub-sector of Left Sector of Divisional Front. Quiet Tour. Active Patrolling from every night. Night of 3rd/4th Relieved by 2/7th R.War.R. and withdrew to Support in MAISSEMY.	62.b. S.W. 1/20,000.
	4th		In Support. Work on Redoubt Line. Night of 4th/5th Raided Wood in M.17.c. Found to be unoccupied by enemy.	62.c. S.W 1/20,000 62.b. S.W 1/20,000
	5th - 7th		In Support. Work on ESSLING REDOUBT. Night of 7th/8th Relieved 2/7th R.War.R. in Front Line.	
	8th - 11th		Front line trenches. Enemy inactive. Fighting Patrols occupied NO MAN'S LAND nightly, but did not encounter enemy. Night of 11/12th Relieved by 1/8th Argyll & Sutherland Highlanders 183rd Infantry Brigade. Moved by march route to billets at VAUX.	62.b. S.W. 1/20,000
	12th		In billets at VAUX – rested.	62.D. 1/40,000.
	13th - 18th		Work on improving Defences of Battle Zone. 15th. 2/5th R.War.R. disbanded. Draft of 17 Officers and 350 O.R. transferred to this Unit.	
	19th		Prepared for trenches. Night of 19/20th Relieved 2/4th O.B.L.I. 184th Infantry Brigade,in Support of Right Sector of Divisional Front. in Dug-outs HOLNON and SAVY WOODS.	62.c. S.W. 1/20,000
	20th & 21st		Work on Burying cable to Front Line Battalion H.Q.	
	22nd		Moved to Dug-out M.D.E. HOLNON WOOD.	
	23rd - 26th		Work on improving defences of the Battle Zone.	
	27th		Prepared for Front line trenches. Night of 27/28th Relieved 2/8th Worcs. in Right Sector of Divisional Front.	62.3. 1/20,0
	28th		In front line trenches. Work on improvements of Defences.	

Fighting Strength – Officers 55. O.R. 1044.

[signature]
Lieut.-Colonel,
Comdg., 2/6th R.War.R.

A3834. Wt. W4973/M687 750,000 8/16 D. D. & L.Ltd. Forms/C.2118/13.

Army Form C. 2118.

WAR DIARY
or
INTELLIGENCE SUMMARY.
(Erase heading not required.)

Instructions regarding War Diaries and Intelligence Summaries are contained in F.S. Regs., Part II. and the Staff Manual respectively. Title pages will be prepared in manuscript.

Place	Date 1917	Hour	Summary of Events and Information	Remarks and references to Appendices
Field	Feby. 1st-3rd		Front Line trenches in Left Sub-sector of Left Sector of Divisional Front. Quiet Tour. Active patrolling each every night. Night of 3rd/4th Relieved by 2/7th R.War.R. and withdrew to Support in HAISBURY.	62.b.S.W. 1/20,000.
	4th		In Support. Work on Redoubt Line. Night of 4th/5th Raided Todd in H.17.c. Found to be unoccupied by enemy.	62.c.S.W. 1/20,000. 62.b.S.W. 1/20,000.
	5th – 7th		In Support. Work on FUSLING REDOUBT. Night of 7th/8th Relieved 2/7th R.War.R. in Front Line.	
	8th – 11th		Front line trenches. Enemy inactive. Fighting Patrols occupied NO MAN'S LAND nightly, but did not encounter enemy. Night of 11/12th Relieved by 1/8th Argyll & Sutherland Highlanders 183rd Infantry Brigade. Moved by march route to billets at VAUX.	62.b.S.W. 1/20,000.
	12th		In billets at VAUX – rested.	62.D. 1/40,000.
	13th – 18th		Work on improving Defences of Battle Zone. 15th. 2/5th R.War.R. disbanded. Draft of 17 Officers and 350 O.R. transferred to this Unit.	
	19th		Prepared for trenches. Night of 19/20th Relieved 2/4th O.B.L.I. 184th Infantry Brigade,in Support of Right Sector of Divisional Front. In Dug-outs HOLMON and SAVY WOODS.	62.c.S.W. 1/20,000.
	20th & 21st		Work on burying cable to Front Line Battalion H.Q.	
	22nd		Moved to Dug-out M.D.B. HELMON WOOD.	
	23rd – 26th		Work on improving defences of the Battle Zone.	
	27th		Prepared for Front line trenches. Night of 27/28th Relieved 2/8th Wores. in Right Sector of Divisional Front.	62.b.S.W. 1/20,000.
	28th		In Front line trenches. Work on improvements of Defences.	

Fighting Strength – Officers – 55. O.R. 1044.

[signature] Lieut. Colonel,
Comdg., 2/6th R.War.R.

182nd Brigade.
61st Division.

2/6th BATTALION

ROYAL WARWICKSHIRE REGIMENT

MARCH 1918. & APRIL

Army Form C. 2118.

2/6 R. Warwickshire
Mar & April

WAR DIARY
or
INTELLIGENCE SUMMARY.
(Erase heading not required.)

Instructions regarding War Diaries and Intelligence Summaries are contained in F. S. Regs., Part II. and the Staff Manual respectively. Title pages will be prepared in manuscript.

Place	Date	Hour	Summary of Events and Information	Remarks and references to Appendices
Field	1.3.18		In front line outside ST.QUENTIN, quiet time, two casualties from indirect M.G.fire.	
	6.3.18		Relieved by 2/7th R.War.R. and went to GERMAINE for training.	
	14.3.18		Relieved 2/8th WORCESTERS at M.D.E. and M.D.C. West of HOLNON in BATTLE ZONE, the Battalion consisting of 21 Officers and 700 other ranks.	
	20.3.18		Two Companies 'A' & 'C' raided the enemy lines in front of ST.QUENTIN from FAYET and took 12 prisoners and 1 machine gun, our casualties 1 killed and 4 wounded.	
	21.3.18		Enemy bombardment commenced at 4.45 a.m. and continued till 11.30 a.m.	
	22.3.18		Battalion ordered to retire about 12 noon, Col.DAVIDSON formed an extended line with his men from ATTILLY in a northern direction joining on his right the 2/7th R.War.R., and kept up a slow rearguard fight to the ARMY LINE, which the remains of the Battalion reached about 4.30 in the afternoon: a further retirement was made at about 6.0 p.m. to BEAUVOIS, where Col.DAVIDSON collected 40 men and occupied an old French trench: at 7.30 p.m. he sent 2/Lieut.F. HARDY away to get orders, but he did not return and has not since been seen; at 9.30 p.m. Col.DAVIDSON collected his men with the intention of endeavouring to re-occupy the Line, he went forward himself with the R.S.M. and taking a rifle, sniped at the enemy whom he found occupying the line, he returned to the trench by the Village and collected some stragglers of other units, making his force about 80 strong. At 10.45 p.m. he sent another officer back for orders, as his right flank was then being attacked but this Officer reached H.Q. too late for retirement Orders (which should have reached Col. DAVIDSON at 9.30 p.m.) to be sent him.	
	25.3.18		Being almost surrounded, Col.DAVIDSON withdrew his force at 2.0 a.m. They rested at MATIGNY and reached VOYENNES without loss at 8.0 a.m., they then joined a further party of the 2/6th R.War.R. at BILLANCOURT at about 2.30 p.m. This further other party of about 120 men under 2 Officers was collected at VOYENNES and at 4.30 a.m. on the 23rd was marched to LANGUEVOISIN reaching there about 5.0 a.m. At 10.30 a.m. they were sent to BREUIL, but found it occupied by our troops, they then made for BILLANCOURT, where they arrived at 2.30 p.m.	

APPENDIX 'B'
Brief Summary of Operations by surplus personnel of Battalion from night of March 21st.

21.3.18. All O.Rs under Major H.N. DAVENPORT M.C., proceeded to UGNY and all surplus Officers (9) under Capt. A.D. WILLCOX proceeded to Corps Reinforcement Camp at ESTOUILLY, near HAM, and returned to UGNY with a draft of approximately 60 O.R. the same day. This composite force dug in as a defensive measure, and remained until ordered to retire to VOYENNES. About 200 O.R. of the Battalion were picked up en route, but proceeded in the direction of NESLE, under 2/Lt. J. McDONOUGH.

22.3.18. Surplus personnel took up defensive position at Bridge-head at VOYENNES until 5.0 a.m., and proceeded to NESLE, where they were ordered to barricade the streets round Church and prevent enemy advance through town. Brig-Gen. SPOONER and two other Generals were present at this operation.

23.3.18. The force was ordered to proceed to BILLANCOURT, where the Battalion also arrived same evening.

24.3.18. Surplus moved to GRUNY under arrangements.

25.3.18. Force proceeded to DAMERY under Brigade and 6.0 p.m. same night to FOLIES.

26.3.18. Our patrols were fired on while moving along ROYE-AMIENS road in direction of ROYE. Stores etc., moved off at once. Remainder took up a defensive line through WARVILLERS and ROUVROY, until relieved by 89th and 90th Brigades at 4.0 pm same day.
Force then withdrew to MEZIERES and met rest of Battalion, and dug defensive positions.

Army Form C. 2118.

WAR DIARY
or
INTELLIGENCE SUMMARY.
(Erase heading not required.)

Instructions regarding War Diaries and Intelligence Summaries are contained in F.S. Regs., Part II. and the Staff Manual respectively. Title pages will be prepared in manuscript.

Place	Date	Hour	Summary of Events and Information	Remarks references to Appendices
Field	24.3.18		At 11.50 a.m. the Battalion then about 140 strong, left BILLANCOURT under Col. DAVIDSON, and occupied the CANAL du NORD on the West Bank behind BUVERCHY.	
	25.3.18		At 5.0 p.m. when forces on our right gave way they had to retire. Col. DAVIDSON collected all the troops he could in MOYENCOURT, and put up a fight until wounded. The remainder of the Battalion retired to VILLERS aux ERABLES, arriving there on the 26th.	
	26.3.18		In evening marched and dug in, in front of MAISON BLANCHE, where they were joined by the details from the rear, consisting of 8 officers and about 140 men.	
	27.3.18		At 3.0 a.m. the Battalion marched to LE QUESNEL arriving there about 4.0 a.m. and dug in, leaving at 11.0 p.m., the Battalion was sent by lorry to MARCELCAVE, where after fighting in front of the village and in the Railway cutting, dug in 800 yards in rear of the village.	
	1.4.18		Marched to GENTELLES.	
	3.4.18		The Battalion was sent in lorries to SAISSEVAL.	
	4.4.18 to 12.4.18 see Appendix 'A'			
	13.4.18		About 2.0 p.m orders were received ordering amalgamation of 24th Entrenching Battalion and this Battalion under the name of 182nd Composite Battalion. Relieved 2/7th R.War.R. in Right sub-sector of Brigade Front on night of 13th/14th. N. boundary stream in Q.7.b. - S.boundary Q.14.c.6.3. (Ref: Map 36A S.E.1/20,000)	
	14.4.18		Hostile Artillery active, no infantry action. Prisoner captured belonging to 2nd Bav.R.I.R., 1st Bav. R. Div: on night of 14th/15th. Active patrolling throughout the night and casualties inflicted on the enemy in one encounter.	
	15.4.18		Quiet day. Relieved by 2/7th R.War.R. on night of 15th/16th, and withdrew to Brigade Reserve in HAMET BILLET.	
	16.4.18		Rested and reorganized in HAMET BILLET. Reinforcements received. 24th Entrenching Batt. became separate unit again.	

Army Form C. 2118.

WAR DIARY
or
INTELLIGENCE SUMMARY.

(Erase heading not required)

Instructions regarding War Diaries and Intelligence Summaries are contained in F. S. Regs., Part II. and the Staff Manual respectively. Title pages will be prepared in manuscript.

Place	Date	Hour	Summary of Events and Information	Remarks and references to Appendices
Field	17.4.18		Continued reorganization and refitment. Relieved 2/8th WORCESTERS in Left sub-sector of Brigade Front night of 17th/18th.	
	18.4.18		Enemy shelled LA HAYE continuously from 1.0 a.m. to 6.0 a.m. with gas and H.Es. Enemy attack on Left Company of Battalion on right at 4.0 a.m. repulsed with losses.	
	19th/20th		Trenches, Quiet during day, active patrolling at night.	
	21.4.18		Trenches. Relieved by 2/7th R.War.R. on night of 21st/22nd. Withdrew to Brigade Reserve in HAMEL BILLET.	
	22.4.18		Reinforcements received and Battalion reorganized into 4 Companies.	
	23.4.18		Reorganization and refitment continued. Relieved 2/8th WORCESTERS in right sub-sector of Brigade Front.	
	24th/26th		Trenches. Quiet during day. Active patrolling at night.	
	27.4.18		Trenches. Relieved by 2/7th R.War.R. on night of 27th/28th. Withdrew to Brigade Reserve in HAMEL BILLET.	
	28.4.18		Rested.	
	29.4.18		Prepared for trenches. Relieved 2/8th WORCESTERS in Left sub-sector of Brigade Front on night of 29th/30th.	
	30.4.18		Trenches Quiet day.	

Casualties March 21st to April 5th 1918. 16 Officers - 450 O.Rs. (approx).

Major
Commanding 2/6th Battn.R.War.R.

APPENDIX 'A'

Sheet
LACOUTURE 1/30,000

Entrained at ST ROCH AMIENS having marched from SAISSEVAL. detrained at BERGUETTE at 5.30 p.m. orders from G.S.O. 111 3rd Corps to bus to MT BERNECHON and come into Corps Reserve. Embussed at 7.45 p.m. reached MT BERNECHON about 9.30 p.m. transport marching. Troops no food since breakfast at 2.15 a.m. No orders and no Infantry Commander at MT BERNECHON. I reported to Hdqrs 51st Div: at ROBECQ and was ordered to move to LE CORNET MALO Q.28.d where Battalion would come under orders of G.O.C. 153rd Inf: Bde: Battalion reached LE CORNET MALO at 2.30 a.m. G.O.C. 153rd Bdge ordered preparation for a counter-attack on approximate front R.15 Central - R.21.c.9.5. with possible alternative of holding a defensive position from Q.23.d. central (PACAUT) to Q.35.d. central. The situation at that time was not sufficiently clear to enable reconnaissance to be made. Battalion concentrated in Q.28.d central with Hdqrs at Q.29.c.0.3. ready for counter-attack if ordered. At 7.30 a.m. orders were received to hold a defensive position from Q.23.central to Q.29 central. Battalion was in position at 8.15 a.m. with 'A' Coy on left, 'C' Coy centre, 'D' Coy right and 'B' Coy in reserve about Q.29.c.3.7.
A number of M.G.'s of 39th Batt: M.G.C. moved forward with the Battalion and took up a position 200-300 yards in advance of position held by Batt: Patrols were pushed forward and detachments of infantry went forward to support of M.G's.
At 11.30 a.m. orders were received to readjust the line with our left at Q.11.d.2.0. and our right at the present right of 'A' Coy Q.29 central. Orders were issued for Reserve Company to move at once with its left at Q.11.d.0.2. and right on the ditch at Q.23.b.2.9. and for 'D' Coy to move into gap between 'B' & 'A' Coy and for 'C' Coy to move into Reserve near Q.22.b. and d. central. There were a certain number of reorganised troops of 51st Div: h-ing a line parallel with our new line and with a switch running S.E. towards Q.23.b.7.2.
At 6 p.m. 11th April dispositions were as shown on attached map "A" Touch was lost with 5th D.C.L.I. during afternoon and a unit of troops from 51st Div: came in on our left.
At about 12 midnight touch was lost with units on our left. 153rd Bdge were informed and at once issued orders to move up a detachment of 100-150 men. Pending their arrival a strong patrol was moved into this gap from Reserve Coy and later into outskirts of PARADIS. They reported no signs of enemy.
Disposition about 2 a.m. on 12th April were as shown on Map "B". Patrols were out on Battalion Front but did not return.
About 6.0 p.m. on 12th I drew attention of 153rd Bdge to the extended front held by the Battalion and the weakness of the defensive dispositions on the right flank.

At about 5 a.m. Artillery fire noticeably increased in the South. 5.15 - 5.20 Capt. B.K. PARSONS reported our troops retiring past Batt: Hdqrs. I went to investigate and found a large number going backwards, did my best to stem the retreat, and succeeded in throwing a few into trenches with some men of 'C' Coy. Enemy Very Lights were falling between Hdqrs and the nearer buildings of PACAUT and were some 500yds distant on the left. M.G. fire opened from general direction of PACAUT - well in enfilade and sweeping our men retiring. I went into H burned my maps and papers and attempted to send warni 153rd Bdge but found lines gone. Enemy fire was com House from both flanks. I went out again and found disappeared. This was about 5.30. Enemy infan buildings on my return. With the Adjutant and Ca decided to withdraw. Soon after this we came up 'D' Coy with Lt. V.H. TRIPP. 2/Lt. C.C. HARPER and 2/ 2/Lt. F.B. GORE. Enemy were at this time firing l outskirts of LA PIERRE AU BEURE and rifle and M.G.

from that direction. An attempt was now made to effect an orderly withdrawal to railway line which runs about Q.15.central in a N.E. direction. A party under 2/Lt.C.C.HARPER and 2/Lt.F.B.GORE was sent to hold farm buildings at Q.21.a.0.6. and a pary under 2/Lt.F.G.LEE to line Railway Embankment about 15 central, to cover withdrawal of main body (some 50 men in all) to line of railway and there to farm buildings and orchard Q.14.d.8.3. Here were found some forward posts of 2/7th Warwicks. Some stragglers of THE ROYAL SCOTS and 1 M.G. were found about Q.15.c.5.6. At this time quite an accurate M.G. fire was being brought to bear on area between railway bank and road from LES RUES DES VACHES southwards, party from Q.21.a.0.6. withdrew in good order to our posts at Q.14.a.9.3. losing 2 Officers and several men. Party under 2/Lt.F.G.LEE also withdrew in good order to orchard where they dug in. When all were in touch with 2/7th WARWICKS with my Adjutant I went to find 2/7th WARWICK Hdqrs going by road in Q.14.d. towards BAQUEROLLES farm at road junction Q.14.c.9.1. Enemy patrol with L.M.G. opened fire at short range from BAQUEROLLES farm buildings. We withdrew, runner being killed en-route. At this time this flank was entirely exposed. I warned 2/7th WARWICK platoon in Q.14.d.9.3. and withdrew remnants of 2/6th WARWICKS from orchard and formed a line from farm at Q.14.c.9.3. N.E. across CLARENCE towards 1 platoon of 2/7th WARWICKS which were dug in about Q.14.c.4.3. L left 2/6th WARWICKS under command of 2/Lt.H.A.TETLEY and placed him under orders of Coy Commander. of 2/7th WARWICKS. He was subsequently killed with 15 or 20 men in this position. With my Adjutant I went towards 2/7th WARWICK Hdqrs and from there to Hdqrs 182nd Inf: Bde: then at P.11.d.1.2. and reported the situation. I was then ordered to come under orders of the Bde and take up a position on right of 2/8th WORCESTERS from P.12.d.8.4. to FARM buildings at LES AMUSOIRES. At 5 p.m. commenced digging in with some 63 men who had been collected. Remained in this position with Hdqrs at P.11 central until night of 13/14th. At this time Battalion was organised into 2 Coys.

On 13th/14th Battalion relieved 2/7th WARWICKS in right sector.

The casualties of the Battalion between 10th and 14th April inclusive were 9 Officers and 133 other ranks.

Major,
Commanding 2/6th Battn.R.War.R.

APPENDIX to WAR DIARY 182 Bde

61st Division.   XVIII Corps No. G.a.155/5.

Orders having been received for the transfer of the 61st Division from the XVIII Corps to another Corps I wish to place on record my high appreciation of the services rendered by the Division during the recent strenuous fighting and to narrate in proper sequence and perspective the events in which the Division played a part from 20th March to 1st April, 1918. The scene of action lay between ST. QUENTIN and the river AVRE, North of MOREUIL, and the following brief notes will no doubt be of particular interest to the 61st Division.

(1) By mid-March the possibility of a German attack at an early date was indicated on the Corps front by air photographs and other sources of information, but it was not till the 19th of the month that its imminence became pronounced. To clear up the situation a raid had been carefully prepared by the 61st Division. It was launched under cover of a heavy artillery bombardment at 10 p.m. on 20th March and was completely successful. Two companies of the 2/6th Warwicks penetrated the German trenches opposite FAYET, inflicted many casualties upon the enemy, brought back three machine guns and 15 prisoners, and established the fact that another fresh German division had recently arrived in the trenches. As a result of this valuable raid all the troops in this and adjoining army corps were warned before 2 a.m. on 21st March to expect an attack in force on the morning of 21st March, and at 4.30 a.m. the order to "Man Battle Stations" was also sent out from XVIII Corps Headquarters to all concerned. As the FORWARD ZONE was always permanently manned, this warning applied only to the BATTLE ZONE which was over 6,000 yards from the front German trenches.

(2) On the 21st March in a dense mist three battalions (2/8th Worcesters, 2/4th Oxford and Bucks and 2/5th Gordon Highlanders) were holding a front of 6,000 yards in the FORWARD ZONE and occupied ground to a depth of some 1,500 yards in rear of their outposts. These heroic battalions were first subjected to intensive bombardment by all calibres of guns and trench mortars for a period of five hours, and were then overwhelmed by not less than three German infantry divisions which assaulted at about 10 a.m. The fog prevented our "S.O.S." rockets being seen and deprived our artillery and machine gunners of distant targets. Desperate fighting took place all day in the FORWARD ZONE, whose redoubts remained in telephonic communication with us until 4.10pm. by means of cables buried 8 feet deep. At that hour the garrisons were told they might cut their way out at night, but except a few odd men, no one returned from the three battalions whose duty it was to garrison the FORWARD ZONE. They simply fought it out on the spot and their heroism will live for ever in the annals of their regiments. They undoubtedly accounted for very great numbers of the enemy but details are necessarily lacking. All we know for certain is that three battalions held up three enemy divisions all day on the 21st March and prevented them from assaulting the BATTLE ZONE of the 61st Division. Moreover, their left flank was turned early in the forenoon when the enemy captured MAISSEMY and pressed on to VILLECHOLLES, both of which places were in the BATTLE ZONE of an adjoining division. To retrieve this local situation the 2/4th Battalion Royal Berkshire Regiment in reserve at MARTEVILLE undertook a counter-attack against the high ground south of MAISSEMY at 6.10pm. and was most gallantly led by its Commanding Officer. He was killed, and the attack was only partially successful owing to his loss. Col DIMMER V.C.

Nine of our guns belonging to two 18-pdr. batteries which had been over-run by the enemy between MAISSEMY and VILLECHOLLES were fought for and recovered early on 22nd March and the remainder of the BATTLE ZONE was intact in our hands until the afternoon.

(3) From 8 a.m. till 11 a.m. the left flank of the BATTLE ZONE was again heavily attacked from MAISSEMY, but was stoutly held by the 8th battalion Argyll and Sutherland Highlanders, assisted by another counter-attack by the Royal Berkshire Regiment. In fact the enemy gained no success whatever against any part of the BATTLE ZONE even after he had penetrated to VERMAND and west of it, which he did at about 12 noon. The 9th Battalion at VILLEVEQUE was detailed to watch and counter this considerable movement of enemy forces proceeding westwards along the

P.T.O.

-2-

the northern slopes of the OMIGNON Valley in the direction of CAULAIN-COURT. It thus safeguarded the left flank of the Corps.

(4) But late in the afternoon this deep penetration and the consequent massing of hostile guns across the valley compelled the 61st Division to withdraw to a prepared position between VAUX and VILLEVEQUE. This was done in good order by 5.40 p.m. on 22nd March, on instructions from the Corps and these instructions were partly influenced by the fact that ESSIGNY and the ground south-west of it had been captured by the enemy early on this date (22nd.). The choice lay between sacrificing the 61st Division in its BATTLE ZONE or withdrawing it to conform to the deeply penetrated British line on its left. It withdrew fighting to the last.

(5) The Division was subsequently attacked in its new position, was subjected to severe and accurate artillery fire, but held its front line with success until 2.30 a.m. on 23rd March, when the 2/5th Gloucesters of the 184th Infantry Brigade retired through the 20th Division to take up a position behind the SOMME. The enemy's fire was so heavy in the neighbourhood of BEAUVOIS that movement became almost impossible at that important road junction during the night.

(6) The subsequent retreat under enemy pressure afforded the 61st Division two good opportunities of rounding on the enemy and inflicting further heavy casualties upon him in the following actions :-

(a) On the 24th March the Pioneer Battalion and part of the Reinforcement Battalion joined in a successful counter-attack in the direction of HAM and restored our line in conjunction with the 20th Division.

(b) On the same date, and also in co-operation with the 20th Division, the 183rd Infantry Brigade counter-attacked at BETHENCOURT and drove the enemy back across the river SOMME.

(7) On 25th and 26th March the Division supported the 20th and 30th Divisions on the line HANGEST - LE QUESNOY and also on the line MEZIERES - DEMUIN. On the 27th it was transferred in a hurry to retrieve a critical situation in another Corps area. Here, on the 28th March, the 183rd and 184th Infantry Brigades attacked LAMOTTE, captured it and held it for six hours under heavy shell and machine gun fire. On 1st April the Division was relieved at MARCELCAVE, where it was put in to hold the line as a temporary measure.

(8) Throughout this period of sleepless fighting and constant movement, the Royal Artillery, the Royal Engineers and the Pioneer Battalion were all put through a severe test of endurance and courage. They acquitted themselves well. The 61st Division has thus established for itself a high reputation for its fighting qualities and gallant spirit, and I wish to thank all ranks for their cheerful alacrity whenever they were called upon to make a special effort.

I would also remind them that even greater exertions will be required of them during the coming months, and I am convinced that they will respond to the call as readily as they have done in the past. May good fortune and success attend the 61st Division in the future.

Ivor Maxse

Lieutenant-General,
Commanding XVIII Army Corps.

10th April, 1918.

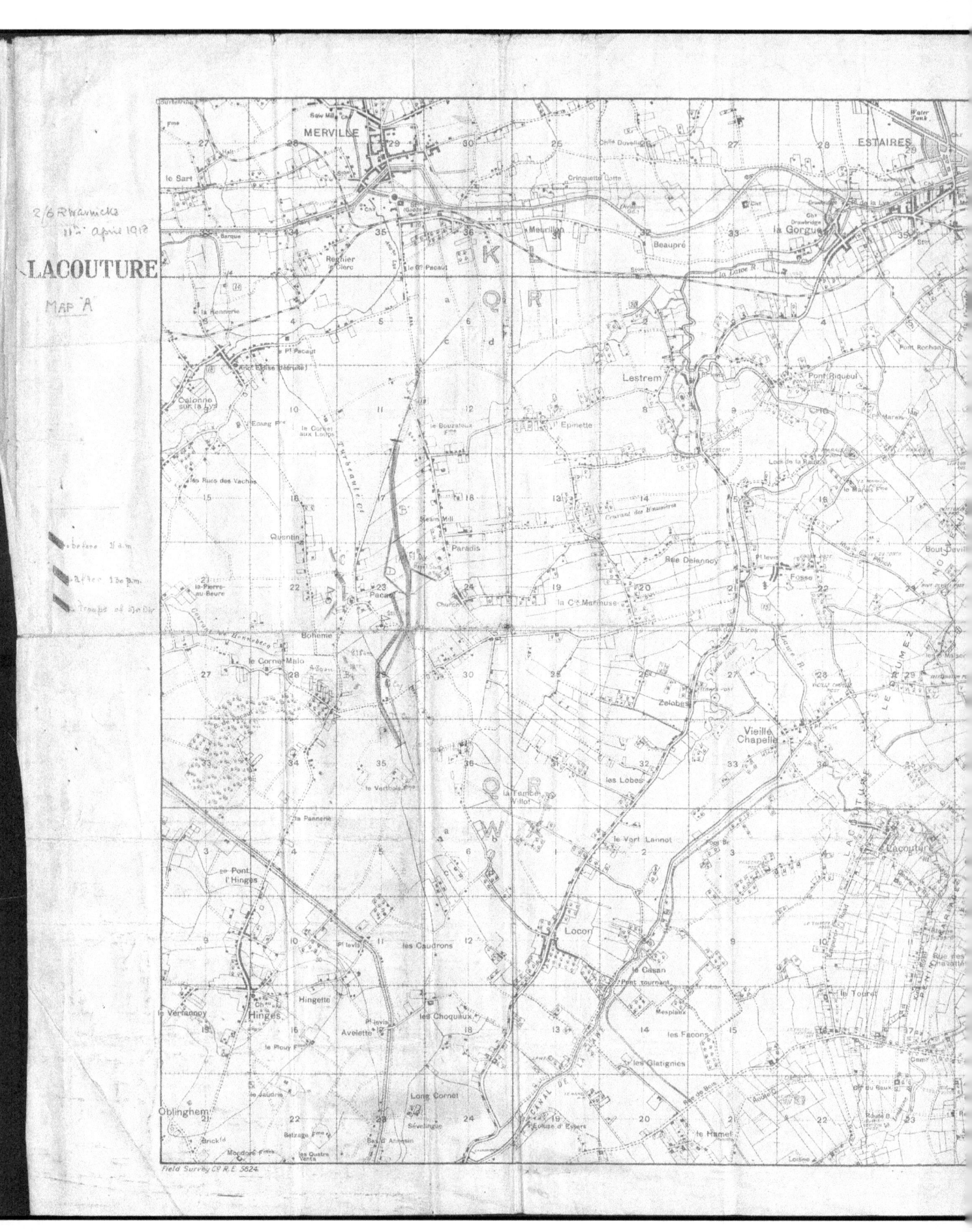

LACOUTURE

MAP "A"

2/6 R Warwicks
11th April 1918

Vol 25

CONFIDENTIAL.

WAR DIARY
of
2/6TH BATTALION ROYAL WARWICKSHIRE REGIMENT.
From May 1st to May 31st, 1918.

@@@@@@@@@@@@@
@   @
@ VOLUME XXV. @
@   @
@@@@@@@@@@@@@

Army Form C. 2118.

WAR DIARY
or
INTELLIGENCE SUMMARY.
(Erase heading not required.)

Instructions regarding War Diaries and Intelligence Summaries are contained in F. S. Regs., Part II. and the Staff Manual respectively. Title pages will be prepared in manuscript.

Place	Date	Hour	Summary of Events and Information	Remarks and references to Appendices
Field. 36A.S.E. 1/20,000.	1.5.18.		In forward system - Left subsector of Brigade front. Quiet day - patrolling and improvement of defences at night.	AA
	2.5.18.		Trenches. A raid by two patrols of 1 Officer and 14 O.R. each, was attempted on the night of 2nd/3rd May, under cover of a creeping barrage, on Posts situated 100 yards East of stream running North and South through Q.2.c. Enemy was found to have established himself in Posts 50 yards West of stream, and raid was repulsed by Machine Gun fire.	AA
-do-	3.5.18.		Trenches - quiet day. Relieved by 2/7th R.War.Rgt. on night of 3rd/4th, and withdrew to Brigade Reserve in HAMET BILLET.	AA
-do-	4. & 5. 5.18.		In billets. Resting, re-fitting and bathing.	AA
-do-	5.5.18.		Relieved 2/8th Batt. Worcester Regt. in right subsector of Brigade front, on night of 5th/6th. Dispositions :— 'B' Company - Left front. 'D' " - Right front. 'C' " - Reserve. 'A' " - LES AMUSOIRES - HAVERSKERQUE Line.	AA
-do-	6. to 9. 5.18.		Trenches. Active patrolling at night. No enemy patrols encountered. Work on improvement of defences during hours of darkness. Relieved by 2/7th R.War.Rgt. on night of 9th/10th and withdrew to Brigade Reserve in HAMET BILLET.	AA
-do-	10. & 11.5.18.		Resting and bathing. Relieved 2/8th Worcester Regt. in Left subsector of Brigade front on night of 11th/12th. Dispositions :— 'A' Company - Left front. 'C' " - Right front. 'D' " - Reserve. 'B' " - LES AMUSOIRES - HAVERSKERQUE Line.	AA
-do-	12. to 14.5.18.		Trenches. Quiet. Usual patrolling activity, and work on wire and trenches at night. Two strong fighting patrols, under cover of a creeping barrage, raided enemy Posts West of stream running North and South through Q.2.c. on night of 14th/15th. Enemy forced to evacuate Post at Q.2.c.10.30. by barrage. Prisoner of 25th R.I.R. 15th Reserve Division, captured in Post at Q.2.c.15.40.	AA

A5834 Wt.W4973/M687 750,000 8/16 D.D. & L. Ltd. Forms/C.2118/13.

Army Form C. 2118.

WAR DIARY
or
INTELLIGENCE SUMMARY.

(Erase heading not required.)

Instructions regarding War Diaries and Intelligence Summaries are contained in F.S. Regs., Part II. and the Staff Manual respectively. Title pages will be prepared in manuscript.

Place	Date	Hour	Summary of Events and Information	Remarks and references to Appendices
36a.S.E. 1/20,000.	15.5.18.		Trenches. Quiet. Relieved by 2/7th R.War.Rgt. on night of 15th/16th and withdrew to Brigade Reserve in HEMET BILLET.	
-do-	16. & 17.5.18.		Cleaning and resting. Relieved 2/8th Worcester Regt. in right subsector of Brigade front on night of 17th/18th. Dispositions :- 'D' Company - Right front. 'B' " - Left front. 'C' " - Reserve. 'A' " - LES AMUSOIRES - HAVERSKERQUE Line.	
-do-	18. to 21.5.18.		Trenches. Quiet. Patrolling and improvement of trenches, shelters, etc., throughout hours of darkness. On night of 21st/22nd, Inter-Battalion boundary was adjusted, 2/8th Worcesters taking over all ground North of line running through Q.8.a.10.15 - Q.7.c.00.25. - Q.18.a.70.35.-- Q.18.a.40.30. - Q.18.c.00.90. - Q.17.d.00.80.	
-do-	22.5.18.		Trenches. Quiet day. Relieved by 2/5th Gloucester Regt. (184th Infantry Brigade), on night 22nd/23rd, and withdrew to Divisional Reserve in LA MIQUELLERIE.	
36a. 1/40,000.	23.5.18.		Cleaning of billets, re-equipping and resting.	
-do-	24.5.18.		Training - Close Order Drill, P.T. and B.F., Musketry, wiring and sandbagging.	
-do-	25.5.18.		Training - Close Order Drill, P.T. and B.F., Musketry, Specialist Training, visual signalling Demonstration. Bathing.	
	26.5.18.		Training :- Physical drill and B.F., Musketry, Specialist training. Bathing. Sports :- Inter-Coy. competition and baseball exhibition match.	
-do-	27.5.18.		Battalion parade. Training :- P.T. and B.F. Sandbagging and wiring. Relieved 2/7th R.War.Rgt. in the forward system on night 27th/28th.	

Army Form C. 2118.

WAR DIARY
or
INTELLIGENCE SUMMARY.
(*Erase heading not required.*)

Instructions regarding War Diaries and Intelligence Summaries are contained in F. S. Regs., Part II. and the Staff Manual respectively. Title pages will be prepared in manuscript.

Place	Date	Hour	Summary of Events and Information	Remarks and references to Appendices
36a.S.E. 1/20,000.	28.5.18.		Trenches. Quiet day. Patrolling and work carried on throughout the night.	
–do–	29.5.18.		Increased hostile artillery activity. Patrolling and work carried on throughout the night. Enemy shelled the whole of the forward system from 10 p.m. 29.5.18 to 12.30 a.m. 30.5.18 with Green Cross Gas shells.	
–do–	30.5.18.		Hostile artillery again active. Usual work and patrolling at night.	
–do–	31.5.18.		Quiet day. Relieved by 2/7th R.War.Rgt. on night 31st May/1st June, 1918.	
			Fighting Strength of Battalion – 41 Officers. 962 Other Ranks.	

W. R. Phillis
Lieut–Colonel,
Commanding 2/6th Batt. R. War. Rgt.

Vol 26

CONFIDENTIAL.

WAR DIARY of

2/6TH BATTALION ROYAL WARWICKSHIRE REGIMENT

From June 1st to June 30th, 1918.

@@@@@@@@@@@@
@   @
@ VOLUME XXVI @
@@@@@@@@@@@@@

Army Form C. 2118.

WAR DIARY
or
INTELLIGENCE SUMMARY.
(Erase heading not required.)

Instructions regarding War Diaries and Intelligence Summaries are contained in F.S. Regs., Part II. and the Staff Manual respectively. Title pages will be prepared in manuscript.

Place	Date	Hour	Summary of Events and Information	Remarks and references to Appendices
In the Field.	1.6.18.		In billets in Brigade Reserve at HAMET BILLET. Resting and re-equipping.	
	2.6.18.		Specialist Training. Bathing. Aquatic Sports held in LA BASSEE canal.	
	3.6.18.		Resting and preparing for the Line. Relieved 2/8th Worcesters in the Front Line, Left Sub-Section, ST. FLORIS Section, on night of 3rd/4th inst. Dispositions :-	
			Left Front - 'D' Company.	
			Right Front - 'B' "	
			Left Support - 'A' "	
			Right Support- 'C' "	
	4.6.18.		Lieut-Colonel W.R. PHILLIPS, M.C. granted 14 days leave, and Major J. DIGBY WYATT, M.C. assumed Command.	
	4.6.18 to 9.6.18.		Trenches. Quiet. Work on improvement of Defences in the Forward System throughout the hours of darkness. Active patrolling nightly. 183rd Infantry Brigade relieved 182nd Infantry Brigade night of 9th/10th. Came into Divisional Reserve, the Battalion moving by march route to billets at GUARBECQUE.	
	10.6.18.		Billets. Inspection Parades and resting.	
	11.6.18 to		Section, Platoon, Company, Specialist Training. Night Operations 13th and 17th. Corps Commanders inspection 18th. Brigade Horse Show and Sports 19th inst.	
	21.6.18.		Battalion concert 15th. Cricket in the afternoons. Lieut-Colonel W.R. PHILLIPS, M.C. returned from leave,	
	22.6.18.		Inoculation. Bathing and resting. and assumed Command of the Battalion.	
	23.6.18.		Church Parade. Resting.	
	24.6.18.		Resting and preparing for move. 182nd Infantry Brigade relieved 184th Infantry Brigade night of 24th/25th in the ROBECQ Section, the Battalion moving to LA MIQUELLERIE into Brigade Reserve.	
	25.6.18		Section and Platoon Training.) Working Party of 200 Other Ranks worked on the LES AMUSOIRES - Football in the afternoons.) HAVERSKERQUE Line, night of 26th/27th inst.	
	26.6.18. & 27.6.18.		Section and Platoon Training.	

A5834 Wt.W4973 M687 750,000 8/16 D.D.&L.Ltd. Forms/C.2118/13.

Army Form C. 2118.

WAR DIARY
or
INTELLIGENCE SUMMARY.
(Erase heading not required.)

Instructions regarding War Diaries and Intelligence Summaries are contained in F. S. Regs., Part II. and the Staff Manual respectively. Title pages will be prepared in manuscript.

Place	Date	Hour	Summary of Events and Information	Remarks and references to Appendices

In the Field.	28.6.18.		Resting and preparing for the line. Relieved 2/8th Worcesters in the Left Sub-Section, ROBECQ Section, night of 28th/29th inst. Dispositions :-
			     Left Front - 'A' Company.
			     Right Front - 'C' "
			     Reserve - 'D' "
			                           'B' "	

	29.6.18. & 30.6.18.		LES AMUSOIRES-HAVERSKERQUE Line - Work on improvement of defences in the Forward System during the hours of darkness. Trenches. Quiet day. Active patrolling at night.	
			FIGHTING STRENGTH - 43 Officers and 894 Other Ranks.	

July 1st, 1918.

W.E. Phillips
Lieut-Colonel,
Commanding 2/6th Batt. R. War. Regt.

Vol 27

CONFIDENTIAL.

WAR DIARY OF

2/6TH. BATTALION THE ROYAL WARWICKSHIRE REGIMENT.

From July 1st to July 31st 1918.

oooooooooooooo
o
o VOLUME XXVIII o
o   o
ooooooooooooooo

Army Form C. 2118.

WAR DIARY
or
INTELLIGENCE SUMMARY.
(Erase heading not required.)

Instructions regarding War Diaries and Intelligence Summaries are contained in F.S. Regs., Part II and the Staff Manual respectively. Title pages will be prepared in manuscript.

Place	Date	Hour	Summary of Events and Information	Remarks and references to Appendices
In the Field 48A 36A 32 J.10.070. 4 36 A J.10.500	1.7.18		Trenches. Left Sub-section of the ROBECQ Section. Quiet day. Work on improvement of defences in the Forward System and active patrolling during the hours of darkness. Divisional Commander visited portion of Section.	A.D.
	2.7.18		Trenches. Quiet day. Inter-company relief night of 2/3rd. Dispositions:— Left front, "D" Company Right Front, "B" " Reserve, "A" " "C" "	A.D.
			LES AMUSOIRES—HAVERSKERQUE line, the Forward System, also active patrolling at night. Work continued on improvement of defences in the Forward System, also active patrolling at night. Incidence of "3 day" fever appears to have reached its maximum. Figures to the present date to show numbers with "3 day" fever retained with unit:—	
			<table><tr><td>16th</td><td>17th</td><td>18th</td><td>19th</td><td>20th</td><td>21st</td><td>22nd</td><td>23rd</td><td>24th</td><td>25th</td><td>26th</td><td>27th</td><td>28th</td><td>29th</td><td>30th</td><td>1st</td></tr><tr><td>11</td><td>36</td><td>27</td><td>76</td><td>1-66</td><td>1-72</td><td>1-52</td><td>8-165</td><td>5-148</td><td>9-144</td><td>9-174</td><td>5-175</td><td>5-220</td><td>5-234</td><td>5-211</td><td>3-208</td></tr><tr><td>2nd</td><td>3rd</td><td></td><td></td><td></td><td></td><td></td><td></td><td></td><td></td><td></td><td></td><td></td><td></td><td></td><td></td></tr><tr><td>3-208</td><td>3-208</td><td></td><td></td><td></td><td></td><td></td><td></td><td></td><td></td><td></td><td></td><td></td><td></td><td></td><td></td></tr></table>	
	3.7.18		Divisional Commander visited Headquarters 8.15 a.m. Trenches. Quiet day. Hostile shelling more active at night. Continuance of usual night work and patrolling. Two O.R. wounded.	A.D.
	4.7.18		Trenches. Enemy artillery very active during the early hours, otherwise quiet day. Usual night work and patrolling. M.G's. less active.	A.D.
	5.7.18		Trenches. Quiet day. Hostile artillery fairly active throughout the day. Continuance of work on defences in the Forward System and active patrolling at night.	A.D.

Army Form C. 2118.

WAR DIARY
or
INTELLIGENCE SUMMARY.
(Erase heading not required.)

Instructions regarding War Diaries and Intelligence Summaries are contained in F. S. Regs., Part II. and the Staff Manual respectively. Title pages will be prepared in manuscript.

Place	Date	Hour	Summary of Events and Information	Remarks and references to Appendices
In the Field	6.7.18		Trenches. Quiet day. Relieved by 2/7th R.War.R. night of 6th/7th and withdrew to LA MIQUELLERIE, into Brigade Reserve.	
	7.7.18		In billets at LA MIQUELLERIE. Resting, re-equipping and bathing.	
	8.7.18		-do- Resting, and preparing for raid on enemy's trenches by "D" Coy. Orders attached. Raid unsuccessful. One O.R. slightly wounded. No prisoners or identifications.	App.
	9.7.18		Resting and Training. Working party of 200 other ranks found at night for work on Forward Defences.	
	10.7.18		Relieved 2/4th Ox. & Bucks. Light Infantry at LA PIERRIERE in the morning. Remainder of day – Resting.	
	11.7.18		In billets at LA PIERRIERE. Resting. Relieved in Brigade Reserve by the 10th Battalion The Buffs Regt. night of 11th, and proceeded by march route to QUERNES, where Division comes into G.H.Q. Reserve. Orders attached.	App.
	12.7.18		In billets at QUERNES. Resting.	
	13.7.18		Battalion Parade. Training under Company arrangements.	
	14.7.18		Resting.	
	15.7.18		Section, Platoon and Company Training in the morning. Specialist Training in the afternoon. Bathing. Lectures.	
	16.7.18		Training as for 15th. Staff Ride for Company Commanders in the afternoon.	
	17.7.18		Section, Platoon and Company Training in the morning. Football Match, versus 2/7th R.War.R. Tactical Scheme carried out with	
	18.7.18		-do-	
	19.7.18		Transport Section. Night operation for Signallers. Commanding Officer, Company Commanders Section, Platoon and Company Training in the morning. and Intelligence Officer reconnoitred the Forward Area.	
	20.7.18		Section, Platoon and Company Training. Range practice. Specialist Training. Staff Ride for Company Commanders in the afternoon.	
	21.7.18		Resting and Training.	
	22.7.18		61st Division transferred from XIth Corps to XVth Corps. Battalion marched to billets at LYNDE.	
	23.7.18		In billets at LYNDE. Resting. Medical Inspection.	
	24.7.18		Training and Cleaning Parades under company arrangements. Specialist Training in the afternoon.	

Army Form C. 2118.

WAR DIARY
or
INTELLIGENCE SUMMARY.
(Erase heading not required.)

Instructions regarding War Diaries and Intelligence Summaries are contained in F. S. Regs., Part II. and the Staff Manual respectively. Title pages will be prepared in manuscript.

Place	Date	Hour	Summary of Events and Information	Remarks and references to Appendices
In the Field	25.7.18		In Billets at LYNDE. Training under company arrangements. Inspection by the Army Commander in the afternoon.	
	26.7.18		At LYNDE. Training under company arrangements.	
	27.7.18		-do- -do- Football in the afternoon.	
	28.7.18		-do- Church Parade at 11.0 a.m. Football in the afternoon. Commanding Officer reconnoitred the Forward Area.	
	29.7.18		At LYNDE. Training under Company arrangements. Specialist Training in the afternoon. Commanding Officer reconnoitred part of the line. Warning Order received t'at Brigade was moving to QUERNES on night of 31st July/1st August.	
	30.7.18		AT LYNDE. Battalion Parade and training under Company arrangements.	
	31.7.18		At LYNDE. Battalion Inspection Parade, and preparing for move to QUERNES.	

FIGHTING STRENGTH - 43 Officers and 906 Other ranks.

August 1st 1918.

W.R.Mullen
Lieut. Col.
Commanding 2/6th Bn. Royal Warwick.Regt.

APPENDIX 'A'

SECRET.   2/6TH. BN. ROYAL WARWICKSHIRE REGIMENT

Order No. 115. dated 7/7/18.

Reference Maps - Sheet 36.a. S.E. Edn.6. 1/20000
              Sketch map attached.
              Air Photo 42. H.A.5

1.   Identifications are urgently required to confirm enemy order of battle opposite this front.

2.   'D' Company will force an entry into the enemy's system of forward posts, and will kill or capture the garrisons, bringing back identifications.

3.   Not more than two platoons (50 all ranks) will be used to carry out this operation.

4.   Operations will commence at ZERO hour on night of 8th/9th inst. ZERO hour will be notified later.

5.   O.C. 'D' Company is responsible that every possible means of identification is removed from his troops, and that raid identity discs are carried.

6.   PLAN.
      (a) Objective. Enemy line between Q.8.c.8.8. and Q.8.c.65.50.

      (b) Details   Two parties, each of two groups.
          of Troops. One covering party.
                      One stretcher squad.

          Right Party. Group 'A' - Sec.Lieut. A.A.WILLIAMS,
                                   2 N.C.Os. 6 O.R's.
                       Group 'B' - 2 N.C.Os. 6 O.R's.

          Left Party. Group 'C' - Sec.Lieut. G.F.FRANKLIN,
                                   2 N.C.Os. 6 O.R's
                       Group 'D' - 2 N.C.Os. 6 O.R's.

          Covering   Groups 'P' & 'Q' - 2 N.C.Os. & 12 O.R's
          Party   2 Lewis Guns.

          Stretcher   1 N.C.O. 8 Stretcher Bearers,
          Party.   4 Stretchers

      (c) Mission. Points of entry are at 'X' & 'Y' (see sketch attached)
                    These points are roughly determined by the ditches leading towards the enemy's line.
                    Right party enters at 'X'; left party enters at 'Y'.

          1. 'A' group forces wire, crosses enemy's line, turns N. works N. in rear and close to enemy's line.

          2. 'B' group follows 'A' group, turns S. works 10 to 15 yards S. searches this area for Germans, and covers flank during operations. 'B' group covers the withdrawal of 'A' group.

          3. 'C' group forces wire, crosses enemy's line, turns S. works S. in rear and close to enemy's line.

          4. 'D' group follows 'C' group, turns N. works 10 to 15 yards N. searches this area for Germans, and covers flank during operations. 'D' group covers the withdrawal of 'C' group.

- 2 -

NOTE:- 'A' & 'C' groups will "mop up" the whole of the enemy's line between their points of entry.
'B' & 'D' groups will be confined by our own barrage to points within 25 to 30 yards of outer flanks of points of entry. They will be available to exploit any opportunity of success in their direction, to assist in the withdrawal of prisoners and to cut off any prisoners who may seek shelter in either orchard, and finally they serve to cover the withdrawal of 'A' & 'C' groups.

7. ASSEMBLY MARCH.
   (a) All personnel taking part in the operation will parade in their raid equipment at Battalion H.Q. LA MIQUELLERIE, at 9.15 p.m. They will be taken by bus to Left Battalion H.Q. They will de-bus and march in groups to the Reserve Line in Q.13.a. central.
   (b) They will complete preliminary organisatin in the Reserve Line, and will move forward so as to reach the Support Line not later than ZERO minus 60.

   (Note:- Preliminary bombardment lasts from ZERO minus 120 to ZERO minus 105.)

   (c) All arrangements will be completed in the Support Line before ZERO minus 30, at which time all groups will move forward to their assembly positions in rear of Nos. 33 and 32 posts, ready to advance to a line not less than 200 yards west of the objective.

   (d) The great importance of making every possible preparation to ensure tha rapid and correct assembly of troops concerned is emphasised, and O.C. 'D' Company will be responsible that these steps are taken.

8. ASSEMBLY POSITIONS.
   All 'D' Company's dispositions for assembly will be complete at ZERO minus 20.
   Assembly will be covered by covering party, Groups 'P' & 'Q' who move to a line as in para. 7 (c) at ZERO minus 30, and make good both flanks.

   NOTE:- Until ZERO hour there will be no shell fire on the actual objective, but the barrage will lie on both flanks and rear.
   Not until ZERO hour will the barrage first fall on the objective, and at ZERO all parties will move forward as close to our barrage as possible, and, if possible, to the enemy wire, and will use the opportunity to cut this wire between ZERO and ZERO plus 3, when the barrage begins to creep forward.

9. WITHDRAWAL.
   The operations of the Right and Left parties after ZERO hour will be totally independent.
   Withdrawal of either party will take place on a pre-arranged whistle signal or order from the commanders of the respective parties. This signal will be three blasts on the whistle, and will be repeated by all leaders. In any case, all parties will withdraw from the enemy's lines not later than ZERO plus 20.
   'B' & 'D' groups cover the withdrawal of 'A' & 'C' groups, and after the latter have withdrawn from the enemy trench, 'B' and 'D' groups will follow.
   'A', 'B', 'C' & 'D' groups will pass through the covering groups 'P' & 'Q' and will proceed to our own lines.
   The covering groups 'P' & 'Q' will be withdrawn by O.C. 'D' Company on pre-arranged light signal fired from our own lines.
   On completion of operations, all personnel will make their

- 3 -

way independently to the H.Q. of the Left Battalion, will be checked, marched to their bus and return to LA MIQUELLERIE.

10. ARTILLERY.
    Artillery co-operation will be divided into phases as follows:-

    1. ZERO minus 2 HOURS.   Fifteen minutes bombardment of flanks of objective.

    2. ZERO minus 4.   Four minutes fire on flanks of objective creeping inwards.

    3. ZERO to ZERO plus 3. Intense bombardment of the objective.

    4. ZERO plus 3 to ZERO plus 20.   A box barrage around objective and bombardment of special points.

    5. ZERO plus 20 to ZERO plus 30. Fire slackens and ceases altogether at ZERO plus 30.

11. PROGRAMME.

    ZERO minus 120 to ZERO minus 105   (A) Flanks of objective bombarded.
                                       (I) All parties in reserve trench

    PAUSE   Parties move to Support Line, to be in position before ZERO minus 60.

    ZERO minus 30   (I) Parties move to position in rear of the front posts.
                     Groups of the covering party move forward

    ZERO minus 10   (I) Parties move to assembly positions forward of our wire, but not less than 200 yards distant from the objective.

    ZERO minus 4.   (A) Bombardment falls on flanks of objective creeping inwards.
                     Box barrage falls in rear of objective.

                     (I) Stands fast. If necessary, groups 'P' and 'Q' adjust their positions to be clear of any short shooting.

    ZERO   (A) Barrage lifts 100 yards off objective.
                     Box barrage still continues on flanks.

                     (I) ALL PARTIES ADVANCE TO THE ASSAULT.

    ZERO plus 20   (I) Withdrawal commences.

    ZERO plus 30   Fire ceases. All parties back in our lines.

12. DRESS & EQUIPMENT.
    Details of dress and equipment are left to the discretion of the Officer Commanding the enterprise, but they will generally follow that laid down in Appendix 'A'

13. MEDICAL ARRANGEMENTS.
    It is intended that the stretcher squad should not go further forward than the line P-Q, and they will evacuate by the main ditch towards our lines, casualties being carried from the enemy's line to them by hand.

- 4 -

These bearers are provided under the arrangements of O.C. 'D' Company.

O.C. 'C' Company will place four men and one trained stretcher bearer at the disposal of O.C. 'D' Company from 12.0 noon 8th inst.

These bearers will carry as far as company headquarters., will hand over to another relay, also provided by O.C. 'D' Company, who will carry to a R.A.M.C. relay post about Q.13.a.5.6., evacuations from there being by wheeled stretcher to the R.A.P.

14. SYNCHRONISATION OF WATCHES.
Watches will be synchronised by the Signalling Officer at Battalion H.Q. at 7.30 p.m.

There will be an artillery feint at ZERO minus 10 opposite the Brigade on our left.

ACKNOWLEDGE.

(Sgd.) D.J.DUTHIE.
Capt. & Adjt.
for O.C. 2/6th R.Warwick.Regt.

APPENDIX 'A'.

	Groups 'A' & 'C'			'P' & 'Q'				Groups 'B' & 'D'		
	1 Off.	2 NCOs.	4 O.R.	2 O.R.	2 NCOs.	1 O.R.	5 O.R.	2 NCOs.	4 O.R.	2 O.R.
Rifle & Bayonet	-	2	4	-	2	-	1	2	4	-
Bayonet	1	2	-	2	2	-	1	2	-	2
Revolver	1	-	-	2	-	1	-	-	-	2
S.A.A.	-	-	120	-	100	-	250	-	120	-
Pistol Amm.	12	24	-	24	-	36	-	24	-	24
No. 23's.	-	4	4	-	6	-	10	4	4	2
Cup attachments	-	-	-	-	-	-	2	-	-	-
Blanks	-	-	-	-	-	-	24	-	-	-
Egg Bombs	2	-	-	4	20	-	-	4	-	4
Whistles	1	2	-	-	2	-	-	2	-	2
Very Pistols 1"	1	-	-	-	-	-	-	-	-	-
Flares	2	-	-	-	-	-	-	-	-	-
Wire Cutters, (hand pattern)	1	2	4	2	2	1	3	2	4	2
Bill-hooks	-	2	-	2	2	-	-	2	2	-
Tape	-	-	-	-	100 yards	-	-	-	-	100 yards
Haversacks	-	-	-	2	-	-	-	-	-	2
L.G.	-	-	-	-	-	1	-	-	-	-
L.G. Magazines	-	-	-	-	-	-	12	-	-	-

Box respirators in "Alert" position.
Magazines charged with ten rounds.
Balance of S.A.A. in pockets.
Bayonet on rifle or carried in scabbard on belt - no other equipment.
Haversacks carried by Intelligence men.
Bill-hook serves as a tool, or as a weapon at close quarters.

APPENDIX 'B'

1. Final organisation of groups must be settled by the immediate commander who is going to lead them, but the following points will be considered:-

    (a) <u>'A' & 'C' Groups.</u>

    1. Two scouts to watch flanks while wire cutting, if necessary, is in progress. All this party have wire cutters.

    2. Where group moves by ditches, scouts move on top and slightly in advance.

    3. Two scouts and four O.R's. search for Germans and kill or capture them.

    4. Two men armed with revolvers specially detailed to search any dead or wounded Germans and to bring back documents etc. These men carry empty haversacks. Or to act as escort to any prisoners who will be handed over to the covering party.

    5. A leader who controls and leads the group.

    (b) <u>'B' & 'D' Groups.</u>

    1. Two scouts who are the N.C.O's in charge.

    2. Two O.R's who remain at the point of entry to guide troops to it during withdrawal.

    3. Four O.R's who, with the leaders, go outwards to search for Germans.

    4. Two O.R's. as in (a) 4.

    (c) <u>Covering Parties - 'F' & 'O'</u>

    O.R's will carry Lewis Gun magazines, wearing panniers as equipment. Magazines can be removed as required. These men then become available as riflemen or rifle bombers, if necessary.

    <u>NOTE</u>:-
    The Officer Commanding the enterprise is reminded that it is of great importance that the role of these covering parties be clearly explained and clearly understood by all concerned.
    Failure on their part will jeopardise the whole enterprise.
    They must know the ground perfectly and must be prepared for any eventuality.

APPENDIX "B"

SECRET.   2/6TH. BN. ROYAL WARWICKSHIRE REGIMENT.

Order No. 117 dated 11/7/18.

Reference Map - Sheet 36.a. 1/40000

1. The Battalion will be relieved in Brigade Reserve tonight 11/12th inst. by the 10th Battalion The Buffs. Regt and on completion of relief will proceed by march route to billets in QUERNES, where the Division will come into G.H.Q. Reserve.

    DRESS - Fighting Order, soft caps will be worn.

    ORDER OF MARCH - Battalion H.Q., Drums, A. B. C. D. Transport.

    ROUTE - Starting Point - HAM-EN-ARTOIS - QUERNES.

    STARTING POINT - O.24.b.60.00

    TIME - To be notified later.

    A distance of 100 yards will be maintained between companies, between Battalion H.Q. and A. Coy., and between D. Coy. and the Transport.
    A distance of 25 yards will be maintained between each section of six transport vehicles.

2. ALL documents, aeroplane photographs, billet stores, etc., will be handed over and receipts obtained.

3. ALL BRIDGE GUARDS will be relieved by the incoming unit by 6.0 p.m. 11th inst., and will return to their companies

4. Battalion H.Q. will close at LA PIERRIERE on completion of relief, and will re-open at QUERNES on arrival.

5. ACKNOWLEDGE.

(Sgd.)   D J. DUTHIE.

Capt. & Adjt.
for O.C. 2/6th R. Warwick. Regt.

Issued at 5.30 p.m. by runner.

DISTRIBUTION.
Copy No. 1 to C.O.
        2 to Second-in-Command,
        3 to Adjutant,
        4 to A. Coy.
        5 to B. Coy.
        6 to C. Coy.
        7 to D. Coy.
        8 to Quartermaster,
        9 to Transport Officer,
       10 to R.S.M.
       11   File.

Army Form C.2118.

2/6 R Warwick Regt
9/8 28

WAR DIARY
or
INTELLIGENCE SUMMARY.
(Erase heading not required.)

Instructions regarding War Diaries and Intelligence Summaries are contained in F.S. Regs., Part II. and the Staff Manual respectively. Title pages will be prepared in manuscript.

Place	Date	Hour	Summary of Events and Information	Remarks and references to Appendices
Sheet 36.a.1.8.18 1/40000	1.8.18		61st Division transferred from XV Corps to XI Corps night of July 31st/August 1st 1918. Battalion returned to billets at QUERNES. Remainder of day devoted to resting and Medical Inspection. Night operations.	
	2.8.18		Section, Platoon and Company training in the morning. Specialist training in the afternoon.	
	3.8.18		Battalion Tactical Scheme in the vicinity of LINGHEM Training Area.	
	4.8.18		Resting. Voluntary Church Services.	
	5.8.18		61st Division relieved the 5th Division in the Left Sub-section of the XI Corps Front. The Battalion relieved the 2/4th Ox. & Bucks Lt Infantry in billets at TANNAY.	
Sheet 36.a.6.8.18 N.E. 1/20000	6.8.18		182nd Infantry Brigade relieved 15th Infantry Brigade in the LE SART Section, the Battalion relieving the 1st Battalion Norfolk Regt. in the Right Sub-section night of 6th/7th inst. Dispositions:-
			Right Front - C.Company.
			Left " - A.Company.
			Centre. B.Company.
			Reserve D.Company.
	7.8.18.		Active Patrolling after completion of relief. Hostile gas shelling of NIEPPE FOREST. Trenches. There being indications of an enemy withdrawal, operations as per Appendix 'A' were carried out.	
		8.30	2/7th Warwicks reported to have captured the whole of their objectives.	
	8.8.18	F.E. a.m.	A.Company reached MOATED GRANGE. Two enemy machine guns captured.	
		8 a.m.	Battalion holding line - Old German Line from ANCHOVY FARM to TOIL CROSS thence due South to Canal Bank K.32.b.6.3. Troops of 183rd Infantry Brigade moved across our front and seen	
		11.30 a.m.	Moving East of LE SART at about 9.30 a.m. Patrols at K.33.b.3.4. report 183rd Infantry Brigade digging in about 100 yards East. Posts established at K.33.a.3.9. to K.33.a.6.2 by noon. Troops of 2/7th R.War.Regt. and 182nd Infantry Brigade 800 to 1000 yards East.	
		3 a.m.	Battalion holding line K.32.b.10.20 - thence follows German Communication Trench eastwards for 50 yards - thence over the LE CORBIE-LE SART road northwards to K.26.d.35.55 - thence in a N.E. direction to junction of ditch and road K.27.a.25.35. Consolidation began at dusk. Active patrolling. Enemy artillery fairly quiet, except for heavy gas shelling of	

Army Form C. 2118.

WAR DIARY
or
INTELLIGENCE SUMMARY.
(Erase heading not required.)

Instructions regarding War Diaries and Intelligence Summaries are contained in F. S. Regs., Part II and the Staff Manual respectively. Title pages will be prepared in manuscript.

Place	Date	Hour	Summary of Events and Information	Remarks and references to Appendices
Sheet 36. N.E. 1/20000	8.8.18 9.8.18		NIEPPE FOREST and back areas at night. Much hostile M.G. activity. Holding line as above. Erection of posts and trenches continued. 182nd Infantry Brigade relieved 183rd Infantry Brigade and 184th Infantry Brigade on the line LYS CANAL – BOURRE RIVER, the Battalion being in support in NIEPPE FOREST. Our artillery very active during the whole of the day. Increased artillery and M.G. activity, especially at night. NIEPPE FOREST shelled with gas shells for several hours.	
	10.8.18		In Support. Day devoted to resting and cleaning up. Hostile artillery and M.G. less active during the day. At night, continuance of gas shelling.	
	11.8.18 12.8.18		-do- -do-	
			Relieved 2/7th Warwicks in Left Sub-section, LE SART Section night of 12th/13th inst. Dispositions:-	

			Left Front, 'A' Coy.
			    Right Front, 'D' Coy.
			    Left Support, 'C' Coy.
			    Right Support, 'B' Coy.	

	13.8.18		Active patrolling after completion of relief. Artillery active on both sides. Hostile M.G's active at night, also usual gas shelling. Our artillery active all day firing on Trenches. Erection and improvement of defences. Hostile gas shelling at night, less machine gun activity.	

	14.8.18		Inter-Brigade boundary changed night of 14th/15th inst. as follows:- MERVILLE Road Trenches. Inter-Brigade boundary as follows:- (as far west as house at K.14.b.1.5 – K.13.b.0.9 – J.17.central (all inclusive to Right Brigade) Battalion boundaries altered as follows:-
			    Northern – Brigade boundary as above.
			              – Road Junction K.26.a.3.3 – GLOSTER ROAD K.27.a.0.3 – thence
			    Southern – GLOSTER ROAD (inclusive).	

	15.8.18		All troops north of the MERVILLE ROAD relieved by the 9th Battalion Northumberland Fusiliers. Our artillery very active all the day firing on selected targets. Less M.G. activity. NIEPPE FOREST heavily shelled with gas at night. Active patrolling. Our artillery Trenches. Improvement of defences in Outpost Line. Active patrolling. Our artillery exceptionally active, firing on selected targets. Normal hostile artillery and M.G. activity. Heavy hostile bombardment with Green Cross gas shells on front system during the greater part of the night.	

Army Form C. 2118.

WAR DIARY
or
INTELLIGENCE SUMMARY.
(Erase heading not required.)

Instructions regarding War Diaries and Intelligence Summaries are contained in F.S. Regs., Part II. and the Staff Manual respectively. Title pages will be prepared in manuscript.

Place	Date	Hour	Summary of Events and Information	Remarks and references to Appendices
Sheet 36.a.1. N.E. 1/20000	16.8.18		Trenches. Active patrolling day and night. Post established in LOXTON HOUSE. Our artillery rather inactive during the day. Usual activity at night. Wiring and improvement of posts.	
	17.8.18		Trenches. Active day and night patrolling. Indications of further enemy withdrawal. 'C' Coy. relieved 'A' Coy. in front line. Artillery less active. Wiring etc. continued.	
	18.8.18		Trenches. Indications seen in MERVILLE in the early morning. Patrols pushed out by front companies. Enemy posts located at K.28.a.50.55 and K.28.a.6.6. and found unoccupied. 'C' Company in conjunction with company of Battalion on left attacked post at K.28.a. Outpost Line established on west bank of BOURRE RIVER. During the night patrols crossed the river in an endeavour to gain touch with troops of 182nd Infantry Brigade at SACHET FARM. No Mans Outpost Line also west bank of BOURRE River. Hostile aeroplane brought down by M.G. and rifle fire. Relieved by 2/9th Worcester Regt. night of 19th/20th inst. and withdrew to NIEPPE FOREST, in Support.	
	19.8.18		In Support in NIEPPE FOREST. Resting and bathing.	
	20.8.18		—do—	
	21.8.18		—do— Corn gathering in the afternoon.	
	22.8.18		182nd Infantry Brigade withdrew to Divisional Reserve. Battalion relieved by 2/4th Battalion Royal Berkshire Regt. and withdrew to billets at STEENBECQUE.	
Sheet 36.a.2. 1/40000	23.8.18		In billets at STEENBECQUE. Resting, Cleaning and Bathing.	
	24.8.18		—do— Individual and Platoon Training under Company arrangements.	
	25.8.18		Range and Fire Practice. Specialist Training. Football and cricket in the evening.	
	26.8.18		In billets at STEENBECQUE. Church Services.	
Sheet 36.a.3. 1/40000	26.8.18		In billets at STEENBECQUE. Training under company arrangements during the morning. Relieved XXXX 2/7th R.Warwick.Regt. at VILLIOFBA CAMP night of 26th inst. 2/7th F.Way.Regt. relieving the Battalion at STEENBECQUE.	
	27.8.18		Individual training under company arrangements in the morning. Specialist training in the afternoon.	
	28.8.18		—do—	
	29.8.18		—do—	
	30.8.18		A. & B. Companies — Company Training. C. & D. Companies – Tactical Scheme. Specialist training in the afternoon.	

Army Form C. 2118.

WAR DIARY
or
INTELLIGENCE SUMMARY.

(Erase heading not required.)

Instructions regarding War Diaries and Intelligence Summaries are contained in F. S. Regs., Part II. and the Staff Manual respectively. Title pages will be prepared in manuscript.

Place	Date	Hour	Summary of Events and Information	Remarks and references to Appendices
Sheet 36.a 1/40000	31.8.18		Training under Company arrangements. Commanding Officer and Company Commanders reconnoitred the line preparatory to relieving the 11th Battalion Suffolk Regt.	

W.E. Mieir
Lieut. Col.
Comdg. 2/6th R.Warwick.Regt.

Appendix 17

SECRET.   2/7TH BN. ROYAL WARWICKSHIRE REGIMENT.   Copy No

Order No. 143. dated 7/9/18.

Map Reference - Sheet 62.a. N.E. 1/20,000 Ed. 7.B.

1. There are indications of an intended enemy withdrawal on this front. South of the river SCARPE our troops have advanced a certain distance.

2. At ZERO hour night of 7th/8th inst. a local attack will be made by the 2/7th Warwicks having for its objective the German front line between K.21.c.2.6 and K.22.b.7.3.
    When this objective is taken posts will be established at K.27.a.3.8 - K.27.a.8.6 - K.21.c.8.4 - K.21.c.3.8 - K.22.b.4.1.

3. Barrage will fall on the line K.22.b.8.1 - K.22.b.7.7 - K.21.c.1.7. at ZERO hour.
    At ZERO plus 8 it will roll forward.
    At ZERO plus 43 a protective barrage will be formed 200 yards clear of the forward posts established by the attacking troops.
    From ZERO plus 43 to ZERO plus 63, there will be a bombardment of selected targets in rear of the enemy's front line. The bombardment will cease at ZERO plus 63.

4. In co-operation with this attack, C.Coy. at ZERO hour will send forward patrols to gain contact with the enemy in his lines south of the WULLEN ROAD. This patrol will reconnoitre his normal front line and, if unoccupied, will establish themselves there.
    Not more than one platoon may be used by O.C. 'C' Company for this operation without reference to Battalion H.Q.
    If the situation demands it, another platoon will be placed at his disposal on reference to Battalion H.Q.

5. O.C. 'B' Company will arrange that two Lewis Guns are available to immediately counter any enemy activity in the vicinity of K.21.c.8.7 from ZERO onwards.
    It is necessary that the fire of these guns be delivered in a direction S.E. by E. or E. in order to clear our attacking troops. These guns will not fire after ZERO plus 60.
    NOTE.
    Lewis guns detailed above must be carefully sited and fire controlled by an officer.

6. When the 2/7th Warwicks have established posts as stated in 4, it is intended to establish ourselves on a general line 50 to 80 yards East of the enemy's present front line, and O.C. A.Coy. will be ordered from these Headquarters to push forward not more than two platoons for the purpose of clearing the enemy front line from ANGIERS FARM south, if possible to gain touch with 4.Coy.
    This operation, when ordered, will be made in close co-operation with the troops of the 2/7th Warwicks.

7. O.C. 'A' Coy. is authorised to use not more than one platoon without orders from these Headquarters provided communication is broken in order to exploit any success which may have been gained by the 2/7th Warwicks.

8. O.C. 'A' Coy. will send a liaison officer to the H.Q. of the right company of the 2/7th Warwicks.

9. ZERO hour will be 9.0 p.m.

- 2 -

10. In the event of conditions being favourable for a general advance and the Battalion is ordered to move forward, orders will be issued from these H.Q. for A. & C. Coys. to advance, B.Coy. taking over present area held by A.Coy. and D.Coy. less one platoon, the area at present held by C.Coy.

11. In the event of such an advance being ordered, the northern Battalion boundary will be the communication trench from ANCHOVY FARM N.E. to K.27.c.7.7.

12. Company commanders in the front line will at once pass back any information to Headquarters as to progress of operations on their front.

                                        (Signed) D.J.DUTHIE,
                                                 Capt. & Adjt.
                                        for O.C. 2/6th R.Warwick.Regt.
2/9/18.

Distribution.
Copy No. 1 to O.C.
        2 to Adjutant
        3 to A.Coy.
        4 to B.Coy.
        5 to C.Coy.
        6 to D.Coy.
        7 to H.Q.
        8 to R.S.M.
        9   File

Vol 29

CONFIDENTIAL.

WAR DIARY OF

2/6TH BATTALION ROYAL WARWICKSHIRE REGIMENT.

From September 1st, 1918 to September 30th, 1918.

&&&&&&&&&&&&&&&&
& VOLUME XXIX &
&&&&&&&&&&&&&&&&

Army Form C. 2118.

WAR DIARY
or
INTELLIGENCE SUMMARY.
(Erase heading not required.)

Place	Date	Hour	Summary of Events and Information	Remarks and references to Appendices
Sheet 36a M.W.1/20,000 Sheet 36 N.W.1/20,000	1.9.18.		182nd Infantry Brigade relieved 183rd Infantry Brigade in Main Line of Retention, the Battalion relieving the 9th Batt. Northumberland Fusiliers, and becoming attached to 184th Infantry Brigade on completion of relief. Hostile activity NIL. Dispositions :- Left Front 'B' Coy.; Right Front 'A' Coy.; Left Support 'C' Coy. Right Support 'D' Coy.; B.H.Q. TEWFI FARM.	
	2.9.18.		182nd Infantry Brigade relieved 184th Infantry Brigade as Advance Guard Brigade, night of 2/3rd, holding Outpost Line from G.13.d.0.0 - G.14.a.5.5. - G.9.a.7.8. Enemy on East bank of Canal River. Enemy M.G. fire intermittent. Dispositions :- Rt. Front 'A' Coy.- Centre 'B' Coy. Lt.Front 'C' Coy. Support 'D' Coy. See Appendix 'A'.	
	3.9.18. to 6.9.18. 7.9.18.		Holding Line 183rd Infantry Brigade relieved the 182nd Infantry Brigade as Advance Guard Brigade night of 7th/8th inst., the Battalion being relieved by the 9th Batt. Northumberland Fusiliers and taking over billets vacated by the 11th Batt. Suffolk Regt. in area L.11.d.2.2. - L.16.c.9.5. - L.11.c.4.2. - L.10.c.8.2.	
	8.9.18.		In billets, shelters etc., in above area. Day devoted to resting, cleaning of equipment and arms and improvement to billeting area.	
	9.9.18.		Two hours training under Company arrangements. Remainder of day devoted to bathing re-equipping and improving billeting area.	
	10.9.18.		Battalion Parade. Training under Company arrangements. Specialist training under Specialist Officers. Bathing.	
	11.9.18.		Training under Company arrangements. Improvement of billets. Specialist Training. Bathing.	
	12.9.18.		Battalion Parade. Training under Company arrangements. Specialist training in the afternoon.	
	13.9.18.		Battalion Parade. Remainder of morning training under Company arrangements. Test carried out of Manning Battle Stations.	
	14.9.18.		Specialist training in the afternoon. Football and concert in the evening.	

Army Form C. 2118.

WAR DIARY
or
INTELLIGENCE SUMMARY.

(Erase heading not required.)

Instructions regarding War Diaries and Intelligence Summaries are contained in F. S. Regs., Part II. and the Staff Manual respectively. Title pages will be prepared in manuscript.

Place	Date	Hour	Summary of Events and Information	Remarks and references to Appendices
	15.9.18.		Resting and preparing for the line. 182nd Infantry Brigade relieved 184th Infantry Brigade as Advanced Guard Brigade, night of 15th inst. The Battalion relieved the 2/5th Gloster Regt. in area L.9.d - G.23.a. - G.18.c. and H.7.d.	
	16.9.18. 17.9.18.		Battalion in Support in above area. In support. 'A' & 'B' Companies moved to area G.29.a. and G.12.c. night of 17th/18th. On completion of relief 'B' Company came under the tactical Command of Officer Commanding 2/7th Batt. R. War. Regt.	
	18.9.13.		In support. B.H.Q. moved to G.20.b.5.7, and 'D' Coy. to G.20.b.9.1. Major J.C. MURIEL, D.S.O. (9th Batt. Inniskilling Fusiliers) assumed Command of the Battalion, vice Major J. DIGBY-WYATT, M.C. (1st Northants Regt.)	
	19.9.18.		In support.	
	20.9.18.		In support.	
	21.9.18.		In support. 182nd Infantry Brigade relieved by 183rd Infantry Brigade as Advanced Guard Brigade night of 21st/22nd. Battalion relieved by 11th Batt.	
Sheets 36 & 36a 1/40,000.			Suffolk Regt., and withdrew to billets vacated by 1st Batt. East Lancs Regt. in the immediate vicinity of ESTAIRES, and became responsible for the Southern Subsection of the Corps Battle Line.	
	22.9.18.		In billets as above. Day devoted to resting, cleaning of arms & equipment, re-equipping and bathing. Voluntary Church Service in the evening.	
	23.9.18.		Training under Company arrangements in accordance with Training Programme. Improving billets. Recreation in the afternoon. Football match. Bathing.	
	24.9.18.		Battalion Parade. Training under Coy. arrangements as per Programme. Improving billets.	
	25.9.18.		Morning - training under Coy. arrangements. Afternoon - Recreational Training. Football match, Officers versus Sergeants. Improving billets.	
	26.9.18.		Battalion Route march in the morning. Route :- ESTAIRES - NEUF BERQUIN - Road Junction K.24.a.90.20 - Road junction K.20.d.20.25 - ESTAIRES. Specialist training in the afternoon. All unoccupied men engaged in billet improvements.	

Army Form C. 2118.

WAR DIARY
or
INTELLIGENCE SUMMARY.
(Erase heading not required.)

Place	Date	Hour	Summary of Events and Information	Remarks and references to Appendices
	27.9.18.		Training under Company arrangements. Specialist training in the afternoon.	
	28.9.18.		Preparing for the line. In view of preparations being made to renew our advance, the Divisional front was re-organised on a two Brigade front. The Battalion relieved a portion of the 9th Northumberland Fusiliers, and a portion of the 11th Suffolks in the Left Subsection of the Left Brigade. Dispositions :- Left Front 'A' Coy. Right Front 'C' Coy. Support 'D' Coy. Reserve 'B' Coy.	
	29.9.18.		Hostile Artillery very active. B.H.Q. at G.12.c.40.55 heavily shelled, necessitating removal to G.12.d.7.3. Active patrolling after completion of relief. Enemy found to be holding his Front Line in force.	
	30.9.18.		Holding Line as above. Enemy artillery very active. Marked decrease in Hostile M.G. activity at night. Active patrolling after dusk, in order to ascertain whether the Enemy was still holding his Front Line. Holding Line as above. Active patrolling at night. Our artillery very active. Marked decrease in Enemy Activity.	

Fighting Strength - 38 Officers 900 Other Ranks.

Majors
Commanding 2/6th Batt. R. War. Regt.

2/6TH. BN. ROYAL WARWICKSHIRE REGIMENT.

Reference Map - Sheet 36 N.W.

Narrative of Events from 3rd to 6th September 1918.

Night of 2nd/3rd September 1918. The Battalion relieved the 2/5th Battalion Gloucestershire Regiment, 184th Infantry Brigade, in the forward line on night of 2nd/3rd September 1918, taking up a position on the left bank of the River LYS and River STILL BECQUE, roughly on the line G.10.central - G.16.a. - G.21.central.

The Battalion boundaries were:-
On the South - E. & W. line through G.22.d.0.3.
On the North -   -do-   G.10.central
Dispositions :-

	Right	Left
Front	B.Coy.	C.Coy.
Support	A.Coy.	D.Coy.

The enemy was holding the east bank of the rivers and all bridges over the River LYS on the Battalion front were destroyed. The Battalion had no special bridging material.

Patrols were at once sent forward all along the line to endeavour to effect a crossing.

ON THE RIGHT.

Sept.3rd At daylight 'B' Coy. found themselves on a forward slope in full view of the enemy.

1.0 p.m. They were unable to cross on their own front, but finally did so over a footbridge on their right about G.21.d.7.5 at about 1.0 p.m. Casualties had occurred, one officer being wounded and one gassed.

They moved to the left and re-organised to W. of road in G.22.a. from which they were fired on.

They advanced about 400 yards working along hedges and ditches and then came under fire from about 6 M.Gs. and some snipers, and had some casualties.

After moving forward another 300 yards they were held up by heavy M.G. fire in enfilade from the right. They were then about 400 yards short of their objective, the railway through G.24.cent. In the meantime, the 2/8th Battalion Worcestershire Regiment, on our right had moved off in a S.E. direction and in consequence touch had been lost. After dark the enemy withdrew. Two platoons of 'A' Coy. went through and held the line. 'B' Coy. finally got the line of the railway in G.24. and established posts in front of it.

8.0 p.m.

ON THE LEFT.

'C' Coy. found it impossible to cross the STILL BECQUE on their front owing to lack of bridges and enemy fire from the east bank.

6.0 a.m. At 6.0 a.m. No. 10 Platoon under Sec.Lieut. M.A.ROSE, crossed in the north of G.10.b. with the Lancashire Fusiliers - the Battalion on our left - and moved forward to CROIX DU BAC which was reached at about 10.0 a.m. They then turned south, working in conjunction with the Lancashire Fusiliers. As a result of this combined movement the enemy retired from G.11. and one prisoner was captured by the Lancashire Fusiliers.

10.0 a.m.

6.0 p.m. At 6.0 p.m. the line north of the river ran from CROIX DU BAC to the river in G.17.b. Company Headquarters moved forward to the Brickfields at G.17.a.2.8.

'D' Coy. received orders at dusk to send patrols through 'C' Coy. and this was done.

'C' Coy. continued to push on and took the post at G.12.c.7.1.

Sept 4th. RIGHT FRONT.

'A' Coy. was ordered to pass through 'B' Coy. at dawn, and advance on the objective, road from H.20.d.2.3. through H.21.a.5.3 to H.15.c.0.0. (the road west of FLEURBAIX).

There was only one man in 'A' Coy. at this time, and the Company Commander therefore ordered his two leading platoons to advance east from their posotion in G.29.b. describing as well as possible from the map the features which they would find on their objective. They were then in touch with the WORCESTERS on the right, but not with their left ('C' or 'D' Coy.)

The WORCESTERS moved in a S.E. direction and 'A' Coy. at first followed, but afterwards realised the mistake and turned further east. They reached ROUGE DE BOUT (G.36.d.8.6) and the Platoon Commander in charge confused this, owing to lack of a map and similarity of features, with his objective in H.21.a and reported his arrival as at the latter place at 8.0 a.m. He was out of touch on both flanks, and had already met and scattered parties of the enemy. The Company Commander followed him and realised the mistake made which he reported to Battalion Headquarters. This message, however, didnot reach Battalion Headquarters until about 9.0 p.m. The two leading platoons had already started to advance up the road N.E. and he decided to continue and try to reach his correct objective. Considerable opposition was met from M.Gs. and snipers, and in addition, the road was shelled and the party came under T.M. fire. By working up hedges and ditches they pushed the enemy back, killing at least one, and reached H.25.d.3.3. Here they came under fire from both flanks and their front, and were held up. An attempt was, however, made to reach the road junction (H.26.a.0.0) with a fresh platoon at dusk, but failed, the crater there being held strongly. In the meantime, the company commander had returned and reported the position to the Commanding Officer personally.

When 'A' Coy. went off to the right in the morning, the Commander of 'B' Coy. realising that a gap was left, filled it, sending two platoons to the left and two platoons to the right.

Those on the right made ground as far east as H.25.a. - the position at dark being that they held four posts in H.25.a. and H.19.c. opposite the close ground in H.25.b.2.8.

Those on the left, starting from the line of railway in G.24.a. tried to push S.E. towards the road in G.24.d. and H.19.c. in order to cut off the enemy, who were known to be in G.24.d. They met strong resistance, and were held up in G.24.b. and were then unable to join up with the platoons on the right as intended.

'B' Coy. had lost another officer during the morning, and the Company Commander was therefore alone. The Commanding Officer, Lieut.Col. W.E.PHILLIPS, M.C. was assisting him to direct the above mentioned operations when he was hit in the leg by a M.G. bullet at about 7.0 p.m. in G.18.c.8.0.

Capt. G.W.ARBELL, M.C. (O.C. 'A' Coy.) assumed command.

During the night two officer reinforcements came up to B.Coy. and were sent by the Company Commander to command his right and left parties.

LEFT FRONT.

6.0 a.m.
Sep. 4th
During the night, 'D' Coy. passed through 'C' Coy. and at daybreak, the right platoon had reached G.18.b.9.3. Coy. H.Qrs. were at G.12.c.8.1. with one platoon in reserve, and the left platoon was advancing on SUFFOLK POST, which was cleared at 8.30 a.m.

No. 16 platoon had been sent round to the south of the river during the night; they found that 'B' Coy. were some way to the south and worked in conjunction with them, and encountered strong enemy opposition in G.24 - being fired on by four M.Gs.

- 3 -

'C' Coy. had managed to bridge the river at G.17.a.5.6. during the night and early morning, and pushed one platoon across to the south.   By 10.30 a.m. 'C' Coy. had got to a line running south from G.12.sentral, to about G.18.c.3.5. with 'D' Coy. in front of them.

The two platoons of 'D' Coy. on the north were under fire from the south of the river, which they could not cross.

At about mid-day, O.C. 'D' Coy. learnt from the Battalion on the left, that they had orders to occupy the line of posts running N.E. from G.12.c.8.1. through SUFFOLK and ESSEX, thus moving south 500 yards over their boundary.   He was therefore ordered to withdraw two platoons from north of the river, leaving his left platoon only, which was then in front of SUFFOLK POST. This move started at 1.0 p.m.   No. 13 platoon crossing by bridge made by 'C' Coy. in G.17.a. - No. 15 platoon by a sluice further east.   These two platoons joined up at about G.18.a.0.0. and got int touch with 'C' Coy's post at G.18.c.3.5.   O.C. 'D' Coy. then ordered his two platoons to work east round the village of BAC ST.MAUR.   They reached a line about G.18.d.central, but were then held up by enemy fire.   No. 14 platoon, left on the north of the river, had worked up to a position in H.7.c. near the river bank, which was being heavily shelled.   When they attempted to advance to the river, they were fired at from the east bank.

7.0 p.m.   At 7.0 p.m. touch had been established with 'B' Coy. on the right, who were also held up in G.24. and No. 16 platoon which had been sent south of the river the previous night, now rejoined.

7.15 p.m.   At 7.15 p.m. an explosion occurred in a house close to 'D' Coy's Headquarters, causing thick volumes of smoke.   This was presumably started by a time fuse, or a wire, and appears to have been the method generally used by the enemy throughout the period, to indicate his withdrawal from any area.

Immediately after the explosion, an enemy aircraft flew low over the place, dropping two green Very Lights - a very heavy barrage followed on the area.

O.C. 'D' Coy. then ordered No. 16 Platoon, in conjunction with the other two platoons, to make another attempt to push through the village, working from house to house.   This they did during the night and managed to reach the eastern end of the close part of the village, being level with the station by the morning.

At nightfall, all the enemy had withdrawn from our area west of the river, but owing to its width and depth, no crossing could be made.

After dark, No. 14 platoon, 'D' Coy. was withdrawn from the west bank of the river, and came into company support at company headquarters.   One platoon of 'C' company replaced it by taking up positions on the river bank at H.7.d.2.3.

Sept. 5th.   The positions at dawn were as follows:- One post in H.7.d and west of the river clear.   We held the village of BAc.ST.MAUR as far east as the Station, but enemy M.Gs. were still firing from just east of this line.

Two platoons of 'B' Coy. had worked up to and held the cross roads at H.13.d.1.0. and the ground in the vicinity.   These platoons now came under the orders of O.C. 'D' Company.   The remaining two platoons of 'B' Coy. were west of the close ground in H.25.a. and H.25.b.

'A' Coy. who had been under continual shell fire during the night made another attempt at dawn to take BARLETTE FARM, but could not advance beyond the road junction at H.26.a.1.1.

After a conference with the Brigade Commander at Battalion Headquarters, orders were issued as follows:-

'D' Coy. to send a platoon to advance from BAC ST.MAUR to H.19. central.

- 4 -

'B' Coy. to work round the left of the close ground in
H.25.a. & b. - these two platoons to join hands with 'A' Coy.
who were to work N.E. up the road to H.26.a.

It was hoped to make the line of the road running from
H.20.c.9.0. N.W. to H.19.b.0.9.

12.0 noon The movement started about 12.0 noon, 'D' Coy. sending a
combined platoon of 'D' and 'C' Coys. to H.19.central, from their
Company Headquarters at G.18.c.3.5. and another two platoons of
'B' Coy. to move S.E. from H.13.d.1.0. The southern of these
platoons reached a point about H.19.central, but then came under
fire from numerous enemy M.Gs. concealed in H.2 O.a. & c. and
H.19.b. & d. The northern platoon of 'B' Coy. came under heavy
fire from the north and east, estimated from about six M.Gs.
as soon as they came into the open, and could advance no further.

'B' Coy. succeeded in driving the enemy out of the close ground
in H.25.a. & c. but could not advance beyond the line of the road
H.25.b. and H.19.c. 'A' Coy. were again held up by BARLETTE FARM.

It now appeared from the increased resistance met when an
advance beyond this line was attempted, that the enemy's tactics were
changed, and that we were nearing some solid line of resistance.

Some slight progress was, however, made, and at dark the line ran
approximately as follows:- From north to south - H.7.d. - road
junction H.13.b.1.4 - road to railway - road junction H.13.d.7.7 -
thence along the S.W. edge of close ground to H.19.a.7.3 - line of
road N.W. and S.E. through H.19.c. and H.25.b. to H.26.d.1.1.

'A' Coy. having failed N.E. up the road to H.25.c. and H.25.d.
were still far south of the Battalion area.

The Brigade, therefore, ordered the WORCESTERS to take over the
front up to the inter-Battalion boundary during the night, and by
dawn they had relieved 'A' Coy. and had a post in the road at
H.25.b.5.5.

'A' Coy. was withdrawn into Support in the area H.24.c.

10.0 p.m. The following orders were issued at 10.0 p.m. :-

'C' Coy. to pass through 'D' Coy. in BAC ST.MAUR and work up to
H.8.central, and send patrols forward from there. 'D' Coy. to
clear the RUE BATAILLE through H.15.d. and H.14.a. as far as the
road junction at H.14.a.6.4. 'B' Coy. to clear the cross roads at
H.19.a.4.0. and gain touch with 'D' Coy. on their left at H.19.a.7.3.
These orders were put into effect during the night. 'C' Coy. made
a considerable advance. 'D' Coy. in spite of two attempts failed
to get up the RUE BATAILLE, meeting strong resistance from the
enclosed ground at the northern end H.14.a. & c. 'B' Coy.
carried out their task successfully.

Septr. 6th. At dawn on the 6th. 'C' Coy. was established at FORT ROMPU
and had posts from the road junction H.7.d.95.40. to the river.
'D' Coy. were in the same position as at nightfall, their men along
the RUE BATAILLE having been shelled heavily during the night.

After a reconnaissance of the position at FORT ROMPU, it
appeared that this was satisfactory and there was a good prospect
of reaching the road junction H.8.central, although enemy M.Gs.
were firing from S.E.

A combined operation between 'C' & 'D' Coys. was therefore
decided on to reach the objectives laid down the previous night.
The details of the scheme were carefully worked out by O's.C.
'C' & 'D' Coys. and time was given to ensure that all concerned
were fully acquainted with all details of it.

The general idea was that 'C' Coy. should send up another
platoon to assist in taking H.8.central, and the copse and houses
to the south which were held by the enemy. As soon as they reached
this, they would send up a light signal which was to be answered
by 'D' Coy. 'C' Coy. would then open fire in a southerly direction
across H.14.central and 'D' Coy. would commence operations.

- 5 -

'B' Coy. were ordered to fire N.E. from the road at H.19.c. and H.15.b. and the artillery also combined by keeping suspected enemy strong points in front under fire.

The two platoons under Sec.Lieut. M.A.ROSE ('C' Coy.) successfully accomplished their task in square 8 and a green Very Light was sent up by them at about 11.30 a.m. This was answered by a red Very Light from No. 15 platoon at about H.13.b.2.2.

Nos. 13 and 16 platoons under Sec.Lieut. A.A.WILLIAMS then worked forward to the S.W. corner of the enclosure in H.14.a. & c. under covering fire from No. 15 platoon and Vickers guns firing from houses in BAC ST.MAUR. A T.M. also fired on the enclosure from road junction at H.13.d.7.7. No. 13 platoon reinforced No. 16 platoon, who started bombing the enemy our of a post he held about H.14.a. 05.10. As a result, the enemy was seen running across the open in all directions from the enclosure and posts to S. & E. of it, also from a post about H.14.b.7.0.

The two platoons of 'B' Coy. under Lieut. MASSEY fired at the retreating enemy from the RUE BATAILLE. Nos. 13 & 16 platoons moved to the S.E. of the enclosure and opened fire with L.Gs. No. 15 Platoon moved east along the railway and joined up on the left of Sec.Lieut. WILLIAMS, and fifteen of the enemy under a Sergeant Major surrendered to them. It is estimated that 120 to 150 enemy were seen to retreat and a great many were hit, one Lewis Gun claiming as many as thirty. Our losses during this operation were very slight, being two men wounded. Great assistance was given by the fire of Vickers guns, four of which were attached to 'C' & 'D' Coys. and the L.T.Ms.

1.0 p.m.   By 1.0 p.m. the RUE BATAILLE area was cleared and a line established as follows:-

In front of the close ground along the RUE BATAILLE, running S.W. from H.14.a.6.0. to H.19.central.

'B' Coy. on the right shortly afterwards slung their left forward and joined up with this new line.

The platoon of 'C' Coy. after reaching H.8.central, was fired at from the wood and houses to the N.E. in H.8.b. but a patrol pushed through here successfully, and cleared the wood establishing a post at H.8.b.5.5. during the morning. This cleared the left flank of the Battalion.

The Battalion on our left had worked round the northern bend of the river in H2. and held the northern bank as far as H.3. This movement was completed by the evening of Sept. 5th, but they did not cross to the south of the river, and in consequence our left flank north of H.8.central, had been unprotected during the day, there being a 1000 to 1500 yards of frontage between us and the river, which should have been occupied by the Division on our left.

By the evening, our line ran as follows from North to South :-
H.8.b.5.5 - H.8.central - H.8.c.95.50 - thence south to railway about H.14.a.8.4 - H.8.a.6.0 - H.19.central - road at H.19.c.8.3 - thence S.E. to junction with WORCESTERS at H.25.b.5.5.

The 2/7th Bn. Royal Warwickshire Regt. passed through our line after dusk, and with the exception of 'C' Coy. who formed a line from the river at about H.1.d.8.0 to their line as given above, as far south as the railway, all coys. were withdrawn, and concentrated in support in areas about 1000 yards in rear of their original line, where they dug themselves in during the night.

The Battalion came into Brigade Support as soon as the 2/7th R.Warwick.Regt. had passed through.

Vol 30

CONFIDENTIAL.

WAR DIARY.

From 1st October to 31st October 1918.

2/6th Battalion The Royal Warwickshire Regiment.

(VOLUME XXX)

WAR DIARY or INTELLIGENCE SUMMARY.

(Erase heading not required.)

Army Form C. 2118.

Place	Date	Hour	Summary of Events and Information	Remarks and references to Appendices
	October			
Sheet 57.	1/10		Holding line running through H9 & H14. Disposition - L.F. "A" Coy, R.F. "C" C, Support "D" Coy., Reserve "B" Coy.	
36 N.W.	2/10		Indications that enemy was withdrawing. "A" & "C" Coys. pushed out daylight patrols and rested the line RUBARBE - BOIS GRENIER without opposition. 182nd Infantry Brigade relieved by 178th Infantry Brigade, the Battalion being relieved by the 36th N.F. & 23rd.R.W.F. and withdrew to billets vacated by the 1st East Lancs. in area around Kennet Cross.	
1/20,000				
Lens 11	3/10		Battalion moved by light railway-march route to billets at TRUIZENNES.	
	4/10		In billets at TRUIZENNES. Day devoted to resting, cleaning of arms and equipment & re-equipping. Concert by Battalion Concert Party in the evening.	
1/100,000	5/10		In billets at TRUIZENNES. Training under Company arrangements. Bathing. 61st Division transferred from XI Corps to XVII Corps, night of 5/6th inst.	
	6/10		The Battalion proceeded by train to billets at GEZAINCOURT.	
	7/10		Arrived in billets at GEZAINCOURT at 1 p.m. Remainder of day devoted to resting. Training under Company Arrangements. Specialist Classes in the afternoon.	
	8/10		do. Concert in the evening.	
Valenciennes	9/10		Battalion moved by rail and route march to area S.W. of MOEUVRES, the Division coming into Corps Reserve.	
12.	10/10		Battalion moved by route march to ANNEUX.	
1/100,000.	11/10		In shelters E. of ANNEUX. Training under Coy. Arr. Working Party of 150 O.R. found in the afternoon.	
	12/10		do. Battn. in attack practice with M.Gs., T.M., & Artillery.	
	13/10		do. Training under Coy. Arr., practising "following up"	
	14/10		do. Specialist training in afternoon.	
	15/10		Batt. took part in Bde Adv Gd Practice Scheme,in area around Bourlon Wood.	
	16/10		Training under Coy. Arr., Lectures in billets owing to inclement weather.Bathing.	
	17/10		Training under Coy. Arr., including elementary tactics, platoon tactics, use of ground, section commanders' initiative, and use of Lewis Guns. Specialist training in the afternoon.	

Army Form C. 2118.

WAR DIARY
or
INTELLIGENCE SUMMARY.
(Erase heading not required.)

Instructions regarding War Diaries and Intelligence Summaries are contained in F.S. Regs., Part II. and the Staff Manual respectively. Title pages will be prepared in manuscript.

Place	Date	Hour	Summary of Events and Information	Remarks and references to Appendices
	18/10		Battalion moved by route march to billets in area S.W. of CAMBRAI (A.26.c & d.) Remainder of day devoted to resting and cleaning up.	
	19/10		Battalion moved by route march to billets in RIEUX. Remainder of day devoted to resting and cleaning up.	
Sheet 57B 1/40,000	20/10		In billets at RIEUX. Church Parade and Foot Washing in the morning. Remainder of day resting.	
	21/10		In billets at RIEUX. Training under Company Arrangements, to include Close Order Drill, tactical scheme, and crossing open country with Box Respirators on. Practice attack on strong point carried out at night.	
Sheet 51A S.E. 1/20,000	22/10		In billets at RIEUX. Training consisted of Practice attack scheme.	
	23/10		Battalion moved to MONTRECOURT WOOD in the morning, prior to relieving the 9th Welch Regt. in the evening just west of VENDEGIES. Dispositions :- L.F. "B" Coy., R.F. "D" Coy., Support "C" Coy., Reserve "A" Coy.	
	24.10	04.00	Under cover of artillery barrage, the village of VENDEGIES was attacked and the river ECAILLON crossed, but the Battalion had to withdraw West of the river, owing to strong enemy resistance. Fighting continued throughout the day, and at about 18.00 hours the en emy withdrew. The village was occupied immediately. Casualties sustained 5 Officers, 182 O.R.	APP:'A'
	25/10		2/8th Worcesters occupied the Left Section of the Corps Main Line of Resistance, E. of VENDEGIES, when the Battalion became Right-S Sub section with H.Q. at VENDEGIES. Captures 2 prisoners, one 4.2 How., 1 Anti-tank Rifle, 11 Heavy and 12 Light Machine Guns.	
	26/10		In support in billets at VENDEGIES.	
	27/10		do. At night, Battalion relieved 2/8th Worcesters in Corps Main Line of Resistance, Batt. H.Q. remaining at VENDEGIES.	
	28/10		Holding Left Section of Corps Main Line of Resistance until evening, when relieved by 2/4th Ox. & Bucks. Light Infantry, the battalion withdrawing to VENDEGIES.	
	29/10		In billets at VENDEGIES. During night of 28/29th, gas shell fell in billets occupied by "C" Coy., causing 78 casualties.	
	30/10		Relieved 11th Suffolk Regt. in left Section of Corps Main Line of Resistance,	

Army Form C. 2118.

WAR DIARY
or
INTELLIGENCE SUMMARY.
(Erase heading not required.)

Place	Date	Hour	Summary of Events and Information	Remarks and references to Appendices
	31/10		B.H.Q. remaining at VENDEGIES. Holding Left Section of Corps Main Line of Resistance.	
			FIGHTING STRENGTH :- 40 Officers, 638 Other Ranks.	
			J. Mins Lieut.-Colonel, Cmdg. 2/6th Battn. R. War. R.	

Appendix 'A'

2/8th BATTALION ROYAL WARWICKSHIRE REGIMENT.   Copy No. 6.

Issued in connection with Order No. 142 d/d 23.10.18.

1. INFORMATION. On the 23.10.18 the Army intend to try to establish a line about –
P.17.central – P.18.c.0.3. – Q.19.a.0.0. –
Q.19.d.1.0. – Q.26.a.1.9. – Q.27.c.0.3. –
Q.33.b.0.3. – Q.34.central – R.31.d.3.0.
This will form a jumping off line for a new advance.
The enemy's moral is poor. Latest prisoners captured have been very young.

2. PROPOSED ATTACK BY 61st DIVISION.

   INTENTION. To press back the enemy in the direction of VALENCIENNES, securing the high ground. MAING (Division on left) – K.19.central – K.26.central (both divisions on left) K.33.Central – Q.3.b.9.0. – Q.10.central – Q.10.d.3.0. – Q.17.a.0.3. (Division on right) – Q.17.d.0.0. – R.19.c.7.0. – R.25.Central – R.31.central – R.31.d.3.0. (all to Division on right.)

3. DETAIL. (a) The 183rd Infantry Brigade will be on the Right and 182nd Infantry Brigade on Left.
   Inter Brigade Boundary will be :-
   Sunken road Q.19.d.1.0. (inclusive to 183rd) to road junction Q.20.a.4.0. (bridge inclusive to 183rd) – X road Q.14.b.9.1. (inclusive to 183rd) – Q.10.central (stream inclusive to 182nd).
   (b) The 2/8th WARWICKS will be on the right of the Brigade front and the 2/7th WARWICKS on the left, the 2/8th WORCESTERS will be in reserve.
   The inter-battalion boundary will be :-
   P.24.b.75.30. – Q.13.d.1.7. (Beetroot factory inclusive to 2/8th) – road junction Q.14.a.3.7. (inclusive to 2/8th) – road junction Q.8.d.9.3. (inclusive to 2/8th) along road (inclusive to 2/8th) to junction of track. Q.9.a.1.8. – Q.4.a.90.05.
   (c) The Battalion will attack on a two company front as under:-
   'D' Coy. Right.
   'B' Coy. Left.
   'C' Coy. In support (To mop up VENDEGIES)
   'A' Coy. In reserve.
   The inter-company boundary will be :-
   Sunken road Q.19.a.9.2. (inclusive to 'D' Coy.) X roads Q.14.d.4.2.0. (inclusive to 'D' Coy.) along road (inclusive to 'B' Coy.)to road junction Q.14.a.95.5. (inclusive to 'B' Coy.) to junction of hedge and sunken road Q.13.a. 30.90. to Q.10.a.3.8.
   (d) 'D' & 'B' Coys. will attack with two platoons in front and two in support. They will follow between 80 to 100 yards behind barrage.
   'C' Coy. The two leading platoons of 'C' Coy will advance close up to 'D' & 'B' Coys into the village of VENDEGIES. 1 section of each platoon will push through to the Eastern edge of the village. The remaining sections will begin mopping up the village.
   The remaining two platoons will push on South of the village and enter the village from Q.13.a. mopping up as they go through.
   When the barrage moves on 'C' Coy. come into reserve N.E. of VENDEGIES in Q.8.d. and Q.13.a. 'A' Coy. will follow close behind 'C' Coy. and will form up during the standing barrage in Q.8.d. and Q.13.a.
   They will reach forming up place by keeping South of the village of VENDEGIES.

-2-

'A' Company will be in Support, (two Platoons behind
'B' Company and two Platoons behind 'D' Company) for the
advance to the final objective.
Should 'B' Company get very much involved in the village,
'A' Coy. will be prepared to fill the gap or any part of it
on 'D' Coy's left.

(e) Four Vickers M.G's will be attached to the Battalion.
They will come under the Command of Capt. M.E. JACKSON, MC.
and will move in the neighbourhood of the Supporting
Platoons of his Company.
Their chief role is to get to the outpost line of resistance
which they will assist in manning. If VENDEUIES offers
resistance, they will assist in overcoming it.

(f) 1 Section R.E's and one Platoon of Pioneers, with four
30 feet bridges will be attached to the leading Companies.
The attack, however, must not be held up while bridges
are erected. The river ECAILLON must be boldly waded.

Q10 c 1.3 - Q16 c
(g) When the final objective is taken, 'B' & 'D' Companies with
each 2 Platoons of 'A' Coy. will man outpost line of
resistance. (Tactical Posts), on the reverse side of the
Q10 c 10.55 - slope Q.3.d.6.2. - Q.3.d.3.0 - Q.10.c.6.6. with an outpost
Q10 a 0.0 - Q9 6.6 line on the actual objective. This Outpost Line must be
Q3 d 8.6 - Q3 6.50.05 held by one or two Platoons per Company according to strength
-Q3 c 0.9 - Q2 6.12 on arrival at objective. The Outpost line of resistance
will be in depth.

'C' Coy. will take up a position about Q.8.d.70.99. to -
Q.9.c.3.5. - Q.9.c.6.6. and will hold the approach to the
village at all costs.

4. ARTILLERY. (a) There will be a heavy artillery barrage at the start,
consisting of about 9 Brigades of F.A. as far as across the
River ECAILLON.
Thence for about 1500 yards the barrage will consist of
6 Brigades F.A. and thence about 4 Brigades.
For the first 1000 yards the barrage will move at the rate
of 100 yards per 3 minutes.
Thence for about 1500 yards the barrage will move at the
rate of 100 yards per 6 minutes.
Thence to final objective, the barrage will move at the rate
of 100 yards per 4 minutes.
The barrage will halt for an hour about the line :-
Q.7.b.9.6. - Q.8.b.7.2. - Q.9.c.4.0.
This is only approximate, the barrage map will be issued later
(b) Caution. When the barrage halts, the leading Companies
will re-organise clear of the village of VENDEUIES.
Men must be warned not to follow any retreating enemy over
the standing barrage line.
(c) Wherever the barrage halts, Thermite will be put down
on the Battalion Boundaries to indicate a lift. Thermite
will be put down along the front to indicate the long halt.

white
5. LIGHT SIGNALS. Green Very Lights will be sent up to indicate the
position of front line. Red flares will be lit to indicate
line to aeroplanes. Every Officer will carry two S.O.S.
Rockets. The S.O.S. is Red, Green, Red.

6. COMMUNICATIONS. Brigade Headquarters will be at Sandpit in V.5.a.
The Brigade Report Centre will be at P.30.c.2.1. and will
probably move to P.30.b.7.4.
Battalion Headquarters will be in Trench at P.24.a.8.4.
and will move to Q.13.b. and later to Q.8.c.

- 3 -

Runners must use roads P.24.b. - Q.15.a. - Q.13.d.3.8. - Road junction Q.8.d.25.20.
Companies must use every endeavour to get into touch by visual, with Battalion Headquarters.
A visual Station will be established about Q.19.a.0.5.
Information by runner must be sent back when the barrage halts.
Battalion Headquarters will be marked by a flag by day, and a lamp by night.

7. COMPASS BEARING. The Compass Bearing of the advance from junction of front Companies on assembly line, to junction on objective is 63 degrees magnetic.

8. FORMING-UP POSITION. The front line of the Forming-up position will be taped out by Capt. J.R. WARTON.

9. R.A.P. The Regimental Aid Post will be at Battalion Headquarters.

October 23rd, 1918.

(Signed) J.C.Muriel.
Lieut-Colonel,
Commanding 2/6th Batt. R. War. Regt.

CONFIDENTIAL

WAR DIARY OF

2/6TH BN. THE ROYAL WARWICKSHIRE REGT.

FROM:- NOVEMBER 1st TO 30th 1918.

VOLUME XXXI

Army Form C. 2118.

WAR DIARY
or
INTELLIGENCE SUMMARY.
(Erase heading not required.)

Instructions regarding War Diaries and Intelligence Summaries are contained in F. S. Regs., Part II. and the Staff Manual respectively. Title pages will be prepared in manuscript.

Place	Date	Hour	Summary of Events and Information	Remarks and references to Appendices
Brigl.S.tA	11/1/18	02.00	Moved into assembly positions for attack on MARESCHES. Battalion in Brigade Reserve with Headquarters at Cat. c. 40.60.	
		05.15	Attack commenced with 2/6th Bn Norths Regt on right and 2/6th Bn Royal Warwickshire Regt to left. All objectives taken by 0600 hours.	
		09.00	Orders to consolidate line K.30.b.60 – K.24.c.O.4. Headquarters established in railway bank at K.25.a.30.	
		10.40	Enemy counter attack developed with tanks.	
		11.00	1/5 Regt ordered to establish line K.29.b.50.20 – L.19.a.20.10 to protect left flank of Division. Enemy counter attack held on line L.13.a.00 – L.19 central. K.26.c. central.	
		18.50	An attempt made to regain lost objective by 2/4 W. Bn Yorkshire Regt and one Battalion from 189th Infantry Brigade failed.	
	21/11/18		An attack by 187th Infantry Brigade at dawn gained all objectives. 1/4th Infantry Brigade held line and 189rd Infantry Brigade withdrew to K.29. and K.30. B Coy with draw and dug in on K.29.b. and K.30.a. in support of A + B Coys.	

Army Form C. 2118.

WAR DIARY
or
INTELLIGENCE SUMMARY.
(Erase heading not required.)

Instructions regarding War Diaries and Intelligence Summaries are contained in F. S. Regs., Part II. and the Staff Manual respectively. Title pages will be prepared in manuscript.

Place	Date	Hour	Summary of Events and Information	Remarks and references to Appendices
Nov 61A	2nd	11.30	197th Infantry Brigade marched to billets in ST AUBERT. Battalion all billeted at 01.30 (3rd) in billets at ST. AUBERT.	
	3rd		Day devoted to getting cleaning & washing equipment etc.	
	4th		Battalion moved to billets at HAUSSY. Remainder of day spent in this and general re-organisation.	
	5th		Battalion Parade 09.30 hours. Remainder of morning at disposal of Company Commander. N.C.O. class and Lewis Gun classes held in the afternoon.	
	6th		Battalion Parade 09.30 hours. C.R.T. lecture drill followed by Company drill carried out by companies for the remainder of morning.	
	7th		Physical training, Bayonet fighting, Elementary Musketry, Box Respirator drill. Platoon & Company drill under Company arrangements from 09.00 to 12.15 hours. N.C.O. class under the R.S.M. and Lewis Gun instructors class under Battalion Lewis Gun instructor from 14.00 to 15.00 hours.	
	8th		Battalion moved to billets at VENDEGIES-SUR-ECAILLON.	
	9th		Physical training, Musketry, Platoon Open drill and demonstrating tactical handling of Platoon in attack. Specialist training (N.C.Os - Lewis Gunners Stretcher Bearers)	
	10th		Battalion Parade 6.45 E. Service.	

WAR DIARY
or
INTELLIGENCE SUMMARY.
(Erase heading not required.)

Army Form C. 2118.

Place	Date	Hour	Summary of Events and Information	Remarks and references to Appendices
VALENCIENNES	11		O.C. B"n" Musketry (as observer) with demolishing company in attack. A Coy employed on salvage work. Specialist training (NCOs, Lewis Gunners, Stretcher Bearers)	
	12		Company Drill. Physical training. Musketry on company ranges to include application and snap shooting. NCOs class. Afternoon - recreational training.	
	13		Morning - Battalion route march. Afternoon - recreational training.	
	14		Battalion Parade - Physical training - Bill work - NCOs class under the R.S.M.	
			Afternoon - Semi-final inter-platoon football matches.	
	15		Battalion moved by march route to CHISRM.	
	16		Company inspections - work on billets - NCOs class under the R.S.M. Afternoon - recreational training.	
	17		Church Parade. Non-conformist and Roman Catholic Services.	
	18		Steady Drill. Saluting. Games. Bathing.	
	19		Marching. Saluting. Games. Practice of March Past in column of Platoons.	
	20		Battalion Drill on Battalion Parade Ground. Special Thanksgiving Service.	
	21		Marching. Saluting. Games. Practice of March Past in column of Platoons.	
	22		Battalion employed on salvage work in neighbourhood of CHISRM.	

Army Form C. 2118.

WAR DIARY
or
INTELLIGENCE SUMMARY.
(Erase heading not required.)

Place	Date	Hour	Summary of Events and Information	Remarks and references to Appendices
VALENCIENNES	23rd		Battalion employed on salvage work in neighbourhood of CAMBRAI.	
LENS	24th		182nd Infantry Brigade moved by tactical trains and march route to the BERNEVILLE area. The Battalion were billeted at YVRENCH.	
	25th		In billets at YVRENCH.	
	26th		Platoon Cleaning Parade. Commanding Officer's inspection of billets.	
	27th		Kit inspection under Company arrangements. Special Medical class & P.B.T. class. Inspection of Lewis Guns.	
	28th		Resting & Recreation	
	29th		Company route marches. Special Medical class & P.B.T. class	
	30th		Inspection Parade under Company arrangements. Billet inspection by the Commanding Officer.	

Strength of Battalion — 43 Offrs. 832 O.R.

1/2/16.

R. Warwick
Lieut Col
Comdg 10th R. Warwick R.

WO 32

Confidential

War Diary of
2/6th Battalion Royal Warwickshire Regiment.
from December 1st 1916 to December 31st 1918.

Volume XXXII.

WAR DIARY or INTELLIGENCE SUMMARY

Army Form C. 2118.

(Erase heading not required.)

Instructions regarding War Diaries and Intelligence Summaries are contained in F.S. Regs., Part II. and the Staff Manual respectively. Title pages will be prepared in manuscript.

Place	Date	Hour	Summary of Events and Information	Remarks and references to Appendices
Guos Novvea	1/12/18		In billets at YVRENCH. C. of E. service under Coy arrangements. Recreational training in the afternoon.	
	2/12/18		Inspection Parades under Coy arrangements. Battalion Ceremonial Drill & march discipline. Special N.C.O.s class & P.T.& T. class. Recreational training in the afternoon.	
	3/12/18		6.0 a.m. inspection of billets. Remainder of day devoted to resting and recreational training.	
	4/12/18		Coy. Inspection Parades. Educational Classes. Battalion Ceremonial Drill & march discipline. Recreational training in the afternoon.	
	5/12/18		Coy. Inspection Parades. Educational Classes. Battalion Route March.	
	6/12/18		Battalion Ceremonial Drill and march discipline.	
	7/12/18		Recreational training in the afternoon.	
	8/12/18		Coy. inspection parades. Educational Classes. Billet inspection by the C.O.	
	9/12/18		Church Parade at 11.00 hours. Remainder of day devoted to resting & Recreational training.	
	10/12/18		Coy. inspection parades. Educational Classes. Battalion Ceremonial Drill & march discipline. Recreational training in the afternoon.	
	11/12/18		Coy. inspection parades. Educational Classes. Platoon Lectures in billets owing to inclement weather.	
	12/12/18		Coy. inspection parades. Educational Classes. Guard Mounting practice under Coy. arrangements in vicinity of billets. Inclement weather.	
	13/12/18		Coy. inspection parades. Educational Classes. Company & Platoon training under Coy. arrangements.	
	14/12/18		Coy. inspection parades. Educational Classes. Remainder of morning devoted to Recreational training owing to inclement weather. Lecture to all Platoon Officers on Recreational training by Major Digby Wyatt, M.C.	
	15/12/18		Coy. inspection parade. Battalion Ceremonial Drill & march discipline. Educational Classes.	

Army Form C. 2118.

WAR DIARY
or
INTELLIGENCE SUMMARY.
(Erase heading not required)

Instructions regarding War Diaries and Intelligence Summaries are contained in F. S. Regs., Part II. and the Staff Manual respectively. Title pages will be prepared in manuscript.

Place	Date	Hour	Summary of Events and Information	Remarks and references to Appendices
	15/12/18		Parade Service at 11.00 hours. Remainder of day devoted to Recreational training	
	16/12/18		Coy. Inspection Parades – Educational Classes – Battalion Ceremonial Drill & march Discipline. Recreational training in the afternoon	
	17/12/18		Lecture – Farm Settlement & popular Zoology	
	18/12/18		Coy. Inspection Parades – Educational Classes – Route March. Recreational training in the afternoon	
	19/12/18		Coy. Inspection Parades – Educational Classes – Company Drill and Platoon training. Recreational training in the afternoon	
	20/12/18		Coy. Inspection Parades – Educational Classes – Coy. Cross-country run. Afternoon Recreational training	
	21/12/18		Coy. Inspection Parades – Educational Classes – Route March. Inspection of Billets.	
	22/12/18		Parade Service at 11.00 hours. Remainder of day devoted to Recreational training	
	23/12/18		Educational Classes – Battalion Drill and Artillery formation. Recreational training.	
	24/12/18		Educational Classes – Route March – Recreational training in the afternoon	
	25/12/18		Christmas Day – Church Parade	
	26/12/18		Boxing Day – Cross-country Run – Football Match, Officers & Sergeants (mast in Chimney)	
	27/12/18		Educational Classes – Lectures in billets by Platoon Officers	
	28/12/18		Educational Classes – Battalion Ceremonial Drill & march Discipline	
	29/12/18		Church Parade. Remainder of day devoted to resting.	

Army Form C. 2118.

WAR DIARY
or
INTELLIGENCE SUMMARY.
(Erase heading not required.)

Instructions regarding War Diaries and Intelligence Summaries are contained in F. S. Regs., Part II. and the Staff Manual respectively. Title pages will be prepared in manuscript.

Place	Date	Hour	Summary of Events and Information	Remarks and references to Appendices
	30/12/18		Educational Classes - Battalion Drill & march Discipline - Recreational Training	
	31/12/18		Educational Classes, Lectures by Platoon Officers on questions affecting Demobilisation - Inclement weather.	
			Fighting Strength, 44 Officers, 801 O.R.s	

R. Davidson Lieut. Col.
Cdg. 16 R. Irish Regt.

WD 33

2/6TH BN ROYAL WARWICKSHIRE REGIMENT.

Copy of
War Diary
for the month of January 1919

VOLUME XXXIII

Confidential

Army Form C. 2118.

WAR DIARY
or
INTELLIGENCE SUMMARY.
(Erase heading not required.)

Instructions regarding War Diaries and Intelligence Summaries are contained in F. S. Regs., Part II. and the Staff Manual respectively. Title pages will be prepared in manuscript.

Place	Date	Hour	Summary of Events and Information	Remarks and references to Appendices
VRENCH	1/1/19		New Years Day devoted to resting & recreation. Battalion from empty river.	
(LENS/10000)	2/1/19		Coy Inspection Parade. Battn. Route March. Educational Classes. Recreation.	
	3/1/19		do	
	4/1/19		P.B.T. training. Educational Classes. Recreation.	
	5/1/19		Cross Country Run in connection with Brigade Competition. B/B Coys tie for first place.	
	6/1/19		Church Parade. Remainder of day devoted to resting and recreation.	
	7/1/19		Coy Inspection Parade. Battn. Ceremonial Drill. Education. Recreational training.	
	8/1/19		do	
	9/1/19		Battn. Route March. Educational Class. Recreational training.	
	10/1/19		Battn. Ceremonial Drill. Educational. Recreational training.	
	11/1/19		Battn. Route March. Educational. Recreational training.	
	12/1/19		Commanding Officer's Inspection of Billets, by clothing and kit inspection. Educational & Recreational training.	
	13/1/19		Coy Inspection Parade. Recreation of Glean Up. Divisional Commander.	
	14/1/19		Church Parade. Remainder of day devoted to resting and recreation.	
	15/1/19		Coy Inspection Parade. Battn. Ceremonial Drill. Educational Recreational training.	
	16/1/19		do	
	17/1/19		do	
	18/1/19		Battn. Route March.	
	19/1/19		Battn. Ceremonial Drill.	

Army Form C. 2118.

WAR DIARY
or
INTELLIGENCE SUMMARY.
(Erase heading not required.)

Instructions regarding War Diaries and Intelligence Summaries are contained in F. S. Regs., Part II. and the Staff Manual respectively. Title pages will be prepared in manuscript.

Place	Date	Hour	Summary of Events and Information	Remarks and references to Appendices
WRENCH (LENS area)	16/1/19		Inspection Parade. Training under Coy arrangements Educational & Recreational Training	
	17/1/19		do Battalion Drill	
	18/1/19		do Commanding Officer's Inspection of Billets	
	19/1/19		Church Parade. Remainder of day devoted to resting & Recreational Training	
	20/1/19		Inspection Parade. Training under Coy arrangements Educational Recreational Training	
	21/1/19		do Bathe. Route March.	
	22/1/19		do Training under Coy arrangements	
	23/1/19		do do	
	24/1/19		do Coy route march	
			Lecture by Commanding Officer to "B" & "D" Coys. Training under Coy arrangements to "A" & "C" Coys. Educational & Recreational training	
	25/1/19		Coy & Inspection Parades. Lecture as above to C & D Coys. Kit inspection for A & B Coys. Educational Recreational Training	
	26/1/19		Church Service. Remainder of day devoted to resting and recreation	
	27/1/19		Inspection Parades. Training under Coy arrangements Educational & Recreational training	
	28/1/19		do Bathe. Route March. Educational Recreational Training	
	29/1/19		do Training under Coy arrangements	

Army Form C. 2118.

WAR DIARY
or
INTELLIGENCE SUMMARY.
(Erase heading not required.)

Instructions regarding War Diaries and Intelligence Summaries are contained in F. S. Regs., Part II. and the Staff Manual respectively. Title pages will be prepared in manuscript.

Place	Date	Hour	Summary of Events and Information	Remarks and references to Appendices
XRENCH	30/1/17		Coy etc Inspection Parades. Coy Route Marches Educational & Recreational training	
(LENS 110000)	31/1/17		Battalion moved by march route & train to AHNRE and came under the command of Col. 98th Infantry Brigade.	
			Strength of Battalion 41 officers 801 Other Ranks	

J.V. Davidson. Lieut Col.
Comdg 1/4th Royal Warwick Regt.

WO 34

2/6th Bn The Royal Warwickshire Regt.

CONFIDENTIAL

War Diary For The Month Of

FEBRUARY
1919.

Volume XXXIV

Army Form C. 2118.

WAR DIARY
or
INTELLIGENCE SUMMARY.
(Erase heading not required.)

Instructions regarding War Diaries and Intelligence Summaries are contained in F. S. Regs., Part II. and the Staff Manual respectively. Title pages will be prepared in manuscript.

Place	Date	Hour	Summary of Events and Information	Remarks and references to Appendices
Harfleur	1/2/19 to 28/2/19		Units comprising 99th Infantry R.E. Battalion engaged in staffing Demobilisation Camps and disposed as follows:-	A.
			No.1. Reception Camp SANNIC	
			No.1. Despatch Camp SANNIC	
			B Coy. Attached to 4th Bn. "The King's Regt" HARFLEUR	A.
			C Coy. " " 1st Bn. "The Queen's Regt" HARFLEUR	A.
			E Coy. No.13 Camp HARFLEUR	A.
			Battalion Headquarters.	
	20/2/19		Draft of 2 Officers and 99 O.Rs arrived from the 1st Bn Royal Warwick Regt.	
	25/2/19		Draft of 2 Officers and 153 O.Rs arrived from 3rd Bn. Royal Warwick Regt.	
			Strength of Battalion - 34 Officers, 752 O.Rs	
	28/2/19			

F. Hume
Major.
Comdg 99th Royal War. Regt.

Vol 35

2/6TH BATTALION THE ROYAL WARWICKSHIRE REGIMENT.

CONFIDENTIAL.

War Diary for the month of

MARCH, 1919.

VOLUME XXXV.

WAR DIARY
or
INTELLIGENCE SUMMARY.
(Erase heading not required.)

Army Form C. 2118.

Place	Date	Hour	Summary of Events and Information	Remarks and references to Appendices
HARFLEUR	1/3/19.		Staffing Embarkation Camp. Companies disposed as follows:- A and B Companies SANVIC Camp. C Company attached 4th KINGS REGT., HARFLEUR, D Company attached 1st QUEENS REGT., HARFLEUR.	
HARFLEUR.	2/3/19.		Battalion moved by rail from HAVRE to DIEPPE and came under the orders of G.O.C. 100TH INFANTRY BRIGADE. Billetted in D Block, Embarkation Camp, DIEPPE.	
DIEPPE.	3/3/19.		Resting and making preliminary arrangements for taking over 'A' Block from 16th Batt. K.R.R. Draft of 2 Officers and 198 O.Rs arrived from 1/8th Batt. R. War. R.	
	4/3/19.		Resting and making preliminary arrangements for taking over 'A' Block from 16th Batt. K.R.R.	
	5/3/19.		Relieved 16th Batt. K.R.R. and took over working of 'A' Block. Companies disposed as follows:- Group No.1 A Company, Group No.2 C Company. Group No.3 D Company. Delouser B Company. Command of Embarkation Camp passed to G.O.C. 182ND INFANTRY BRIGADE on 5/3/19.	
	6/3/19.		Staffing Embarkation Camp.	
	7/3/19.		Staffing Embarkation Camp.	
	8/3/19.		Staffing Embarkation Camp. Football match v 9TH NORTHUMBERLAND FUSILIERS. Lost 4 - 1.	
	9/3/19.		Staffing Embarkation Camp.	
	10/3/19.		Staffing Embarkation Camp.	
	11/3/19.		Staffing Embarkation Camp.	
	12/3/19.		Staffing Embarkation Camp.	
	13/3/19.		Staffing Embarkation Camp. Football match v H.L.I. Won 3 - 2.	
	14/3/19.		Staffing Embarkation Camp.	
	15/3/19.		Staffing Embarkation Camp.	

Army Form C. 2118.

WAR DIARY
or
INTELLIGENCE SUMMARY.
(Erase heading not required.)

Instructions regarding War Diaries and Intelligence Summaries are contained in F. S. Regs., Part II. and the Staff Manual respectively. Title pages will be prepared in manuscript.

Place	Date	Hour	Summary of Events and Information	Remarks and references to Appendices
DIEPPE.	16/3/19.		Staffing Embarkation Camp. Football match v101 Field Ambulance. Won 3 – 1.	
	17/3/19.		Company Route Marches via ARQUES – DIEPPE – MARTIN EGLISE.	
	18/3/19.	09.00 to 12.00 hours.	Close Order Drill, Arms Drill, Saluting. Prospective N.C.Os.class under R.S.M.	
	19/3/19.	09.00 to 10.00 hours. 10.30 to 12.00 hours.	Kit Inspections. Arms Drill, Platoon and Company Training. N.C.Os. class under R.S.M.	
	20/3/19.	09.00 to 12.00 hours.	Physical Drill, Saluting Drill with and without arms, Arms Drill, Platoon and Company Drill. Football match v R.E. Won 10 – 0.	
	21/3/19.	09.00 to 09.30 hours. 10.30 to 12.00 hours.	Company Inspection Parades. 09.30 to 10.30 hours. Battalion Drill, Company Drill.	
	22/3/19.	09.00 to 09.30 hours. 11.00 to 12.00 hours.	Company Inspection Parades. 09.30 to 10.30 hours Battalion Drill, Lecture by Medical Officer.	
	23/3/19.		Voluntary Church Parade. Remainder of day Holiday.	
	24/3/19.		Lectures by Platoon Commanders. Lewis Gun Class under Batt. Lewis Gun Officer. N.C.Os.class under R.S.M.	
	25/3/19.		Company Route Marches. Route:– MARTIN EGLISE – ST.NICHOLAS – ARCHELLES. Lewis Gun & N.C.Os. Classes.	
	26/3/19.		Company Parades. Lewis Gun and N.C.Os. Classes. 25 men per Company for training for Guard of Honour.	
	27/3/19.		Company Parades. Lewis Gun Class. Guard of Honour training.	
	28/3/19.		Company Parades. Lewis Gun Class. Guard of Honour training.	
	29/3/19.		Company Parades. Lewis Gun Class. Guard of Honour training. Battalion found Guard of Honour on the occasion of the presentation of the M.B.E. to the Mayor of DIEPPE by G.O.C., L. of C.	

Army Form C. 2118.

WAR DIARY
or
INTELLIGENCE SUMMARY.
(Erase heading not required.)

Place	Date	Hour	Summary of Events and Information	Remarks and references to Appendices
DIEPPE.	30/3/19.		Voluntary Church Parades. Rest of day devoted to resting and Recreational Training.	
	31/3/19.		Cleaning of Equipment etc. for Divisional Commander's Inspection. N.C.Os. Class.	
			Strength of Battalion:- 32 Officers, 848 O.R.	

J. V. Davidson

Lieut-Colonel,
Comdg. 2/6th Battalion Royal Warwickshire Regiment.

2/6TH. BATTALION THE ROYAL WARWICKSHIRE REGIMENT.

―――――ooOoo―――――

C O N F I D E N T I A L

WAR DIARY FOR THE MONTH OF

A P R I L, 1 9 1 9

VOLUME XXXVI

Army Form C. 2118.

WAR DIARY
or
INTELLIGENCE SUMMARY.
(Erase heading not required.)

Instructions regarding War Diaries and Intelligence Summaries are contained in F. S. Regs., Part II. and the Staff Manual respectively. Title pages will be prepared in manuscript.

Place	Date	Hour	Summary of Events and Information	Remarks and references to Appendices
DIEPPE	1/4/19	09.30 to 10.30 hours.	Battalion Parade. 10.30 to 12.15 hours. Cleaning Parade.	
	2/4/19	11.15 hours.	Divisional Commander's Inspection.	
	3/4/19	09.15 to 12.15 hours.	Company Parades. Lewis Gun and N.C.O's Classes.	
	4/4/19	-do-	Company Parades. N.C.O's Class. Bathing of Battalion and delousing of Blankets.	
	5/4/19	-do-	Company Parades. N.C.O's Class. Draft of 27 O.R's arrived from 1st Bn. R.War.Regt.	
	6/4/19.		Voluntary Church Services. Recreational Training in the afternoon. Draft of 5 officers and 141 O.Rs. arrived from 1st Battalion Hampshire Regiment.	
	7/4/19		Battalion Route March. Commanding Officer's inspection of Draft.	
	8/4/19		Close Order Drill – Company Drill – Musketry. Specialist Classes. Lectures by Platoon Officers.	
	9/4/19		-do-	
	10/4/19		-do-	
	11/4/19		Bathing. P. & R.T. – Musketry – Close Order Drill – Company Drill. Specialist classes.	
	12/4/19		Kit inspections. P. & R.T. – Musketry – Close Order & Company Drill – Specialist classes.	
	13/4/19		Voluntary Church Services. Afternoon, recreational training.	
	14/4/19		Inspection Parades. Musketry – Judging Distance – Educational & Recreational training. -do-	
	15/4/19		-do-	

Army Form C. 2118.

WAR DIARY
or
INTELLIGENCE SUMMARY.
(Erase heading not required.)

Instructions regarding War Diaries and Intelligence Summaries are contained in F. S. Regs., Part II. and the Staff Manual respectively. Title pages will be prepared in manuscript.

Place	Date	Hour	Summary of Events and Information	Remarks and references to Appendices
DIEPPE	16/4/19		Inspection Parades – Musketry – Close Order & Company Drill – Educational and Recreational Training – Specialist Classes.	
	17/4/19		– do –	
	18/4/19		GOOD FRIDAY – H O L I D A Y.	
	19/4/19		Inspection Parades – Musketry – Close Order and Company Drill – Educational and Recreational Training – Specialist Classes. Draft of 3 officers and 56 O.Rs. arrived from 14th Bn. R.War.Regt.	
	20/4/19		EASTER SUNDAY. Voluntary Church Services.	
	21/4/19		EASTER MONDAY – H O L I D A Y.	
	22/4/19		Inspection Parades – Company route marches – Educational & Specialist classes.	
	23/4/19		Inspection Parades – Close Order & Company Drill – Musketry – Educational & Recreational training – Specialist classes.	
	24/4/19		– do –	
	25/4/19		– do –	
	26/4/19		– do –	
	27/4/19		Parade Church of England Service at 10.30 hours. Draft of 162 O.Rs. proceeded to join 2/8th Battalion Worcestershire Regiment at CHERBOURG. Remainder of day, Recreational training.	
	28/4/19		Inspection Parades – Close Order and Company Drill – Musketry – Educational & Recreational training. Specialist classes.	
	29/4/19		Lectures by Platoon Commanders in billets. Educational Training.	

Army Form C. 2118.

WAR DIARY
or
INTELLIGENCE SUMMARY.
(Erase heading not required.)

Place	Date	Hour	Summary of Events and Information	Remarks and references to Appendices
	30/4/19		Inspection Parades. Cleaning of huts. Educational Classes.	
			STRENGTH OF BATTALION - 41 Officers, 952 Other ranks.	
			P. Davidson.	
			Lieut. Col.	
			Commanding 2/6th Bn. Royal Warwickshire Regiment.	

2/6TH BATTALION THE ROYAL WARWICKSHIRE REGIMENT.

—ooOoo—

CONFIDENTIAL.

WAR DIARY FOR THE MONTH OF

MAY, 1919.

VOLUME XXXVII

Army Form C. 2118.

WAR DIARY
or
INTELLIGENCE SUMMARY.
(Erase heading not required.)

Instructions regarding War Diaries and Intelligence Summaries are contained in F.S. Regs., Part II. and the Staff Manual respectively. Title pages will be prepared in manuscript.

Place	Date	Hour	Summary of Events and Information	Remarks and references to Appendices
DIEPPE.	1/5/19		Inspection Parades. Close Order Drill, Musketry, Educational and Recreational Training. Commanding Officer's Inspection of Billets.	
	2/5/19.		Inspection Parades. Bathing. Close Order Drill, Company Drill, Education and Recreation.	
	3/5/19.		Inspection Parades. Scrubbing of Huts and Inspection by Commanding Officer.	
	4/5/19		Voluntary Church Services. Remainder of day - Holiday.	
	5/5/19		Inspection Parades. Close Order and Arms Drill, Musketry, Education and Recreational Training. 'D' Company on range.	
	6/5/19.		Inspection Parades. Company Route Marches. Education. 'C' Company on range.	
	7/5/19.		Inspection Parades. Extended Order Drill, Education and Recreational Training. 'D' Coy. on range.	
	8/5/19.		Inspection Parades. R.S.M's Parade. Education and Recreation.	
	9/5/19.		Inspection Parades. Bathing - Educational and Recreational Training.	
	10/5/19.		Inspection Parades. Cleaning of Huts and Inspection.	
	11/5/19.		Voluntary Church Parades. Remainder of day holiday.	
	12/5/19.		Inspection Parades. Platoon and Company Drill, Education and Recreation.	
	13/5/19.		Inspection Parades. Close Order Drill, Arms Drill, Musketry, Education and Recreational Training.	
	14/5/19.		Inspection Parades. Battalion Route March, Education.	
	15/5/19.		Inspection Parades. Musketry, Juicing Distances, Education and Recreation.	
	16/5/19.		Inspection Parades. Extended Order Drill, Company Drill, Education and Recreation.	
	17/5/19.		Inspection Parades. Cleaning of Huts and Inspection. Education.	

Army Form C. 2118.

WAR DIARY
or
INTELLIGENCE SUMMARY.
(Erase heading not required.)

Instructions regarding War Diaries and Intelligence Summaries are contained in F. S. Regs., Part II. and the Staff Manual respectively. Title pages will be prepared in manuscript.

Place	Date	Hour	Summary of Events and Information	Remarks and references to Appendices
DIEPPE.	18/5/19.		Voluntary Church Services. Remainder of day holiday.	
	19/5/19.		Inspection Parades. Judging Distance, Musketry, Education and Recreational Training.	
	20/5/19.		Inspection Parades. Extended Order Drill, Musketry, Education and Recreational Training.	
	21/5/19.		Inspection Parades. Kaxgexikax Close Order Drill, Musketry, Education and Recreation.	
	22/5/19.		Inspection Parades. Extended Order Drill, Musketry, Education and Recreational Training.	
	23/5/19.		Inspection Parades. Bathing, R.S.M.'s Parade, Judging Distance, Education and Recreational Training.	
	24/5/19.		Inspection Parades. Cleaning of Huts and Inspection. Education.	
	25/5/19.		Church Services. Remainder of day holiday.	
	26/5/19.		Inspection Parades. Judging Distance, Musketry, Education and Recreational Training.	
	27/5/19.		Inspection Parades. Extended Order Drill, Musketry, Education and Recreational Training.	
	28/5/19.		Inspection Parades. Close Order Drill, Musketry, Education and Recreational Training.	
	29/5/19.		Inspection Parades. Extended Order Drill, Musketry, Education and Recreational Training.	
	30/5/19.		Inspection Parades. Bathing, R.S.M.'s Parade, Judging Distance, Education and Recreational Training.	
	31/5/19.		Inspection Parades. Cleaning of Huts and Inspection. Education.	

STRENGTH OF BATTALION - 44 Officers, 952 Other Ranks.

Commanding 2/6 H. . . . . Lancashire Regiment.

2/6TH BATTALION THE ROYAL WARWICKSHIRE REGIMENT.

———————00000———————

C O N F I D E N T I A L.

WAR DIARY FOR THE MONTH OF

JUNE, 1919.

VOLUME XXXVIII.

Army Form C. 2118.

WAR DIARY
or
INTELLIGENCE SUMMARY.
(Erase heading not required.)

Instructions regarding War Diaries and Intelligence Summaries are contained in F. S. Regs., Part II. and the Staff Manual respectively. Title pages will be prepared in manuscript.

Place	Date	Hour	Summary of Events and Information	Remarks and references to Appendices
DIEPPE.	1/6/19.		Church Parades. Remainder of day - holiday.	
	2/6/19.		Inspection Parades, Musketry, Education and Recreational Training. L.G. and Signalling Classes.	
	3/6/19.		King's Birthday. General Holiday.	
	4/6/19.		Inspection Parades, Close Order Drill, Musketry, Education and Recreational Training, Lewis Gun and Signalling Classes.	
	5/6/19.		Inspection Parades, Bathing, Extended Order Drill, Education and Recreational Training, Lewis Gun and Signalling Classes.	
	6/6/19.		Inspection Parades, R.S.M's Parade, Judging Distance, Educational Training. L.G. and Signalling Classes.	
	7/6/19.		Inspection Parades, Fire Control and Discipline, Close Order Drill, Educational Training, Lewis Gun and Signalling Classes.	
	8/6/19.		Church Parades. Remainder of day - holiday.	
	9/6/19.		Whit Monday. General Holiday.	
	10/6/19.		Inspection Parades, Battalion Route March.	
	11/6/19.		Inspection Parades, Close Order Drill, Rapid Aiming, Loading and Firing, Education and Recreational Training. Lewis Gun and Signalling Classes.	
	12/6/19.		Inspection Parades. Bathing, Extended Order Drill, Description and Recognition of targets, Recreation and Educational Training. Lewis Gun and Signalling Classes.	
	13/6/19.		Inspection Parades, R.S.M's Parade, Judging Distance, Recreation and Educational Training, Lewis Gun and Signalling Classes.	
	14/6/19.		Inspection Parades, Lecture by Army Lecturer, Cleaning and Inspection of Billets, Lewis Gun and Signalling Classes.	
	15/6/19.		Church Parades. Remainder of day - holiday.	

Army Form C. 2118.

WAR DIARY
or
INTELLIGENCE SUMMARY.
(Erase heading not required.)

Instructions regarding War Diaries and Intelligence Summaries are contained in F.S. Regs., Part II. and the Staff Manual respectively. Title pages will be prepared in manuscript.

Place	Date	Hour	Summary of Events and Information	Remarks and references to Appendices
DIEPPE.	16/6/19.		Inspection Parades, Platoon and Company Drill, Rapid Aiming and Loading, Educational Training, Lewis Gun and Signalling Class.	
	17/6/19.		Battalion Route March.	
	18/6/19.		Inspection Parades, Close Order Drill, Artillery Formations, Recreation and Education, Lewis Gun and Signalling Classes.	
	19/6/19.		Inspection Parades, Bathing, Extended Order Drill, Guard Duties and Mounting, Recreation and Educational Training. Lewis Gun and Signalling Classes.	
	20/6/19.		Inspection Parades, R.S.M's Parade, Outpost Scheme, Education and Recreational Training. Lewis Gun and Signalling Classes.	
	21/6/19.		Inspection Parades, Cleaning of huts and inspection by Commanding Officer.	
	22/6/19.		Church Parades. Remainder of day - holiday.	
	23/6/19.		Inspection Parades. Fresh Lewis Gun and Signalling Classes, Artillery and Fighting Formations, Consolidated and Counter attacks. Platoon and Close Order Drill, Lecture on "Attack on a strong point".	
	24/6/19.		General Holiday.	
	25/6/19.		Inspection Parades, Lewis Gun and Signalling Classes, Outpost scheme, Ceremonial Drill, Lecture on Outpost scheme.	
	26/6/19.		Inspection Parades, Baths, Education, Advance Guard scheme, Lewis Gun and Signalling Classes.	
	27/6/19.		Inspection Parades, Battalion Route March, Education.	
	28/6/19.		Inspection Parades, Company and Close Order Drill, Outposts and Patrols, Platoon in attack scheme, Ceremonial, Education, Lewis Gun and Signalling Classes.	
	29/6/19.		Voluntary Church Parades. Remainder of day - holiday.	

Army Form C. 2118.

WAR DIARY
or
INTELLIGENCE SUMMARY.
(Erase heading not required.)

Instructions regarding War Diaries and Intelligence Summaries are contained in F. S. Regs., Part II. and the Staff Manual respectively. Title pages will be prepared in manuscript.

Place	Date	Hour	Summary of Events and Information	Remarks and references to Appendices
DIEPPE.	30/6/19.		Inspection Parades, Education. Guard and Sentry Drill. Recreational Training, Lewis Gun and Signalling Classes.	
			STRENGTH OF BATTALION – 46 Officers, 1350 Other ranks.	
			P. v. Swilson Lieut-Col., Commanding 2/6th Battalion Royal Warwickshire Regiment.	

2/6TH BATTALION ROYAL WARWICKSHIRE REGIMENT.

————ooOoo————

CONFIDENTIAL.

WAR DIARY FOR THE MONTH OF

JULY, 1919.

VOLUME XXXIX

Army Form C. 2118.

WAR DIARY
or
INTELLIGENCE SUMMARY.
(Erase heading not required.)

Instructions regarding War Diaries and Intelligence Summaries are contained in F. S. Regs. Part II. and the Staff Manual respectively. Title pages will be prepared in manuscript.

Place	Date	Hour	Summary of Events and Information	Remarks and references to Appendices
MARTIN EGLISE	1/7/19.		Route March.	
Training Coy. – "A" Coy.	2/7/19.		Inspection Parades, Sentry and Patrol Duties, Principles of Outposts, Outpost scheme and lecture, Ceremonial, Education, L.G. and Signalling Classes.	
	3/7/19.		Inspection Parades, Advance Guards, Education, Bathing, L.G. and Signalling Classes.	
	4/7/19.		Inspection Parades, Company Close Order Drill, Outpost scheme and patrols, Platoon in attack, Ceremonial, and Education, L.G. and Signalling Classes.	
	5/7/19.		Inspection Parades, C.O's Inspection, Guard and Sentry Drill, Education, Scrubbing of huts.	
	6/7/19.		Church Parade. Special Thanksgiving Services.	
Training Coy. "A" Coy.	7/7/19.		Inspection Parades, Education, Explanation of Training, Fire Control & Discipline, Artillery & Fighting Formations, Lecture :- Elementary Outposts, Ceremonial, L.G. and Signalling Classes.	
	8/7/19.		Route March.	
	9/7/19.		Inspection Parades, Education, Artillery and Fighting Formations, Fire Control and Discipline, Section rushes – covering fire, Mutual Support, Bayonet Fighting, Ceremonial, L.G. and Sig. Classes.	
	10/7/19.		Inspection Parades, Education, Artillery and Fighting Formations, Attack on a strong point (Lecture) Bombing lecture, Bathing, Lewis Gun and Signalling Classes.	
	11/7/19.		Inspection Parades, Education, Sentry and Patrol Duties, Outpost scheme and lecture, L.G. & Sig. Classes.	
	12/7/19.		Inspection Parades, Education, Rapid sitting and digging of Trench line, Wiring, Scrubbing of huts.	
	13/7/19.		Church Parades. Remainder of day – holiday.	
	14/7/19.		French Peace Celebrations – General Holiday.	
Training Coy. "C" Coy.	15/7/19.		Inspection Parades, Education, Explanation of Training Fire Control and Discipline, Artillery & Fighting Formations, Elementary Outposts, Ceremonial, L.G. and Signalling Classes.	
	16/7/19.		Inspection Parades, Education, Artillery & Fighting Formations, Lecture on attack on a strong point, Bombing lecture, L.G. and Signalling Classes.	

Army Form C. 2118.

WAR DIARY
OR
INTELLIGENCE SUMMARY.
(Erase heading not required.)

Instructions regarding War Diaries and Intelligence Summaries are contained in F. S. Regs., Part II. and the Staff Manual respectively. Title pages will be prepared in manuscript.

Place	Date	Hour	Summary of Events and Information	Remarks and references to Appendices
MARTIN EGLISE.	17/7/19.		Bathing. Scrubbing of huts and Improvement of lines.	
	18/7/19.		Inspection Parade. Education. Sentry and Patrol Duties. Outpost scheme and lecture. Ceremonial. L.G. and Sig. Classes.	
	19/7/19.		British Peace Celebrations - General holiday.	
	20/7/19.		Church Parades. Remainder of day - holiday.	
Training Coy - 'C'	21/7/19.		Inspection Parades, Education, Artillery & Fighting Formations, Lecture on attack on a strong point. Consolidation and Counter attacks and Lecture. Platoon Close Order Drill, Ceremonial, L.G. & Sig. Classes.	
	22/7/19.		Inspection Parades, Education, Lecture on Anti-Bolshevism, Sentry and Patrol Duties, Principles of Outposts, Ceremonial. L.G. & Signalling Classes.	
	23/7/19.		Route March.	
	24/7/19.		Bathing. Lecture on 'Nature Study' L.G. and Signalling Classes.	
	25/7/19.		Inspection Parades. Education. Half hour at disposal of Coy.Commanders. Outpost scheme and patrols. Platoon in attack. Ceremonial. L.G. and Signalling Classes.	
	26/7/19.		Education. 10.15 Commanding Officer's Inspection. Remainder of morning - cleaning of huts and lines.	
	27/7/19.		Church Parades. Remainder of day - holiday.	
Training Coy - 'D'	28/7/19.		Inspection Parades. Lecture on Education in the Army. Fire Control. Artillery Formations. Recreational Training. Ceremonial. L.G. & Signalling Classes. Medical Inspection for 'A' Company.	
	29/7/19.		Route March. Medical Inspection for 'B' Company.	
	30/7/19.		Inspection Parades. Education. Mutual Support & Covering Fire. Fire Control and Discipline. Platoon Drill. Ceremonial. L.G. & Signalling Classes. Medical Inspection for 'C' Company.	
	31/7/19.		Bathing. Education. Attack on a strong point. Company Drill, L.G. & Signalling Classes. Medical Inspection for 'D' Company.	

STRENGTH OF BATTALION - 41 OFFICERS 1075 O.R.

S. Boyle.
Lieut-Col.,
Commanding 2/6th Battalion Royal Warwickshire Regiment.

2/6TH BATTALION ROYAL WARWICKSHIRE REGIMENT.

―――――ooOoo―――――

CONFIDENTIAL.

WAR DIARY FOR THE MONTH OF

AUGUST, 1919.

VOLUME XL

Army Form C. 2118.

WAR DIARY
or
INTELLIGENCE SUMMARY.
(Erase heading not required).

Instructions regarding War Diaries and Intelligence Summaries are contained in F.S. Regs., Part II. and the Staff Manual respectively. Title pages will be prepared in manuscript.

Place	Date	Hour	Summary of Events and Information	Remarks and references to Appendices
MARIEH MELIISE.	1/8/19.		Inspection Parades, Consul, Close Order Drill, Outpost Scheme and Patrols, Platoon in attack, Ceremonial Drill, Education, A.C. & Specialist Classes. Lieut.Col. S BOYS, M.C., A.O.S.B. in command vice Lieut.Col. P.V.DAVIDSON, D.S.O.	
'D' COMPANY.	2/8/19.		Battalion Sports.	
	3/8/19.		Church Parades.	
	4/8/19.		August Bank Holiday - General Holiday.	
	5/8/19.		Route March.	
	6/8/19.		Inspection Parades, Arthur & Fighting Formation, Attack on strong point, Recreational Training, Ceremonial (March Past) Education, Specialist Classes.	
	7/8/19.		Inspection Parades, Education, Setting up Drill, Duties, Principles of Outposts, Advance Guards, Musketry (Rapid Loading) Bathing.	
	8/8/19.		Inspection Parades, Education, Company Drill, Platoon in attack, Recreational Training, Ceremonial.	
	9/8/19.		Inspection Parades, Education, Conf. Officer N.C.O's Inspection, Guard & Sentry Drill, Cleaning of Huts & Lines.	
	10/8/19.		Church Parades.	
All ranks logged Ben.	11/8/19.		Inspection Parades, Education, Physical Training, Rail Loading Practice, Arms Drill, Ceremonial, N.C.O's Class.	
	12/8/19.		Inspection Parades, Education, Artillery & Fighting Education, G Tac Drill, Platoon & Recreational Training, Ceremonial, N.C.O's Class.	
	13/8/19.		Inspection Parades, Education, Rail Loading, Arms Drill, Recreational Training, Ceremonial, N.C.O.s Cl ss.	
	14/8/19.		Inspection Parades, Education, Rail Loading, Arms Drill, Recreational Training, Guard & Sentry Drill, Ceremonial, N.C.O's Class.	
	15/8/19.		Inspection Parades, Education, Platoon in attack, Company Drill, Bayonet Fighting, Ceremonial, N.C.O's Class.	
	16/8/19.		Inspection Parades, Billet Inspection by Comd. Officer, Lecture on Peace Treaty.	
	17/8/19.		Church Parades.	
	18/8/19.		Inspection Parades, Education, Select A/of Personnel for Guard of Honour.	
	19/8/19.		Inspection Parades, Arms Drill, Guard of Honour, Lecture on Peace Treaty.	
	20/8/19.		Inspection Parades, Arms Drill and Inspection of Guard of Honour, Guard of Honour furnished for the Battalion on inspection and on return of the 39th French Infantry Battalion OIBPPFB.	
	21/8/19.		Inspection Parades, Education, N.C.O's Class under the R.S.M., L.G. and Signalling Classes.	
	22/8/19.		Inspection Parades, Education, N.C.O's Class under the R.S.M. L.G. & Signalling Classes.	
	23/8/19.		Inspection Parades, Education, Cleaning of Billets and lines and inspection by Comd. Officer.	
	24/8/19.		Church Parades. Remainder of day a holiday.	
	25/8/19.		Inspection Parades, Education, N.C.O's Class under the R.S.M.	
	26/8/19.		Inspection Parades, Education, N.C.O's Class under the R.S.M.	

Army Form C. 2118.

WAR DIARY
or
INTELLIGENCE SUMMARY.
(Erase heading not required.)

Instructions regarding War Diaries and Intelligence Summaries are contained in F. S. Regs., Part II. and the Staff Manual respectively. Title pages will be prepared in manuscript.

Place	Date	Hour	Summary of Events and Information	Remarks and references to Appendices
	27/8/19.		Inspection Parade, Education, N.C.O.'s Classes under R.S.M.	
	28/8/19.		Inspection Parade, Education, Bath's, N.C.O.'s Classes under R.S.M.	
	29/8/19.		Inspection Parade, Education, N.C.O.'s Classes under R.S.M.	
	30/8/19.		Inspection Parade, Education, Lectures on "Europe" "The Russian Revolution".	
	31/8/19.		Church Service, Bathing of Battalion.	

STRENGTH OF BATTALION - 41 OFFICERS, 850 O.R.

Comprising 2/6" Batt. Roy. Warwickshire Regiment.

2/6TH. BATTALION THE ROYAL WARWICKSHIRE REGIMENT.

CONFIDENTIAL

WAR DIARY FOR THE MONTH OF SEPTEMBER 1919.

VOLUME - XLI.

Army Form C. 2118.

WAR DIARY
or
INTELLIGENCE SUMMARY.
(Erase heading not required.)

Instructions regarding War Diaries and Intelligence Summaries are contained in F. S. Regs., Part II. and the Staff Manual respectively. Title pages will be prepared in manuscript.

Place	Date	Hour	Summary of Events and Information	Remarks and references to Appendices
MARTIN EGLISE	1st		Inspection Parades. Available men engaged on improving Camp.	
	2nd		-do- Lecture on "Lessons from Roman & Venetian History"	
	3rd		-do- Lecture on "Street Fighting"	
	4th		-do- Lecture by Platoon Commanders on Military News.	
	5th		-do- Draft of 180 O.R's despatched to P.of W.Coys., 24 N.C.O's to Chinese Labour Corps	
	6th		-do- All unemployed men at disposal of Quartermaster.	
	7th		-do- Church Parades.	
	8th		-do- Changing of Company lines.	
	9th		-do- All unemployed men at disposal of Quartermaster.	
	10th		-do- -do-	
	11th		-do- Recreational Training.	
	12th		-do- All unemployed men at disposal of Quartermaster.	
	13th		-do- Draft of 120 O.R's to P.of W.Coys.	
	14th		-do- Draft of 110 O.R's to P.of W.Coys.	
	15th		-do- Draft of 60 O.R's to P.of W.Coys.	

Army Form C. 2118.

WAR DIARY
or
INTELLIGENCE SUMMARY.
(Erase heading not required.)

Instructions regarding War Diaries and Intelligence Summaries are contained in F. S. Regs., Part II. and the Staff Manual respectively. Title pages will be prepared in manuscript.

Place	Date	Hour	Summary of Events and Information	Remarks and references to Appendices
MARTIN EGLISE	16th		Inspection Parades. Unemployed men at the disposal of the Quartermaster.	
	17th		-do-	
	18th		-do-	
	19th		-do-	
	20th		-do-	
	21st		Church Parades.	
	22nd		Remaining Personnel posted to P.of W.Coys. & Chinese Labour Corps. Colour Party under Lieut. S.R.BOX, M.M. proceeded to England. Cadre under Lieut. W.J.WINTER, M.C. proceeded to England.	

S. Boyle Lieut.Col.

Comdg. 2/6th Bn. Royal Warwickshire Regt.

www.ingramcontent.com/pod-product-compliance
Lightning Source LLC
Chambersburg PA
CBHW080848230426
43662CB00013B/2049